This Book is dedicated to the late Mr Alan Littlewood of Buck Wood Cottage Dog Sanctuary and to Lou Parson, the most fantastic Jack Russell any man can ever hope to share his life with.

Front cover photograph is the Hewenden Railway Viaduct near Cullingworth.

I have always enjoyed walking and dabbling in history of one kind or another. More years ago than I can remember I completed an A level course in Modern International History at Bradford College, but I found that local history is more appealing and inspiring than matters involving The Schlieffen Plan, the advent of The League of Nations or the rise of Adolf Hitler. Merge together walking and local history and it almost becomes an addiction. One can connect with this type of history. You can see it, feel it, breathe it and immerse yourself in it.

With this in mind I embarked on my odyssey of discovery of the rich and varied historical past that the city of Bradford and its environs has to offer. I have not been disappointed as I have learnt many things about fine old Victorian houses, romantic alluring cottages, strange old characters and long gone railways and their station houses. And that's just in the village of Thackley never mind all the other wonderful districts in my home city.

My companion on these walks has been my beloved three year old female Jack Russell Tallulah Parson, or Lou if you want her every day moniker. She has chased rabbits over Haworth Moor, squirrels through the ruins of old Milner Field, and scoffed more sandwich crusts than is good for her. She has walked at my side for every single step of the way and lapped it up like a good Jack Russell Terrier should. Everyone ought to have a dog like this at their side at least once in their life. I have indeed been blessed as I have had four of the buggers.

The walks were planned with almost military precision using Google Earth, old Ordnance Survey maps dating back over 150 years, ideas I had gleaned from the Facebook group Banter about Bradford (BAB) and my sometimes lucid and vivid imagination. The remit of BAB is to discuss only matters relating to Bradford and the official Bradford area and I have done my upmost to stick to this and not stray outside. I have, on a couple of occasions stepped outside and onto foreign territory but I make no excuses as it had to be done for reasons of necessity. It's my party and I'll stray if I want to. I used the great local bus services for all my travels as I refuse to own or drive one of those new-fangled Motor vehicle things any longer. I love the sense of personal freedom this affords me and besides the old man with the big white beard upstairs didn't give us legs for nothing you know.

All the forthcoming walks were carried out between April 2nd 2014 and 25th July 2015.

Contents

1)   Idle Village to Shipley- Canal Walk   4
2)   Eldwick Bottom to Tong Park via Baildon   14
3)   Allerton to Denholme   20
4)   Tong Street to Wyke via Birkenshaw   27
5)   All Alone Road to Wrose Road via Idle Hill   33
6)   Keighley to Sandbeds via Riddlesden   40
7)   Shelf to Wellheads Thornton   47
8)   Bolton Woods to Northcliffe Park Shipley   54
9)   The Salt Mansion Trilogy   60
10)   Thackley Corner to High Esholt   74
11)   Hodgson's Fold to Walnut Farm via Peel Park   82
12)   Baildon to Menston Village   94
13)   Drighlington to Black Carr Woods via Tong   102
14)   Eccleshill To Spink Well Canal Lock   110
15)   Fagley to Apperley Bridge   116
16)   City Centre to Tong Village via Raikes Lane   124
17)   Denholme to Bingley via Harden   132
18)   High Eldwick to Baildon via Weecher Reservoir   141
19)   Greengates to Thackley Corner via Little London   147
20)   High Eldwick to Crossflats via Bradup Bridge   154
21)   Keelham Crossroads to Scarlet Heights   161
22)   Cutler Heights Lane to Greengates via Calverley   170
23)   Manningham and the Ghost of Len Shackleton   177
24)   Keighley to Haworth with The Bronte's   186

The twenty eighth of February 2015 was the first day in three weeks that had promised any sort of sun. I had been cooped up in Magpie Cottage for what seemed an age so after checking the weather forecast I decided a good walk to blow away the cobwebs was in order. Nothing complicated just a fairly simple linier stroll down through the village of Idle and then along the Leeds-Liverpool Canal to Shipley. Nice, simple and straight and just what the Doctor ordered.

Just for a change I was planning to take my other Jack Russell, the rather elderly Missy Moo Flint but she didn't seem all that interested so it was the usual team of Lou and I that set out at dinnertime on this bright sunny Saturday in February. So we set off up to the sometimes dangerous Five Lane Ends roundabout then down the familiar Bradford Road to Idle village. The huge roundabout of Five Lane Ends is manic at the best of times and I have to have eyes in the back of my head when navigating it with either of my dogs.

We passed by the former Jowett car factory which is now of course a William Morrison's supermarket. Jowett's had begun as a company elsewhere in Bradford in 1901 and was founded by the brothers Benjamin and William Jowett. They were among the early pioneers of car manufacturing in Britain, with their emphasis being on the production of light, affordable cars. The company moved to the Springfield Works site in Idle in 1919 and, for the next 35 years cars and vans were produced there, including many that have become collectors' items since. Many models of cars and vans were made at the factory. Amongst them was the Kestrel, the Ken, the Jupiter and the Javelin, and these still evoke fond memories among car enthusiasts. After the Second World War the company was sold, but by the mid-1950s it was in financial difficulties. Jowett's stopped making cars at the Idle factory in 1954, but continued in business for a while, making aircraft parts and spare parts for Jowett's vehicles at a site elsewhere in Yorkshire. However, the Idle site was sold to Harvester International who produced tractors there until the early 1980s. The factory was demolished in 1983 and the site is now a large retail park dominated by the Morrison's supermarket and a drive-in MacDonald's.

Lou and I arrived at The Springfield pub and I remembered that I helped out for a while many years ago at an animal sanctuary on Arthur Street that runs down the side of the pub. I wondered if it was still there so we walked down the street and onto a still partially cobbled track that once led to Friar Mill. I remembered the smart whitewashed cottage and sheds down at the end but there was no sign of the sanctuary. Going back thirty years it was all a bit hazy but as I stood there looking around all I could see in my mind's eye was the giant Turkey which I had to feed every time I was there. It was massive enough but when it spread its feathers and wings its size increased tremendously. Gordon as he was known used to get really excited when it was feeding time and this scared the hell out of me. There were all kinds of other animals there at this sanctuary but it was Gordon who stuck in my mind and I used to think of him when eating my Christmas dinner every year for ages afterwards.

Back on the main road we made our way past where the old railway line used to cross then on towards Idle village. The historic village of Idle is located to the north of Bradford and to the east of Shipley. The place-name Idle probably relates to the Old English term Idel meaning an empty place or an uncultivated area. In 1583-4 the Manor is portrayed as containing mostly uncultivated land and woodland, with some quarries for wall stones and slates. Idle lordship comprised the settlements of Idle, Thorpe, Wrose, and Windhill. Open fields were situated immediately south and west of Idle with Thackley Common, and the East and West Woods to the north. Idle Mill, comprising a water corn mill and fulling mill with two stocks, stood on the south bank of the River Aire, the river forming the northern bounds of the lordship.

Moorland and the hamlet of Wrose, with its fields systems, were situated on the south and southwest bounds of the estate. Industrial activity in this period included The Iron Smithies, powered by a water mill situated to the southwest of Windhills, on the east side of Bradford Beck. Earlier industries included tanning as did many areas of Bradford during this period. Inhabitants of Idle comprised 21 tenants and 14 cottagers, the majority of tenants each residing in smallholdings or farmsteads consisting of a house, barn, and outbuildings, with a croft or parcel of land to the rear of the property. The cottagers' lived in a cottage with a garden, and had rights of Common Land.

Around 1837 Idle was a populous clothing village with a long main street. A number of scribbling and fulling mills and a few worsted mills were situated within the general area; a cattle-market was established at Idle in 1836. The Settlement had mostly remained clustered around the five routes leading to the village and the increase of population and industrial activity, including

Union Mill (woollen) and Castle Mills (Worsted), had been absorbed in development to the south and east of the original village core. The growth of industry and population resulted in the opening of a railway station. The Great Northern Railway operated the first passenger train to Idle in 1875.
This station closed in 1931 with the line finally closing in 1968. The station, bridge and tracks were dismantled in 1972 and replaced by Idlecroft Road.

Walking down Croft Street we passed a tiny disused Wesleyan Methodist graveyard. This piece of consecrated ground stands right at the side of the road in front of a beautiful row of 18th century former weavers cottages. Looking sadly neglected today it contains behind its locked gates one Commonwealth War grave. Passing by more rows of these same cottages we turned onto Apperley Road and headed towards the former coaching inn known today as The George Inn. The Shipley Bantams Supporters Club used to hold their meetings here and as a member I can recall having many good nights in there.

One fellow club member from those days was nicknamed "The Rabbi" due to his unfeasonably long and bushy black beard. He was only in his late twenties and a beard like his would surely have taken some forty years to grow so what exactly was going on we never knew. On the occasions when a player would attend the meetings to give a talk, The Rabbi would stand right at the front on one leg listening intently like a demented Stork. I met some weird characters following Bradford City over the years but he was surely the strangest.

Leaving The George Lou and I passed by the late 18th century, Grade II listed former Miln Holme Farm before arriving at Milman swing bridge. Built in 1810 and formally named Kitman Bridge, this canal swing bridge is surrounded by a grouping of mainly Grade II listed cottages originally built for canal workers. Alongside these cottages there once was a series of three wharves and one of only four maintenance yards on the whole Leeds-Liverpool canal. One of the cottages, built in 1776 served as the Toll House for the bridge.

A short walk in the direction of Apperley Bridge is the marina. Built on the site of the former canal basin, this is one of the few marina's on the whole canal. The basin served Oaklea Mills, a three storey former Worsted mill constructed in 1896. Today the marina is used as a housing point for a number of canal houseboats and has its own Chandler shop which sells all manner of items for use by people enjoying the life of a canal boat owner. I have always found the kind of freedom that Canal boats offer attractive so we stayed here a while to sit and ponder. Some years ago I did dabble with the idea of selling my cottage and buying one of these fine narrowboats but sadly it never got beyond the planning stage. Maybe when Iam older I may have the courage to make what would for me be a big step and take the plunge.

We started along the canal towards Shipley and crossed over by the swing bridge. The howling of the dogs from the kennels alongside the far bank was music to my ears. They run a good ship there as I have trusted them with my own dogs on many occasions in the past when I have jetted off to Amsterdam amongst other places. Just past the kennels the fields lie flat and run right down to the bank. Horses grazed lazily in the early summer sun safe in the knowledge that the humans and dogs on the other bank cannot trouble them. Before long Lou and I had reached Dobson Lock. This traditional and well-kept Grade II listed lock was constructed in 1777 with its adjacent canal company warehouse alongside, and raises the canal by some twenty feet. The former warehouse was converted into three beautiful cottages one of which today houses a British Waterways office. I mounted the top of the lock to look over the fields towards the estate of Esholt and Rawdon beyond.

Just beyond the lock is a workshop and fitting area for the various maintenance tasks that British Waterways have to carry on out this stretch of the canal. As always it was a hive of activity with all manner of trucks and vans parked alongside. Sparks from some frantic welding spat out onto the path through an open door. Dancing around to avoid being incinerated we walked on for a short distance before reaching Bottom Farm and its quaint friendly tearoom. This is the only place on this stretch of the canal where weary travellers can take refreshment and today it was packed even though it was still early.

Up ahead I could see the twin iron riveted railway bridges that cross the canal at this point. The line was constructed in 1846 as the Bradford-Shipley-Leeds line with just the nearside and oldest bridge being built at this time. The railway was extended in the early 20th century from two lines to four and this necessitated the widening of a tunnel, embankment and the construction of the second bridge. Sometime afterwards the older pair of lines closed, the rails removed and the Southern bridge was allowed to deteriorate. As I passed underneath the remaining bridge I looked above and marvelled at the thousands of rivets in their perfect uniform lines. Painted in a dark colour the bridge looked as though it had been built only the day before.

Across on the far bank the flat meadows had given way to dense woodland. This I knew to be Dawson Wood which was once part of the privately owned Esholt Estate and contains trees of many species and ages, most going back hundreds of years. Here on the still water's surface paddled a pair of Ducks followed by their family of Ducklings. Mum and Dad were obviously teaching their children all about life on the water, and although Lou showed her usual interest in all things that moved the Ducks were unconcerned. The canal continued to wind and snake its way past the woods as we approached Esholt Sewage plant. I knew it was not far away long before I saw any evidence as the smell was overpowering. My nostrils twitched and danced around on my face before I gave up and covered up with my hand. Sometimes it is not so bad and it depends on which way the breeze is blowing. Today I was just unlucky as the smell was so bad I could almost see it.

The woods on the far bank had become so dense now that they appeared almost inpenatratable to all creatures but the resident animals. Hollins Wood gave way to Field Wood then this area became the famous Buck Wood. I passed underneath the rusting steel structure of the former narrow gauge bridge which used to carry the Sewage plant railway over the canal and into Buck Wood. On the Thackley side of the canal at this point is Yorkshire Water's storm water tanks and waste water screening plant. Nearby is another magnificent set of canal locks named Field Locks. A 3-rise lock constructed in 1774-77 and designed by the engineers James Brindley and John Longbotham this structure comprises three adjoining wide chambers of coursed dressed stone with stone coping, the walls of the upper two curving out at their tails, with stone steps to either side. The lock consists of two pairs of late 20th century wooden gates to top chamber with one pair of the same to each of the lower ones. Each pair has integral rack and pinion paddle gearing and adjacent boxed ground paddles, with the exception of the middle chamber, where the ground paddles have been removed. Each chamber has a wooden plank footbridge across its tail. There is an overflow weir to offside from the towpath, with channels leading into it from two lower chambers.

The canal towpath wound onwards towards Shipley between the now dense Buck Wood on one side and a thinner stretch of wood leading down to the river Aire on the nearside. Buck Wood lies to the north of Thackley and covers an area of fairly level high ground, as well as the steep north-facing slope down to the Leeds and Liverpool canal. Above this valley Buck Wood forms a broad semi-circular zone of woodland, adjoining other similar woods that are part of a woodland corridor stretching along the Aire Valley. Covering 42 hectares, this wood is bordered by the curving route of the canal at its lower perimeter around 60 m above sea-level. Its highest boundary 135 m above sea level, is shaped by the tree-lined sweep of Ainsbury Avenue leading from Thackley through to Esholt.

Buck Wood lies above a layer of millstone grit rock with numerous rocky outcrops, especially on the steeper slopes, where quarrying has taken place. The wood contains a mixture of habitats, with areas of both broad-leaved woodland and mixed deciduous and coniferous plantations. It has patches of marshland created by the many springs occurring throughout the Wood. There are fields scattered within the woodland, some used as pasture for grazing. With its variety of habitats it is an important reservoir for wildlife in Thackley and the surrounding area, and an area for walking and other leisure activities.

As I stood next to Buck Mill Bridge I remembered there was once a quite sizable and longstanding mill of the same name nearby. Situated between the canal and the river Aire the mill belonged to the Lord of the Manor, and everyone in the area was required to take their corn to the mill for grinding. Some of the tracks and paths that exist today were probably formed by generations of local people carrying their annual harvest of grain to the Mill to be ground into flour. The Lord of the Manor received rent from the miller who was his tenant, and the charge for grinding the corn provided income for the miller. It is also recorded that as early as 1567 the Mill had diversified, and was also being used for processing woollen cloth. By 1584 the corn and fulling mills and the house attached to it were occupied by the Buck family, which led to the Mill becoming known as Buck Mill. At that date they also held various pieces of land nearby and by the mid-eighteenth century the Mill no longer had a monopoly for grinding corn, so the emphasis of its production changed towards the wool trade, as part of Bradford's rapidly increasing primary industry.

The Stansfield family rebuilt the Mill around 1800, adding a scribbling mill to the corn and fulling mill. Benjamin Thornton, who also owned Bowling Green Mill in Thackley and Albion Mill in Idle, rented Buck Mill in the 1860s. He built a new warehouse and wool-washing room, which consisted of two large four-storey blocks, along with a boiler house, engine and chimney. By this time the machinery was powered by steam rather than a water wheel. To conserve water for the boiler a dam was made in a field across from the mill. The remains of this can still be seen as a rectangular shape in the field on the opposite side of Buck Mill Lane.

By 1905 the Mill was described as 'Disused' on official maps. For some years before the 1914-18 War the mill was empty and becoming increasingly derelict. Finally, in 1923 the buildings were blown up and a quantity of the stone was used to pave Buck Mill Lane which climbs the hill to Thackley. Foundation stones of the mill complex are still visible but are now more or less completely overgrown, and the area has become unsafe because of long term problems with water leakage from the canal directly above. When the river level is low it is possible to see some early stonework, and elements of the goit and its construction.

But as I stood there on the bridge something else caught my attention. Across the canal from the towpath lies the narrow cobbled Buck Mill Lane. Only a short distance up the lane stands an old cottage which I had noticed some time before on a previous canal side walk. It looked like just any other old cottage but now I could see that the windows and doors were covered with the metal shuttering that usually denotes an empty dwelling. This change in appearance invoked my curiosity and I crossed the canal to have a closer look at the now deserted cottage.

This secluded and romantic building sits quietly amongst the trees atop a short banking a few yards from the lane. The cottage is located up a setted footpath and was once two dwellings which shared the central corniced chimneystack. The house retains a stone roof, indicating its construction in the first half of the 19th century, although traditional window details are absent. Obviously it was now empty and fearing no rebuke from an angry inhabitant I moved closer to investigate.

It was quite a large cottage built of local gritstone and it stood within a clearing in the trees. A weather-beaten stone statue of an Afghan hound guarded the metal shuttered front door. All the windows were boarded up in the same manner and this puzzled me. The building itself appeared to be in good condition so it was not earmarked for demolition due to any poor state of repair. The metal covering over the front door had a gap around the edge and I peered through it to see just an empty cottage inside. The carpeted stairs rose up in front of my eyes and I could see inside the empty sitting room to the side. Apart from being empty it appeared almost perfect and lived in.

Still puzzled I walked round to the side to see a collection of outhouses and sheds. Most of these small individual buildings stood around the edges of a small yard. They each contained a large dog bed and were separated from each other by wire fencing. Was it a dog boarding kennel I mused as I moved around the yard?

Feeding bowls were scattered about on the concrete floor of the yard. I thought I knew all the local boarding kennels as I had used most of them over the years for my own dogs when I had gone away. I started to feel a strange sensation, a feeling of sadness in some way. Not knowing why as it was not a dark brooding place but I was defiantly getting a vibe of loss and sadness. There were no signs of overgrowing vegetation or neglect, no weeds breaking through the concrete. The place looked like it had been vacated only recently and in something of a hurry. I was not scared or anything only puzzled as to why such a fantastic secluded place was empty and unused. Later that evening whilst doing my usual post walk research I found out why.

The report from the local Bradford newspaper The Telegraph and Argus dated 11th April 2014 said "The man behind Buck Wood Animal Sanctuary in Bradford was found dead at his home surrounded by his dogs. Alan Littlewood, 69, was discovered by police after a friend became concerned because she had been unable to contact him by phone. Long-time friend Sue Wood, of Doncaster, told the newspaper how she had been receiving daily texts from Mr Littlewood but these had ended causing her to alert the police. "He told me he was not very well and that he was going to send me a text every day. For about three days up to April 1, I hadn't heard anything. I kept texting him back but my gut instinct was that something was wrong. I rang the police to say I am very concerned about this man who lives in an isolated cottage." she said.

Mr Littlewood was found dead, laid on the settee in the kitchen with his three dogs. A post-mortem examination revealed Mr Littlewood died of pneumonia and died alone in his cottage. He ran the dog rescue operation for more than twenty years and funded it out of his own pocket. Sitting back in my chair in front of my PC I now knew why I had the feeling of sadness. I looked once again at Mr Littlewood's photo on my screen. It was taken in 1993 out amongst the kennels at the side of the cottage. He would have been around the age that Iam now I thought. He looked like a kind and compassionate man, a man who loved his animals and his dogs. I felt an affinity and a connection with him and thought that's the way I want to go when my time comes, surrounded by my beloved dogs.

I left the cottage to take the short distance back down to the canal side and moved off once again towards Shipley. I passed by the site of the long demolished Canal Tavern opposite Thackley West Wood and then followed the towpath past where the Airedale Iron Works once stood. From here the canal side scenery changed from a pastoral to an industrial setting. Small quarries and ironworks once lay all around this area with Dockfield Road as its centre.

Small industrial units gave way to the massive Junction Mills. This gargantuan building was constructed in several phases with the earliest section being built alongside the canal. It is here where The Bradford Canal branched off form the Leeds-Liverpool canal to make its short two mile journey to the basin in Bradford city centre. This short canal closed in 1922 and is today stagnant, overgrown and littered. Beside is the derelict and forlorn Junction House, a former Toll House and warehouse. Built in 1774 this building had two gable end loading doors but is set back from the canal bank so it would appear that cargo would have been brought onto the bank before being hoisted inside for storage. Alongside Junction House and crossing the Leeds-Liverpool canal is the beautiful and famous Junction Bridge. Constructed in 1774 this Grade II listed single arch bridge with a stone walkway screams packhorse at you. Visions of labouring, sweating beasts piled high with bales of cloth filled my mind as I passed beneath it on my way towards Shipley. This area has seen some development in recent years with a block of fine canal side apartments opposite Junction Mills being the most noteworthy. The view from the balconies whilst sipping Prosecco must be invigorating.

Shipley town centre was looming in the middle distance as Lou and I passed over the point where Bradford Beck drains into the river Aire below us. Its journey that begins as a series of small streams and individual becks in the high hills surrounding Bradford ends here. I always stop to admire the tiny cottage aside Gallows Bridge just a short distance from here. This early 18th century cottage sits snug alongside the canal towpath and despite its unsecluded position I have always liked this spot. The area around Gallows Bridge itself was once home to several wood framed mills. Hence the name

"Gallows" and contrary to what I always thought it has nothing to do with the apparatus for hanging people.

Crossing over the small footbridge here Lou and I walked the short distance along Briggate to the bus stop where we could catch our usual bus back to Wrose and home. I had done this particular canal walk a couple of times in the past so most of it was not new to me but the one thing I did take away from today was Buck Wood Cottage and Mr Littlewood. I will never forget the unexplained feeling of sadness that I felt whilst at his former dog sanctuary, but knowing what I now know it all makes sense. I dearly wish that I had known the man whilst he was alive.

It was a bright sunny late morning when the bus that had chugged up the valley from Bingley deposited Lou and I in what is known as Eldwick Bottom. This ancient hollow between two small hills was originally a bridging point over Eldwick Beck with no permanent settlement surrounding it. The enclosure of the land around Eldwick Hall was created in the late 16th century. Eldwick Spring Farm, originally established in 1588 dates from this time. At this time the only building on the valley floor was Eldwick Beck Mill. Built in 1800 this mill was for a short time used for Scribbling (the processing of raw fleeces) but converted to use as a corn mill in 1828.

The building of this mill provided the impetus for further development. Cottages were constructed as well as a Wesleyan Methodist Church and Sunday school. We walked the short distance along The Green in the direction of the magnificent Compensation reservoir and stopped outside The Acorn Inn. Built in 1820 this fully licensed inn, with accommodation for guests and lodgers was used for a time around 1841 to house Navvies who were working on the construction of nearby Compensation reservoir. Towards the end of the 19th century it also became a popular destination for workers enjoying the local scenery. With some degree of difficulty I resisted the lure of a lunchtime pint of well-kept locally brewed ale and pressed on towards the old packhorse trail that follows the length of Eldwick Beck towards Tewet House and the famed "Paved Causeway".

The Green is a well surfaced and smooth road with a gentle ascent which after a short distance turns steeper and into a much rougher cobbled narrow track that was obviously a packhorse trail in the past. I paused for breath and admired the vista across the undulating fields towards the approaching majestic Compensation Reservoir. Turning to the right to join The Monks Way, as the paved causeway was once known, I started to ascend down the well-worn and weathered flat stones that had been used in centuries past by Medieval religious men. Flanked on either side by high stout dry stone walls the track undulated up and down like a roller coaster till we reached the Eldwick Beck overflow from the reservoir.

As we passed by Compensation reservoir I noticed the many signs warning against swimming in the cold and algae ridden water. Across the fields in the distance I could see the outline of Eldwick Hall which we would soon pass on our way back to Eldwick Bottom after joining Otley Road.

Eldwick Hall is a Grade II listed house at Lane Head. The Hall is initialled and dated "R L 1696" (Richard Longbottom) but the first floor doorway to the right bears the inscription "IHS 1716". Built of dressed gritstone with a stone slate roof Eldwick Hall combines classical features with the local vernacular style. It was once reputedly owned by The Knights of Jerusalem who gave shelter and food from here to weary travellers. On the front of the hall are thirteen stone steps that once led to an isolated chamber where food and water was provided. In 1755 a Lisbon banker named Benjamin Harboyne saw his home and fortune swallowed up by an earthquake. The shock affected him to such a degree that he became a raving madman. He was brought back to England and spent the rest of his days in chains at Eldwick hall.

Walking back down Otley road towards Eldwick Bottom we passed the farmstead of Crag Top before reaching a small long deserted Sandstone quarry. This quarry provided slabs of Sandstone for local buildings before being abandoned in the late 18th century. Today it is overgrown with Larch and Birch trees and tracts of dense vegetation. Quarries such as this are situated all over the Bradford area and are evidence of the past industrial endeavours of hard working Bradford people.

We soon reached Spring Lane and turned on here to make our way along the valley floor to climb up through open moorland in the direction of Baildon. This section of Spring Lane running from Eldwick Beck to Glovershaw was repaired and widened to 7-8 yards in 1777, suggesting it was a route of some importance, and perhaps like Green Lane it was used by packhorses. I carried on towards the site of the former Eldwick Beck Mill which today has been converted into private houses. The mill pond still remains and is home to a collection of brightly coloured ducks in a peaceful setting.

As Spring Lane becomes Glovershaw Lane it winds gently uphill towards the moor and contains no pavement so I had to reel Lou's extendable lead all the way in to exert full control over her. The last thing I wanted was a semi mental Jack Russell to be wandering all over the road chasing the passing traffic. Lou and I stopped for a while at the side of an ancient old stone roadside drinking trough, and listened intently to the trickle of Eldwick Spring as it filled the void before running off under the road.

In medieval times Baildon Moor and indeed much of this area contained Ironstone pits and small Iron Smelting works. Evidence of early Iron smelting works have been found at Glovershaw Beck and Load Pit Beck. Some evidence of ancient iron smelting was discovered alongside Glovershaw Beck just above Hope farm.

Passing by numerous quaint old 18th century cottages and farmsteads we wound our way along Glovershaw Lane past Low Gate towards the site of the last working coal pit on Baildon Moor at Lobley Gate. This deep shaft mine closed in 1863 due to excessive flooding. We were now at the foot of an area known as Windy Hill. This area once contained many small coal pits and also numerous ancient cup and ring marked rocks. The faint outline of the distant Dobrubben caravan site came into view as we tramped along the moorland road. An elderly couple sat nearby in their car enjoying the view and their sandwiches as the traffic sped by at an illegal pace. The long arm of the law obviously doesn't extend to Baildon Moor unless there are any errant 4x4's carving up the sacred moorland.

The area to the left of what was now Bingley Road is taken up by part of Baildon Golf Course. Iam not a golfer but if I was I cannot imagine a more pleasant arena in which to display my skills with the little white ball. We soon reached Acrehowe Hill, the site of both an ancient Prehistoric Tumulus and a stone cross. The curious remains of the Tumulus earthworks are discernible in the grassland to the left hand side of the road just by a small car park. This is a loose double-ring of stones, fifty feet across, surrounded by a shallow trench which was most notable on the south and east sides. Two urns were also uncovered in the 1800's near the centre of the ring, nearly two feet down, containing the cremated remains of Iron Age people.

The stone cross was on the other side of the road from the prehistoric circle. This old cross was destroyed sometime in the first half of the 19th century by one of the stewards to the Lady of the Manor of Baildon, a Mr Walker. The cross was erected (probably between the 12th and 14th centuries) amidst a cluster of heathen burials and cup-and-rings, many of which would have been known by local peasants as having old lore or superstitions about them.

Dodging the errant flying golf balls Lou and I carried on Bingley road to reach a long disused small Millstone Grit quarry named Eaves Crag. I spent some time searching amongst the rocks for one single rock at ground level that is marked with a Prehistoric cup and ring symbol. Upon giving up my search I decided that both Lou and I should have our packed lunch. I settled down on a large flat piece of rock to enjoy the early afternoon sun and my usual cheese and onion sandwiches. Lou waited patiently at my feet for her turn with the unwanted crusts. She was not to be disappointed as I always share my dinner with her.

Directly across the road stand three Victorian reservoirs. These reservoirs, on a 3.5-acre site, were built in the 1850s by Baildon Urban District Council Water Works to provide the village with fresh water. The village had one of the highest death rates in the country because of water-borne diseases and up to 25 households would use the same toilet. Two of the three structures are devoid of water and have been partially stripped of their stonework. The third contains some water and this allows the superb craftsmanship of the Victorian engineers and stone masons to be seen inside. Sitting there on the side I could almost imagine a rock concert taking place within this magnificent structure. Sadly the reservoirs have become somewhat of a financial liability for their owners Baildon Golf Club and are earmarked for demolition and further redevelopment

From the reservoirs we walked on along Bingley Road to cross over Hawksworth Road and then along Moorside. This track skirts along the edge of the disused Low Eaves Delf, from which high quality Gritstone was extracted in the 18th century. On the right we passed by a lovely old house named Strawberry Gardens. This house was originally known as Lantie Gardens, after its builder. In Edwardian times it was renowned as a local tearoom, and the delights offered could be enjoyed either inside or outdoors. Fresh fruit such as cherries and gooseberries were sold from the orchard, and it is recorded that the owners occasionally supplied the Whitsuntide teas for the local Sunday school. The 1901 census records William and Mary Wilkinson living there, 66 and 70 years old respectively, and describes them as market gardeners.

Carrying on down the well-used footpath between Hazel Head Wood and Willy Wood I had to carefully avoid a group of horses that had been stoked into some degree of anger by Lou parson's incessant aggressive yapping. Like most Jack Russell's she intensely dislikes the vacuum cleaner, sweeping brushes and horses. Why she picks fights with beasts of burden many times her size is a mystery to me as she has been brought up alongside them as there is always a herd in the fields next to our house. These fearless little dogs are a law unto themselves of that there is no doubt, and I have come to understand this in the many years I have lived amongst them.

After outrunning the mad equines for some way across the field I vaulted over a drystone wall to once again join the footpath, and taking on board the wisdom to stay on footpaths and not take short cuts near horses, we walked on for a short while till I reached Tong Park war memorial where I could take a well-deserved breather. This memorial commemorates the residents of Tong Park who were killed or missing in World War I (19 names) and World War II (2 names). It was erected in 1922-3 and was paid for by the Denby family who first came to Baildon in 1853 when William Denby Junior bought Gill Mill. It is situated in a rather strange but quaint position out in the countryside overlooking the Cricket pitch of Tong Park and the mill pond of the Worsted spinning and carding mill.

Gill Mill was built in 1778 and was the first steam powered mill in the Bradford area by some eight years. A small steam engine was installed by Haliday and Watson in 1790 to add to the power already produced by the water from the adjacent mill pond. The Cricket pitch sits in a natural amphitheatre, which in 1914 held a crowd of 3,000 spectators for a cup tie against Windhill. Tong Park Cricket Club was formed in 1880 and this is their third ground.

After our short rest at the War Memorial we pressed on along Lonk House Road and over the railway tunnel to pause briefly at an outstanding row of former mill workers cottages named Primrose Row. Constructed of solid Sandstone blocks these cottages are fairly representative of the type of humble dwellings found all over the Bradford area in the vicinity of the many long since disappeared Victorian mills. From here it was only a short walk downhill to Otley Road where we could catch a bus into Shipley and then back to home in Wrose. So after enjoying a most eventful and informative few hours walking we did exactly that.

Allerton to Denholme

I usually have to take two or even three buses to reach the starting point for my walks and this was no different. Two buses and 45 minutes after leaving home Lou and I were fighting our way through a group of smokers on the pavement outside Bradford Royal Infirmary. Being an ex-heavy smoker I resisted the temptation to preach like John Wesley to these sinners and simply shook my E-Cig at them with a wild manic grin. Many years before I had done just what they are doing and knew what it was like so couldn't be too hard on them.

The city of Bradford's main Hospital replaced the aged Victorian Infirmary on the end of Lumb Lane at Westgate in 1936. Bradford's Lord Mayor in 1908-09 Sir James Hill (11 March 1849 – 17 January 1936) devoted his year in office to raising £100,000 towards the cost of a new infirmary. He himself donated £30,000 but sadly died four months before the new Royal Infirmary on Duckworth Lane was opened. The final cost was £500,000 which was raised by public subscription, and this figure would equate to eighteen million pounds in today's money.

Situated directly across the road from the hospital is the magnificent Gothic entrance arch and lodge of Lady Royd Hall. I was aware that this Gothic style house and its associated buildings were in a state of disrepair and was earmarked for redevelopment, and as I had never visited it before it was one of the main reasons for this particular walk. This brooding Grade II listed Gothic house was designed by Bradford architects Milnes and Francis for the textile magnate Henry Williamson and was constructed in close grained Sandstone in 1865. It was a fine example of a mid-Victorian detached house displaying high levels of craftsmanship throughout.

The house retains much of its original layout including door cases with decorative mouldings, panelled doors, elegant moulded plasterwork to ceilings and cornices in all the principal rooms together with many unique and detailed fireplaces throughout. It sits in an elevated position amidst mature and secluded north-south sloping grounds. In 1929 it was purchased by Bradford Girls Grammar school and has been in their hands until recently when it was offered for sale and redevelopment. The gate lodge was constructed in the same style as were the further outbuildings, cottages and stables connected with the house. During the Second World War the house was used as both an evacuation and reception centre for girls from the south of England.

We entered the grounds via the archway and walked down the leafy carriage drive towards the house. There appeared to be a gang of workmen putting up screens and barriers of some description and one of them shot me a quizzical look from beneath his hardhat. Guessing that maybe I shouldn't have been in the grounds to start with I did an about turn as smart as any private on parade would do, and yanking Lou along scuttled back towards the arch and the semi derelict row of cottages I had seen on my way in.

This small row of cottages was built to accommodate the house and estate workers, but now is in a state of advanced decay and most are boarded up and secure. But perhaps not secure enough to deter the entry of a hardened local historian thought I. So when I saw an open door in the end cottage the chance to explore inside was just too much. Despite assuming that it had become a haven for some local drug addicts I was quite surprised to see that the inside was pretty much just as it had been left when the last occupants moved out. The front room was actually still carpeted with a sickly coloured pink carpet but with no sign of any tramps or druggies having been there.

I stood at the foot of the stairs for a moment mulling over who had lived there and what their position at the grand house nearby would have been when alert as ever, Lou darted headlong up the stairs after a black shape on legs that had been sat there watching us. She was as always on her extendable lead so I had no choice but to fly up the stairs with her.

Whatever she was chasing had leaped up into a void through a hole in the ceiling and as much as a Jack Russell can jump there was no chance she would be following her prey upwards. But her loud yapping would alert the workmen nearby and remembering that I really should not have been there I thought it best that we did the proverbial vanishing act. Besides I was not sure if the shape I saw for a fleeting second was a large cat and not a big fat rat. Jack Russell's tend to chase both avidly, and so reeling Lou's lead in and grabbing her snout to silence her I made a quick exit down the stairs and back out into the sunlight. We gratefully emerged onto Duckworth Lane without encountering any high Vis jacket wearing builders still wondering what the hell it was I had seen in the cottage. And I was quite glad I had a fearless hard little dog with me.

Following the perimeter wall of the grounds along Duckworth Lane and passing the coach house and stables we made our way towards Allerton. After the junction with Crows Trees Lane, Duckworth Lane becomes Pearson Lane and this section of road is lined by a number of magnificent and imposing grand Victorian houses. These houses would have been built for fairly wealthy middle class wool and textile merchants and perhaps the odd Bradford Solicitor or Doctor. Just a short way up Chellow Terrace on the left is a simple and plain Bungalow. What caught my attention was a most unusual large ornate sandstone arch guarding the driveway.

This obviously was once the entrance to a much grander house than a mere bungalow, and as I subsequently discovered this house was named Throstle Nest. Originally the site contained a small farmstead which belonged to a clothier named Richard Tetley, but this was replaced by the smart large Victorian house and attached gardens of Throstle Nest. This was built by a JP from Allerton named James Hill sometime in the 18th century.

Retracing my steps back to Pearson Lane I made my way once again towards Allerton, and after passing by the old Prospect Worsted mill arrived at Allerton's war memorial in Ladyhill Park. I have always had an interest for war memorials and remembered this one from a visit here years ago as it stands in a nice peaceful little park directly opposite from the Prospect Methodist Chapel. The graveyard for the chapel has always puzzled me as it contains very few headstones that remain standing. Amongst those that do still stand in situ are eleven headstones that commemorate Commonwealth war graves.

Most of the remaining headstones are simply propped up against the perimeter wall that surrounds the graveyard. Leaving the graveyard behind me I made my way down Chapel lane and turned onto Grange Road. After passing the cottages that remain near the site of Allerton Grange I walked along Saffron Drive in the direction of Allerton Lanes. I wanted to see the former Allerton Parish Workhouse named Dean House which was nearby. This house was built in 1605 by a Yeoman named Robert Dean. It was constructed in the "Halifax" style of coursed Sandstone and Gritstone, with a triple gabled front and mullioned and transom windows. The corner stone panel on the left hand gable is inscribed with the initials "RD" with a cross of The Knights of Jerusalem. Today it is a private residence of some interest in the local area.

Leaving behind Dean House Lou and I walked up Allerton lane towards Hill Top and after passing by the now derelict Old Kings Head pub turned onto Cote Lane. After walking past a clutch of quaint old 18th century former Weavers cottages it was obvious we had left the urban sprawl of Allerton behind and were starting to hit the countryside at Allerton Road. The only house of any note on this stretch of country road is Smithfield House on the right opposite Moorhouse Moor.

This open moorland is dotted with old disused coal shafts and bell pits including the once quite substantial Allerton and Wilsden Colliery. The road here has no pavement and I had to be vigilant with the dog as the traffic passed by at speed as it always seems to do on open stretches of road like this. I was quite surprised to see an armchair simply plonked in the middle of a field surrounded by a herd of cows. It was positioned in such a way as to afford anyone using it a great view over towards Wilsden. As we approached another sad boarded up local pub the Duke of York (what is it with these Dukes and Kings? no staying power?), we passed by the lane leading to a farm dated 1840 named The Mustard Pot. This Grade II listed building built of Sandstone with square mullioned windows has the most wonderful of names.

Reaching The Duke of York Lou and I turned down Dean Lane towards the small row of former quarry workers cottages called Egypt. Apparently named to commemorate the invasion of Egypt by Napoleon in 1798 but in these parts you never know. Just before we reached the bottom of the hill and the cottages we came across what I can only call carnage. For there on the road before us were six dead and splattered rabbits all in a line. Judging from their condition they were what is known as "roadkill". They looked so fresh that Lou could have eaten their flattened meat there and then but there was no way I would allow that. I know from experience that fresh meat like this does strange things to her insides and I was not prepared to sit next to her on the bus back home whilst she let one out. Besides one has to have respect for the dead and it just wouldn't have been right and correct. So we passed them by and left their carcases for the crows and foxes that would inevitably come looking before too long. The fields beside Dean Lane are pock marked with the familiar scars and bumps of long ago quarrying activity and this was evident as we wound our way down the hill towards Egypt.

Stone was generally used for domestic building in the Bradford area from the mid-seventeenth century. By the eighteenth century, quarry and masonry methods improved and landowners' accounts indicate much rebuilding in stone, and the opening up of delphs for wall stones. From the I790s until the early nineteenth century numerous active delphs were providing stone for enclosure walls, mills and housing. The early quarries at Bell Dean and Egypt probably opened to meet this growing demand. In 1876 there were 30 active quarry's in the Egypt area employing 450 workers some as young as eight years old. From 1860 the stone industry in Bradford boomed giving rise to investment in steam powered machinery for lifting, transporting and sawing the stone. The double sided row of cottages at the bottom of the hill were originally built to house workers and their family's from the nearby quarry's There was a small Methodist Chapel to the rear but this closed in the 1960's. A local man named Arthur Jowett was the secretary of the Chapel for some forty five years till it closed.

The road past the cottages was until quite recently enclosed by massive forbidding high stone walls known locally as "The Walls of Jericho". These were constructed to hold back the massive amounts of rubble and soil which had been hewn from the ground over time in the pursuit of valuable stone. The walls are now gone and the road has been rearranged but one huge sidepiece right next to the end cottage survives, and it was on here that we rested for a while and ate our packed lunch. I sat there dangling my legs over the edge and could almost hear the chip chip chipping sound of the men toiling in days gone by. After our rest we started up the steep winding Egypt Road towards The Rock and Heifer Inn and stopped to admire the nearby row of cottages built by quarry owner Jonathan Ackroyd. A date stone on one of the cottages indicates the date of construction as 1820. We climbed gently up Rock Lane past another clutch of well preserved and loved quarry workers cottages at Back Heights. Small disused quarries were all around us as we approached another tiny hamlet named Moscow. It was here that we turned off the main road and headed down Ten yards Lane. Lou and I were heading for Doe Park Reservoir and then further beyond our final destination of Denholme, but first I wanted to check out something I had seen on Google Earth the night before whilst planning my route.

Passing the ancient and delectable Spring Hall Farm we soon came upon the strange oval shaped object that I had seen the night before. From the photographs taken high up in space I could not make out the purpose of this strange shape, but on the ground it was obvious what it was. It was an oval track with short stout fencing on both the inside and the outside. It looked too small for the racing or trotting of horses or ponies. Not wanting to let it bother me for too long as I could search the Internet when I got home as to its reason we moved on down the long and thankfully level country road towards the reservoir.

Now when two female Jack Russell's come face to face round a corner it usually goes one of two ways. Either they rub noses and make friends and there is loads of playful pawing or they start fighting like two drunken women outside a Bradford nightclub. So when Lou and I turned off the road and onto a small track to reach the reservoir and literally walked into a woman with her Jack Russell bitch I was ready for the worst. Thankfully this woman was of the country type and she was obviously used to handling such fearsome tiny beasts. The woman pulled her Russell to the side and holding her there with some strength the bloodbath was averted. I needn't have worried as both dogs just wanted to play so I started to make small talk with the farmer's wife. "Ooooh arrr aye lad aye what you've just seen is a Greyhound practice track aye arrr aye" (She didn't talk like a Wurzel I've just added that for dramatic effect)

It turned out she lived on the farm next to the track and told me that the owner raced Greyhounds all over the north of England and he used it for himself and his friends to train and exercise their skinny and willowy hounds. I was quite disappointed that I had not thought of that myself. So after bidding farewell to the woman in the flat cap and wellies we continued down the thin rocky track towards the large body of water before us.

Doe Park Reservoir is a mid-size body of water situated to the east of Denholme village. It is surrounded by farmland on three sides and there is a small sewage works between it and Denholme. It is quite an open reservoir with only a few small trees and shrubs to obscure the shoreline. It is higher up the same valley as Hewenden Reservoir and its river outlet eventually becomes Harden Beck. The reservoir is fed by Stubden Beck flowing East down from the Stubden and Thornton Moor Reservoirs and Denholme Beck flowing North down Denholme Clough. There is also a sailing club and a small group of fishermen that use it on a regular basis. Activities on the water include sailing, canoeing, kayaking, dragon boating and raft building. It is also popular with bird watchers. Here birds such as Water Rail, Reed Warbler, Grasshopper Warbler and Pied Flycatcher have been seen among good numbers of common migrants. The Sewage works along the west side attracts Wagtails and Pipits on the filter beds as well as Finches and Warblers in the bushes surrounding them.

We walked across the concrete concourse at the head of the reservoir in the direction of our last stop Denholme. At the end of the concourse stands Reservoir House dated 1858. It is an impressive 3 bedroomed detached property located directly next to the Reservoir and surrounded by stunning rural views. It even has a gym apparently. We walked steadily up Foster Park View towards the village of Denholme where I knew we could catch a bus back to Bradford. As we sat in the bus shelter on the main road an old man sitting next to us enquired where we had been that day. "Oh just to Egypt and then on to Moscow" I replied. He was obviously a local man as he didn't seem that impressed. Anyone else might have thought those many thousands of miles was one hell of a journey to complete in a day.

Tong Street to Wyke via Birkenshaw

The Boomtown Rats didn't like Mondays, so much so they even wrote a song about it. I don't like Sundays and the only things I usually do on such days is either watch Premier League Football on Sky or go down Wetherspoons for a dinner and a belly full of real ale. So just for a change on this Sunday I decided to get out there and let my feet hit the street so to speak. So with that in mind I got up early, had a good breakfast and packed my gear and headed for Bradford Interchange to catch a bus that would drop Lou and I at the end of Tong Street near to the famed Lapwater Hall.

Tong Street itself is a long and straight road and it should come as no surprise that it was once the main Roman road through this area. Many Roman artefacts such as coins and pieces of vases have been found over the years in this area, and there was even a Roman fort at nearby Hunsworth. But such ideas were far from my mind as I alighted the bus by the site of the long gone Newmarket Colliery. Today this area is simply a large field with only the odd bump and scrape on the ground to signify to its past use. It was for a time in the 18th century one of this areas many small coal pits and mines. On the 11th of November 1854 there was a massive explosion caused by a build-up of Methane gas that took the lives of six local miners. Amongst those killed were William Blackburn, John Chadwick, John Runder and Peter Palmer.

After crossing Tong Street we walked down the side of another boarded up Bradford pub, The Old Duke William and made our way down Cross Street towards part of Tong Moor and the site of the disappeared Birkenshaw and Tong Railway Station. This station was on the Gildersome branch of The Leeds and Halifax railway and it opened on the 20th August 1856. It closed to passengers on the 5th of October 1953. Today the site is occupied by small light industrial units and no trace of the station remains.

After this point Cross Lane becomes Station Lane. Lou Parson and I walked past a series of substantial late 18th century Victorian detached houses. Some of these were indeed rather grand and will have been built for high middle class wool and textile merchants based in the city of Bradford or perhaps even Leeds. The road is lined with mature elderly trees and the high solid stone walls that usually denote the presence of houses of this nature. One of these houses, the grand Wynberg was designed and built around the turn of the 19th century and contains many of the fine architectural features of that period. The house is soundly constructed of coursed stone under a multi-pitched slate roof. The generous family accommodation is arranged over 3 floors and includes two generous reception rooms, kitchen and utility arrangements, and six bedrooms and the house bathroom. After a few seconds of dreaming and admiration of such a fine residence I came to my senses and carried on down the leafy road towards the more working class village of Birkenshaw.

Up to the 18th century Birkenshaw was no more than a rural hamlet with a scattering of humble yet functional small cottages. The development of the village came with the purchase of land by the Emmet family and the establishment of a foundry for iron smelting. Although this foundry closed in 1815 the community was already well established and growing with the addition of work in local coal pits and the Woollen mills nearby. The Emmet family made provision by granting, in 1828, land for the building of a church in the village. Parliament granted £3000 and the mock Gothic church of St Pauls was the result. The first Vicar died after only three months but his successor, Rev Henry John Smith, was vicar from 1832-1862. His contribution to the parish was outstanding. He began the Sunday school, and then built two school buildings in the church grounds.

We crossed over the main Bradford Road and entered a small area of tiny but still loved cottages called Furnace Lane. This led us onto open countryside to what is known as Navigation Bank. In 1780-1 John Emmet the Elder, Thomas Holden, William Bolland and William Emmet, iron founders of Halifax, leased land in Birkenshaw for a furnace and foundry, which was operating by 1782. Thomas Holden and William Bolland both withdrew their capital, leaving the company in difficulties, and when the prices of iron goods slumped in 1815 the business closed.

Navigation Bank runs southwards from the foundry site. Little is known about it but there are three theories: that it was a canal to bring in supplies of coal and limestone, or to take away slag (to the 'blue hills', which might have been slag heaps), or that it was a linear reservoir to supply water for the water-wheel on Birkenshaw Beck. It was a strip of water retained by a bank constructed along the hillside, its inner wall faced with stone. Although it could have served as a catch water drain, one would expect it to have had a fall towards the Foundry mill if that was its sole purpose.

To avoid the numerous large herds of aggressive looking cows that populated the fields we walked along the bank for a while. Even though I had done my usual research and planning the night before I knew that the direction we were heading in was taking us away from our next destination which was the village of Oakenshaw. But there was just too many of these mad looking cows for my liking so I thought discretion was the better part of valour and urging Lou onwards with some haste we carried on. This was to prove something of a mistake on my part and was to literally lead to me losing my trousers.

After a short while stumbling through the fields and over more than a few fences, I glanced behind us to noticed with some relief the cows had thinned out somewhat. Down a dip in the field runs Lodge Beck so we made for here and followed it along the contours of the land for perhaps twenty minutes or so. I stopped to check my well-thumbed and dog eared map of the area and realised that we were lost. As I was now in quite dense woodland that surrounded the beck at this point I could not see the far away church spire at Oakenshaw. "Ah right, cross the beck, over this barbed wire fence and through this small field and we'll hit Hunsworth Lane and be back on track" thought I.

I sat at the side of the beck by a grotto like place where the ochre red coloured water ran down through a series of rough stone steps before disappearing away down through the vegetation. The wire fence was only a few feet away up the banking so with some effort in the hot early afternoon sun we crossed the beck and climbed the bank. I lifted Lou up and over the fence and throwing my backpack after her started to climb the sharply barbed wire fence. As I wobbled like a drunken Priest on the apex of the fence I just knew what was coming. The ripping sound of my light canvas army issue trousers told me that what I knew was coming had indeed come. If you picture Robinson Crusoe at this point you'll have some idea of what had happened. Three quarters of one leg of my kegs was swinging in the breeze on the fence and I was miles away from home with only a mad Jack Russell, no money and an all-day bus rider ticket.

But being the resourceful man that Iam I thought I would simply roll up my still complete trouser leg to make a pair of shorts. Ok so one side would look neat and rolled up and the other leg raggy and torn but it would have to do. Problem sorted and if I looked a bit strange I'd fit in well when we got back to Bradford and no one would notice. The field we had landed in was more of a pressing problem though as the grass had to be at least 6 feet tall. So tall in fact that I couldn't see the other side but I knew Hunsworth Lane lay somewhere over that way, so for what seemed like an age we battled through the field and the strength sapping grass. When we eventually reached the road I looked like and felt like an extra from the Bridge on the River Kwai film but we had made it.

After a short march up Hunsworth Lane to make up the lost time we reached Hunsworth Lower Lane and the farmhouse of Lower Copley. I love to see a good old farmyard with its vehicles and assorted equipment. Sometimes you can see very old and ancient ploughs and things like that, but in one corner of this farmyard there were a number of battered and well used military vehicles. A rather strange sight in a West Yorkshire rural farmyard without doubt.

After battling through more long grass fields, across Cockleshaw Beck and through the rather dense Chatts Wood we emerged on Cliff Holmes Lane near to the old Oak Mills at Oakenshaw. Originally a corn mill, Oak Mills was converted to textile use at the beginning of this century. It was previously a multi storey stone built structure which was damaged by fire many years ago. Today only a small single storey former stable building section remains. So far since losing half my trousers we had not seen anyone which pleased me, but now we were entering suburbia and civilisation as we passed through the roadway tunnel under the M606 Motorway and onto Wyke Lane.

A short walk up Wyke Lane brought us to The Oakenshaw Memorial Cross. This fine structure stands right in the middle of the road and traffic has to drive around the side of it to pass by. This large ornamental cross on a base of four steps was erected by the Lord of the Manor Dr Richard Richardson in 1702 in memory of his wife Sarah. Erected on the site of a previous medieval cross, this Grade II listed slender stone column sits on a four step circular podium. It is surmounted by an elaborate finial which has a sundial to each face. In the wall opposite is a stone carving containing the "Arms of Bradford" and the legend "Labor Omnia Vincit". It belongs to Cross House Farm, which was built in 1601. I have been informed that it was brought here from the Bradford slaughter house in Hammerton Street by a previous owner who had a shop and wholesale business there. There is a similar one from the same source outside Cliff Hollins Farm nearby.

The section of Wyke Lane between The Memorial Cross and the disused Oakenshaw Railway tunnel contains a varied selection of 18th century former quarry workers and weavers cottages. There is even a couple of the delectable one storey whitewash walled stone slate roofed cottages. These can be seen all over Bradford mostly in places near to long gone quarries as they were usually home to the workers. We carried on towards Wyke admiring this veritable cornucopia of local vernacular buildings as we went.

We had still not seen a single living person when we reached Oakenshaw railway tunnel. This tunnel was constructed in 1848 to enable the road from Oakenshaw to Wyke to pass over the Low Moor fork of The Spen Valley railway line. This line formed part of the Lancashire and Yorkshire railway, and for much of the way at the Low Moor end it followed the route of the river Spen. In 2001 a stretch of the long disused line was converted to a cycling and walking route named The Spen Valley Greenway by SUSTRANS. The tunnel was constructed using the "cut and cover" method with one end collapsing during the building work.

Lou and I carried on past the tunnel and along Wyke Lane through a stretch of open countryside interrupted only by the cottages of Pearson Fold before reaching the site of the former Ben Ing pit. This pit only operated for a short period from 1896 to 1905. Amongst the various bumps and lumps in the now reclaimed grassland I noticed a small handful of metal vents denoting the sites of the former coal shafts themselves. We turned off up Wilson Road and crossed over the path of a tiny railway as denoted on my map. This narrow gauge rail track was used to transport minerals to the furnaces and factories at Low Moor Chemical Works nearby but as of today has long since disappeared. A short section of the old Wilson Road still shows the original cobbled surface. This whole area is pockmarked with old brickworks and coal shafts providing evidence of its rich industrial past.

It was here that we met our first fellow humans since our walk started back at Tong Street. Perhaps everyone else had been in the pub all afternoon watching the football? The young lad we ran into was leading two enthusiastic and bouncy working Terriers. One a Jack Russell and the other a Border Terrier and they immediately made friends with Lou Parson. His dogs were used for ratting on the local farms and had that knarled and slightly battered appearance that these kind of dogs always have. These breeds of dogs should taste work at some point in their lives as it is in their blood to chase and hunt down quarry and it is always good to meet some that have. Although both my other now elderly and arthritic Jack Russell Missy Moo and Lou have killed the odd rat back at home near our cottage, working in this sense of the word is something they are not accustomed to doing.

So after bidding farewell to the dogs and their owner we carried on towards the village of Wyke where we could catch the bus back to Bradford. At least I wasn't away from home for 28 years like Robinson Crusoe.

All Alone Road to Wrose Road via Idle Hill

For a change no bus journeys were needed for this walk as it was close to my home in Wrose and is what I would term a home game. The area is one that I know so well and it is always a pleasure to walk amongst the many ghosts of the past which surround this historical piece of Bradford. The route of my walk took my through land that still to this day shows evidence of long ago human industrial endeavour in the form of 18th century coal pits and tiny Sandstone delfs. These are of course long gone but the evidence is there if you look for it.

Lou and I started on the Wrose Road end of Westfield Lane and soon passed by the cottages which once belonged to Westfield Farm. Set back slightly from the road these quaint dwellings of simple rustic design are all that remain of a once busy and bustling farm. Moving on we soon arrived at the junction with All Alone Road where the row of cottages named Starting Post stand. Constructed of coursed Sandstone bricks with a solid slate roof this short row of originally two cottages was built circa 1800. The third cottage was added at a later date as was the rear extension of the first two. All Alone Road led originally to the first house to be built on the hillside overlooking Idle, right on the edge of the moor, and from the valley dwellers' point of view below, it must have looked "all alone" up on the hill. But before that area was reached we stopped for a few moments at a point just by the present day motor vehicle repair garage where what was known as the "Starting Stoup" used to stand.

The starting stoup, or post, was the area from which the Idle Moor Horse Races used to run from. In the Leeds Mercury of Tuesday 15th July, 1729, and also on Tuesday 6th of July, 1731, it announces that: "races will be run on Idle over Moor by any horse, mare, or gelding for Plate of the value of £3 and £7." Although the old Ordnance Survey maps show a building on this site I have sadly not been able to find any information to confirm this. Today the area is covered by open fields which contain a handful of old stable buildings and horses belonging to the nearby Roleystone Horse and Pony Sanctuary.

As I sat on the stone wall overlooking Idle Moor my imagination turned to one of the few Second World War occurrences that involved the city of Bradford. The Battle of Britain was over and had been won by the RAF but the odd German Luftwaffe aircraft still roamed above the skies of Britain. On the night of 4th / 5th May 1941 a German Junkers Ju88 M2 twin engine multirole aircraft was tasked with laying mines in the Irish Sea off Belfast. Over the North of England they were intercepted by an RAF Bristol Beaufighter of 25 Squadron flown by P/O Kenneth Hollowell and Sgt Richard Crossman. One of the Ju88's engines was damaged over the Bradford area and after losing height and releasing the bombload, two of the crew bailed out. The aircraft was attacked again which caused further damage and the two remaining crew left by parachute. The aircraft crashed into a wood yard and an adjoining row of houses centred on 13-15 High Street, Idle at around 00.45hrs. Sadly at least three civilians were unfortunately killed and four others injured with one succumbing to his injuries a few weeks later. One of the fatalities was a twelve month old baby girl.

The Luftwaffe airmen landed across the North-Leeds area; in the Guiseley, Otley and the Farnley districts and were taken prisoner. The German pilot one Ernst Jurgens drifted slowly down towards the fields close to the houses on Westfield lane. The pilot landed on Idle Hill near to what was Crockers Farm. According to reports two farmhands from All Alone Farm and other men ran to the field where the pilot was landing. The German, apparently just happy to have survived the shooting down simply walked towards his captors with his hands in the air and surrendered. The houses were never re-built and today the site of the crash has a simple seat with two raised flower beds marking it. There is a possibility that one of the engines remains buried at the crash site.

We turned around and walked down the track next to what appeared to be a graveyard of fork lift trucks and a stone yard towards the empty and disused former home of Israel Newton's Boiler Works. The firm of Newton and Sons took over this building and naming it Summerley Works started to build and repair steam Locomotive boilers in 1906. Prior to this the building was used as a stone sawing mill for the local quarries. The famous steeplejack and television personality Fred Dibnah MBE recorded a program in this building some time ago but today it is empty and almost derelict.

Newtons moved their business to Derbyshire some time ago and still do work for the heritage railways. Although all the doors and entrances had been bricked up there was one small hole in the brickwork which I was sure I could squeeze through. So shoving Lou in before me to scare away any curious rats I pushed my heaving, sweating frame into the tiny gap and with Lou's help pulled myself inside.

Startled Pigeons fluttered in the eaves above me as I moved about the empty and oil stained floor. The smell of past heavy industrial toil filled my nostrils as I stepped across a huge railway sleeper to avoid a pile of old tyres and enter the main workspace. Graffiti adorned the stained whitewashed walls all around us and was only broken by the massive bank of electrical fuses in a box on the far wall. All rusty and broken now they were evidence of the raw power this small building must have consumed in its heyday.

An inspection pit lay nearby filled with all manner of antique oil cans and containers. Pigeon droppings were everywhere as the part open roof had given these creatures access to the sanctuary within. A huge rusty flue exited the roof in one corner, snaking skywards to deposit its noxious fumes out of reach in years gone by. In a corner office I found a small tray containing clocking in cards adorned with the names of craftsmen long since retired. As I thumbed through the cards one name caught my eye. It seems everywhere I go on my rambles a Jowett had walked or worked there before me.

I was glad to see the bright sunlight once again as we exited the old building, and with a nod of respect to the clever men of the past Lou and I re-joined All Alone Road and made for the cottages of All Alone. Walking past the cluster of modern electric gated substantial houses that now adorn this part of All Alone Road we soon arrived at the former farmstead. The house of All Alone farm was almost certainly built in the 18th century, though no records seem to survive of the actual date of its erection. Doctor Samuel Ellis came by the land on which the house stands in 1773, so it must have been built between then and 1777, when he had the land enclosed. At All Alone Doctor Ellis cared for a single patient: the Hon. Luke Plunkett, son of the Earl of Fingall, Lord-Lieut. of Meath. It is unclear how this situation came about; it seems that the doctor was loath to leave his roots to travel to Ireland to attend the gentleman, and so perhaps the Irishman came here instead. Others who have lived here include the White family, of whose son, Mr. John White had his children taught by none other Charlotte Bronte. Over the years the house has changed hands on many occasions, but the name of the building always remains unchanged – All Alone.

I turned around and leaving the cottages behind walked towards Highfield Road to make my way down to the top of Idle village, passing by the Yorkshire stone former Coach house of the long gone grand Summerfield House. The 1901 census records one William Greenwood and his family living here.

Walking along Highfield Road I admired the substantial late Victorian houses Briarfield, Barkhill House, Highfield View and Highfield House. All will have been built for wealthy and successful middle class Victorians and their families and their presence still lends an air of refinement to the area.

Lou and I continued along Highfield Road till we reached Towngate. Here stands what is known as the Chapel of Ease. This Grade II listed building dating from 1630 is currently occupied by the performing arts company of Stage 84. Consecrated in 1692, this course Gritstone stone slate roofed building replaced an earlier chapel. Sometimes called the "Old Bell Chapel" after the first Minister Mr Bell it also housed the village lock up. It was here that I joined Westfield Lane which was to take us up to Idle Hill and Catstones Wood.

Westfield Lane is flanked on either side by numerous marvellous 18th century former weavers and quarry workers cottages, some of them listed buildings. After a short while we reached the ground of Hepworth and Idle Cricket Club. This quaint little village ground is built on the site of what was once Town End Quarry and behind the clubhouse stands the last of the three ventilation stacks for the sewage tunnel running from Frizinghall to Esholt.

Directly opposite the cricket ground is one of the most unusual and perhaps the smallest burial site I have come across on my travels. The ground for this ancient Quaker burial ground was donated by Joshua Bartlett, a prosperous Bradford book-seller, and a noted Quaker himself. Trustees for the plot of land were appointed and for a time a Samuel Drake guarded the spot. Others followed, including Jeremy Grimshaw, Thomas Yewdall, and Benjamin Sandall. The first burials were Jeremiah Yewdall in 1690, son of Thomas (named above) and Benjamin Swaine. The last was his Great Grandson David in 1825.The name "Yewdall" appears on an original memorial stone that has been preserved and set into the ground.

The final body count was 30 I believe. We entered the tiny square walled area by the Grade II listed archway facing onto Westfield Lane. As with all Quaker graves the headstones are laid flat within. Local folklore says that a ghost can be summoned by running around the top of the flat top of the walls seven times "faster than is humanly possible" although I tend to take this notion with a pinch of salt. Carrying on along Westfield Lane past the imaginatively named Carcase End farmhouse on High Busy Lane we soon reached the turn off to Low Ash Road. This is more of a track than a road and would take us between Catstones Wood and Idle Hill up to Wrose Road. As we arrived at the turn off I glanced around and noticed the trademark undulating surface of a former quarry in the field opposite. Although the quarry had been filled in when it was abandoned many years ago the ground had settled over the subsequent years and has left quite a sizable dip. This must have been one of the largest quarries in this area as its remains are larger than most. Over the road just along Westfield Lane is Roleystone Horse and Pony Sanctuary. I worked for six months as a volunteer there a few years ago and have fond memories of the place. I worked like a mad man mucking out the stables and learnt so much from the woman who ran the place. The resident horses have nowhere else to go and it really is the last chance saloon for most of them. I salute all the people involved with this venture and was sad when my time there came to an end.

As Lou and I walked along the track towards Wrose I remembered that we were almost on top of one of my all-time favourite spots for sitting, thinking and peaceful reflection. So making a short detour through a fence on the right hand side I found myself once again perched on a large flat piece of rock on Idle Hill looking down across the magnificent vista before me towards Baildon. From here Charlestown can be seen and even the top of Hollings Hill at Guiseley. Esholt and its awesome woods can be seen in the distance, whilst to the other side my eyes picked out Saltaire and even the faint outline of Milner Field. It was playtime at the junior school down at the bottom of the hill in front of me and I could hear the excited playful screams of innocent young children. I always sit here for too long and time slips past too quickly. It was time to move on so I reeled Lou back in and clambered away back up the hill to the track at the top.

Catstones Wood is an ancient place. Coins and broaches from the First and Second centuries have been found in the vicinity at a nearby quarry. A Quern stone used for milling grain and corn was found was also found here in 1926. Even Roman coins were unearthed just over the track at the top of Idle Hill where the service reservoir now sits. All I ever find there is peace but Iam not complaining as sometimes that is worth more than mere old coins and funny round millstones. We walked along the track towards the site of an old maggot farm and a former Piggery. The smell from this area was appalling when both were in operation from what I have been told, but these days both are long gone and the Piggery itself has been replaced by a smart detached house that continues to use the name "The Piggery" .

We soon reached the small row of 18ᵗʰ century cottages that are situated almost at the foot of the upper part of Idle Hill. They are backed by a massive stone wall that was built to keep the hill from sliding down and crushing them I suspect. Across the track from here land slopes away quite dramatically giving way to a plantation that is thick with mature trees and dense vegetation. Walking on from here we were almost at what was once known as Miserable Corner when I met up with a lady I know from walking the dogs near to where I live. We both get about it seems. She always has with her a Jack Russell imaginatively named "Russell" who as a puppy suffered from a horrid disorder named Strangles. He came through it though and is none the worse for it now as an adult.

After bidding farewell to them we carried on past the house of Low Ash and the quite superb aged Wrose Brow Plantation. I have always found this place somewhat dark and brooding with almost a mystical feeling emitting from it. On the far side of this place is the site of the former Wrose Brow Brickworks. This concern was created for the manufacture of bricks and sanitary tubes to be used in local buildings. Ganister and pipe clay was mined from the hillside and Wrose Hill bricks are common in Shipley and north Bradford. In the years 1901-1927 the company owning the works was known as Wrose Hill Fire Clay. A 1945 list of mines suggests that Wrose Hill was closed in July 1944. Today only the Manager's house, built in 1912 and named The Ridge survives.

By this time Lou and I were almost back in the centre of the modern day Wrose. The Bold Privateer came into view at the end of Low Ash Road. This public house built in 1957 was named after The Earl of Cumberland who at one time owned all the land in the Wrose area at the time of Queen Elizabeth 1. We turned right here and walked along Wrose Road past the site of the demolished Catholic church of Our Lady and St. Anthony. This was demolished in 1995 and replaced by sheltered housing bungalows. The Italianate style Presbytery beside it remains today as a private dwelling.

Our walk today ended at the superb Georgian style house that is the Wrose Bull public house. This building was formally the residence of Dawson Jowett, a well-respected local man who was the Master of The Airedale Beagles which were once kennelled here. The Airedale Beagles were established in 1891 through the co-operation of business and working men. This followed a chance encounter on Ilkley Moor between Dawson Jowett and Tom Clark. Tom became the kennel man and Dawson the huntsman. The Hunt had links to the

Bradford Harriers that had disbanded just a couple of years before, and there was a long tradition of Beagling in the Jowett family. The pub was originally named the Hare and Hounds but was nicknamed The Bull after a bull that was kept in an adjoining field.

Behind The Wrose Bull is the site of the "Wrose Elm". Once a focal point for the whole village it succumbed to Dutch elm disease in 2000 and was replaced with an Ash tree. Seeing as Lou and I were right next to one of my favourite watering holes in the area I decided it was the right time to end our walk and call in for a pint. Even though I knew the area and route of this walk quite well it was still a superb afternoon and what better way to end it than with a pint of ale to toast the Airedale Beagles with.

The only connection I have had to this area was visiting a friend of mine Andrew Hartney at his house in Riddlesden for many years. Apart from that I knew very little about it so when I came across a snippet of information about an 18th century industrial age Lime Kiln by the canal a plan was formed. I naturally did my usual meticulous military style planning a few days before and on a bright sunny June morning packed up my kitbag and got on the road.

Lou and I caught the local bus down into Shipley and then the connection on to Keighley. As it usual with a dog as astatically pleasing as Lou Parson I was made to feel like the Pied Piper of Hamlyn again when a group of children pestered me to allow them to stroke and cuddle her. She is naturally rather timid with anyone else but me but it's hard not to give in to these kind of requests as she obviously brings a little bit of joy to all those who meet her. The children got off the bus a few stops further on and with cheery waves bid us farewell. Down to business then eh?

Not being familiar with Keighley all I knew was that I had to walk along North Street and make for the general direction of Low Utley. Lou and I walked in the warm mid-morning sun past Keighley's small rather worn out looking cinema and past a series of grand, substantial late Victorian terrace houses, until we came to the Gothic Revival entrance arch of Cliffe Castle. As is common with buildings of this age the sandstone is discoloured with age and fumes from the passing heavy traffic. Cliffe Hall was built by Christopher Netherwood between 1828 and 1833, and designed by George Webster of Kendal, a Gothic Revivalist. The Butterfields, a textile manufacturing family, bought Cliffe Hall in 1848. Henry Isaac Butterfield transformed the building by adding towers, a ballroom and conservatories from 1875 to 1880, and renamed it Cliffe Castle in 1878. He decorated the building with the griffin motif, which he had adopted as a heraldic crest. His Son Frederick inherited it in 1910 but allowed it to fall into disrepair.

In 1949 the building and grounds were bought by Keighley Corporation with the assistance of Sir Bracewell Smith, a local benefactor, who in 1955, paid for the conversion of the house for public use. The house had been gabled in the neo-gothic style, with tall towers each end, and conservatories. In the interests of modernisation, the back tower was taken down, and the front one shortened. The high Flemish gables and other decorations were removed from the roof. As we had many miles to go today a visit to this splendid building would have to wait for another day so we pressed on towards Low Utley.

Passing by the roundabout at the edge of the Cliffe Castle grounds we met with Skipton Road and continued along here past a number of sturdy, well designed detached houses. These houses will have originally been constructed away from the late Victorian squalor and grime of Keighley town centre for local businessmen of some position. We were now just over a mile away from Keighley and approaching High Utley and the Victorian masterpiece that is Utley Cemetery. As with most places of burial of this age it emits a feeling of brooding yet at the same time is tinged with one of peacefulness. Opened in 1857 it now contains 57 Commonwealth War graves as well as the usual array of resting places of local dignitary's long deceased. One particular interesting resident is Christopher Ingham who served in The Duke of Wellingtons 95th Rifle Regiment. He fought in ten battles against the French in Spain, France and Belgium and even at the famous Battle of Waterloo. After being awarded The Peninsular Medal he died in 1866 and was buried with full military honours. The Television character "Sharpe" featuring Sean Bean is reputedly based on him. The things this man will have seen and done defy description and are difficult to comprehend.

A short jaunty walk past the cemetery brought us to Keelham Lane, and we turned down here past the smallest fish and chip shop I have ever seen. It is a tiny one pan operation no more than the size of a garden shed, but having said that these kind of places often serve up a far more appealing simple meal than the much larger concerns. The fantastic aroma of fish and chips cooked in the traditional Yorkshire beef dripping almost tempted me but being a traditional Yorkshireman I was most reluctant to waste my fully packed lunch that I had with me. So with nostrils flaring and belly rumbling we carried on down towards the hamlet of Low Utley and from there across the River Aire and onto Keighley Golf Club.

The hamlet of Low Utley has the appearance of a time bubble. A tiny collection of mostly early 18th century humble workers cottages of simple design congregate around the lower end of Keelham Lane, it really is a case of stepping back in time. I had not expected this and found myself walking along the cobbled narrow street like a wandering old Priest who had sampled too much of the local beer. Almost every building was resplendent with aged mullioned windows, sandstone slate roofs and tiny cottage gardens. I stumbled along the cobbles intoxicated with the history of these humble dwellings as grizzled toothless old women hung their washing out to dry in the warm early summer sun. This walk was worth it just to see and walk within this place and everything else would be a bonus.

We exited the time capsule to cross over the railway bridge then over the modern A629 bypass and that brought me back sadly to the present time. We carried on Parkers Lane to cross the River Aire by a metal road bridge and glancing down into the frothy seething water I could see the remains of a weir. Perhaps there had been a mill here somewhere at some point in the past I mused?

Up ahead in the middle distance far beyond the golf course I could see the dense trees of Low Wood where I knew the Leeds and Liverpool Canal would be. We were heading there as it was the site of my first ever visit to a traditional Lime Kiln. Although the road we were taking through the golf course was a public right of way I half expected some well off banker with too much time on his hands to start yelling at the scruffy bearded Hoi Polloi who was transgressing upon his hallowed ground. So when some upper class twit in a Range Rover nearly ran me off the road and into the 16th green he received the traditional working man's two fingered salute.

Lou and I passed right by the clubhouse and attracted stares from the assembled well to do folk enjoying their lunches. I resisted the urge to doff my cap at them as the fact that I would have been taking the Michael would have passed them by so we pressed on towards the canal and Booths Bridge. This small modern bridge over the canal was originally built of timber and is operated manually by a pivot on the north side. The Lime Kiln is situated down a bank at the side of the canal bridge on the south bank. It is accessed by a rough rocky footpath that runs off the towpath. Probably built after the canal was opened it is constructed of rubble stone with an arched opening leading to an arched roof space which contained the opening for the flue. Today it is in poor condition with trees growing out of the roof.

The common feature of early kilns was an egg-cup shaped burning chamber, with an air inlet at the base known as "the eye". Limestone was crushed (often by hand) to fairly uniform 20-60 mm lumps. Successive dome-shaped layers of limestone and coal were built up in the kiln on grate bars across the eye. When loading was complete, the kiln was kindled at the bottom, and the fire gradually spread upwards through the charge. When burnt through, the lime was cooled and raked out through the base. Fine ash dropped out and was rejected with the "riddlings". Typically the kiln took a day to load, three days to fire, two days to cool and a day to unload, so a one-week turnaround was normal. Such kilns were constructed near to the canal for the easy method of transportation of the raw materials and the quicklime that was produced. This was used as fertilizer and in mortar for constructing buildings. The development of the national rail network increasingly made the local small-scale kilns unprofitable, and they gradually died out through the 19th century. They were replaced by larger industrial plants. At the same time, new uses for lime in the chemical, steel and sugar industries led to large-scale plants. These also saw the development of more efficient kilns.

After feeling somewhat disappointed in the feeble condition of the lime kiln but still happy that I had at least seen one for the first time, Lou and I crossed over Booths Bridge to sit astride the stone abutment on the south side to eat our simple peasants lunch of Gruel and potatoes. Iam only kidding here as the cheese and onion sandwiches in home baked Wholemeal bread was a veritable feast, and only served to enforce the notion that to be humble is to not be a Banker. So with both our belly's full and our minds clear Lou and I set off through Low Wood and the number of Sandstone escarpments that make up Carr Delph and onwards in the direction of Riddlesden.

The path stayed near to the canal bank and I saw some coped moorings that indicated that stone was taken from the quarry directly onto the canal boats for transportation elsewhere. Walking along the well-trodden trail through the woodland on the edge of Carr Delph we walked up through the smaller Riddlesden Golf Course on a section that was surprisingly cobbled like the tiny street in Low Utley. We had reached Clough Beck where the area had been littered with small coal pits in the past. Now long gone and forgotten there was little evidence of their industrial past. The previously dense woodland had thinned out around the beck and it was perfect Squirrel territory so although Lou was still (as always) on her extendable lead I had to be careful as she will chase anything.

I followed the beck uphill towards the Bradford Corporation Water Works Barden Aqueduct. This still forms part of the system that brings water to the city of Bradford from far away reservoirs on the moors above. The steady flow of the beck runs over a series of rocks at this point forming a small waterfall. I noticed a large rock in the middle of the beck and leaped from the bank to land squarely on it. Lou was still stood on the bank and like a good Jack Russell always does she tried to give chase to a Squirrel that came from nowhere to dart up a nearby tree. Although the rock was not slippy the force of her lunge towards her prey pulled me right into the cold water. It was all I could do to not laugh at the absurdity of my situation. Sat on my arse in the middle of a beck by a waterfall in the middle of nowhere as a tiny Jack Russell is trying her best to climb a tree. Who cares I was having a ball. It was time though to move on so I trudged out of the beck and collecting Lou, started to move through the trees, over a high drystone wall and off in the direction of Dunkirk Wood.

We followed a track through the fields, past rundown and ramshackle humble homes of horses till we reached the small wood. From there we walked downhill past the vegetation ridden site of a long forgotten small Sandstone delph till we came across a small row of terraced cottages called High Cote. Sat above the canal bank this terrace of stone built cottages occupies an elevated position at the top of a steep wooded bank. Built in the first half of the 19th century of coursed local stone with solid slate roofs these cottages sit in an area of some tranquillity and as we walked past them I got that all too familiar feeling of "ahh if only" once again. Following on along the small road alongside the cottages Lou and I passed by Leach's Bridge and before long came upon West Riddlesden Hall.

Considered to be of national interest, this fine example of a 17th century Manor House stands in well wooded grounds. The Grade I listed building was the long time residence of the Maud family before being passed to the Leach family in the 17th century. Constructed of hammer dressed stone with a stone slate roof it has a south facing front dominated by three gabled bays. The central doorway includes a torus-moulded architrave on plinth blocks. A date stone of 1687 with the initials TL (Thomas Leach) adorns the front. In the Interior there is an oak-panelled hall with dated beam and open-string staircase with turned balusters.

After pausing for a few moments to admire this fine old building we carried on along Limekiln Road and skirting lower Morton Banks arrived at Stockbridge Wharf. This is where the canal takes on an industrial feel due to the tall former warehouses alongside that have been converted into flats. The other side of the canal has houses with gardens that run right down to the water's edge. Although the warehouses still retain the original loading bays the lifting mechanisms have been removed. The wharf was originally built to allow the transportation of goods and materials to Keighley as it was not served by the Leeds and Liverpool canal.

We carried on walking on this side of the canal for a short distance till we reached Banks Bridge. This modern structure carries Granby Lane over the canal and has a stone built overflow on the far side which I found to be most unusual. Lou and I crossed back over the canal at this point as we had to pass the famed and ancient Marquis of Granby public house. This building is of considerable age and may have been constructed along with the canal. Built of dressed deep course stone with a stone slate roof, it has sadly lost some of its original character due to the replacement of multi pane sash windows with more modern UPVC replacements. Next door to the pub is a quaint small single bay shop built in 1880.

We were now on what is known as Hospital Road, and although today there is no Hospital here there once was many years ago. At one time in the past there were many fever or isolation hospitals dotted all around the Bradford area, even one near to Top Withens on Haworth Moor. Before the discovery of Penicillin and the advent of modern health care the world was awash with many contagious diseases. Most of these have now been eradicated or at least brought under some degree of control. Prior to that though it was a different scenario and deadly diseases such as Smallpox, Typhoid, Scarlet fever and Typhus were widely prevalent throughout the Western World. So to aid in the recovery from these type of diseases and to prevent the spread of infection many Isolation hospitals sprang up around this area.

Morton Banks Fever Hospital or The Keighley and Bingley Joint Isolation Hospital as it was also known as was one such place, and it was this establishment that once lay at the end of Hospital Road. Most if not all of these places are long gone but the old Ordnance Survey maps show them still and it was whilst looking at one of these that I came across this particular old fever hospital. The Keighley and Bingley Joint Isolation Hospital opened on "a most eligible site" at Morton Banks, in February, of 1897, and by the end of the year had treated 131 patients with infectious diseases, including two of the nurses, one of whom had contracted scarlet fever and the other typhoid fever. Another 240 were admitted in 1898, including 67 with diphtheria. That year a further smallpox hospital was built a little higher up the hillside. Morton Banks had 746 beds and reportedly dealt with more than 13,000 sick or wounded military men, some of whom came from as far away as Canada and the Fiji islands. There were 114 deaths including 42 Germans in the wake of the great Influenza Epidemic at the end of World War I. The hospital was even visited by American Military surgeons studying developments in military surgery, and advances were made in the treatment of Tetanus, gas poisoning and Gangrene. In 1938 there were 415 admissions, with diphtheria accounting for 286.

So with all this in mind I made my way towards the gated and walled entrance that is all that remains of this weird place. The hospital was a series of buildings and huts contained within a walled compound but a lot of this has now been built on with modern housing. The area that remains is heavily wooded by the passage of time but I was sure I could find some evidence of its former use inside this tree infested area. I could have been rambling around in any number of heavily wooded plantations. I could have been in Esholt Woods or the ruins of Milner Field at Gilstead as there seemed to be no sign of its former grisly use. But I had the knowledge of what it once was and that seemed to give me a sense of respect and I trod the ground carefully. Then I saw a series of red bricks laid in the ground obviously denoting part of the foundations of a building. Then a large cut in the soil containing a protruding sewage pipe. As I walked along through the trees more evidence came into view. Amidst large pieces of broken toilet pottery a whole series of drains and their associated pipework lay before me. Granted it was not much to see but if you have a vivid imagination like me and have the knowledge of what it all once was then you can build a picture and get a feeling.

I'd like to state here that a ghostly figure swathed head to toe in blood stained bandages came out of the trees and stumbled towards me begging for salvation, but alas sadly nothing like that happened and almost before I knew it we had traversed the whole area and were down at the southern wall next to the canal. Sorry to disappoint you like. How beck runs down the other side of the copse so we followed that back uphill to exit the site onto Saxilby Road, then walked through another estate of new build house to join Swine lane and then down onto Bradford Road to wait for the bus back to Shipley.

It had been a long and interesting walk and I had learnt many things. But I made sure I had a hell of a good scrub in the bath that evening in case there had been any lingering particles of some long gone infectious disease skulking around.

Shelf to Wellheads Thornton

Sometimes during my research for these walks I come across a mere snippet of information on a place, a person or an occasion which arouses my interest and sets me off on a tangent so to speak. This could be an old photograph or a simple few words on a document somewhere in the ether of the Internet. The spark that made me construct this walk was a grainy photograph of what was once known as Bradford's last remaining Windmill. Today it is long gone but the adjacent cottages on Burned Road in Shelf remain and this was enough for me to construct a walk that took me from there all the way to the village of Thornton via Mountain.

As is usual two buses were required to deposit Lou Parson and I at our starting point on the road formally known as The Shelf Foundry and Stone Tables Branch of the Leeds and Halifax Trust Toll Road, or Cooper Lane if you want to be lazy. Toll roads or Turnpikes such as this covered the whole area of not just Bradford but most of Wales as well. Turnpike trusts were established in England and Wales from about 1706 in response to the need for better roads than the few and poorly-maintained tracks then available. Turnpike trusts were set up by individual Acts of Parliament, with powers to collect road tolls to repay loans for building, improving, and maintaining the principal roads in Britain. At their peak, in the 1830s, over 1,000 trusts administered around 30,000 miles of turnpike road in England and Wales, taking tolls at almost 8,000 toll-gates. The trusts were ultimately responsible for the maintenance and improvement of most of the main roads in England and Wales, which were used to distribute agricultural and industrial goods economically. The tolls were a source of revenue for road building and maintenance, paid for by road users and not from general taxation. The turnpike trusts were gradually abolished from the 1870s.

So after leaving the bus we started to walk down the slight gradient towards the main road which runs through Shelf village. We passed by a long row of 19th century terrace houses where one of my old friends lives. Chris Ambler is the most knowledgeable man on Bradford City matters and indeed all local sport I have ever known. Some years ago in 2003 before he went modern and bought a computer he commissioned me to bid on eBay for Jimmy Speirs FA Cup winners medal from the 1911 final victory against Newcastle United. His family auctioned this medal with his Military Medal and service medal. The FA

Cup medal was sold for £26,210, a record for a cup medal but I was ordered to duck out at £25,000 and the present day Bradford City co Chairman Mark Lawn eventually won the auction. I remember it as being quite a buzz to play with someone else's money though. I didn't call in as we had no time for the long chat which would inevitably result.

Upon reaching Carr House Road we walked for a short distance before reaching an old Independent Methodist Chapel named The Bethel Chapel. Built in only 139 days and opening in September 1853, this large sombre building enjoys a very large well kept graveyard which contains the graves of some 4944 people. One most interesting grave contains the mortal remains of "the man who broke the bank at Monte Carlo". Joseph Hobson Jagger was an engineer at Bottomleys Mill in Shelf and in the 1870's he went to Monte Carlo to visit the casinos. Using his engineering skills he studied the Roulette wheels and devised a method with which to beat it. On July 7th 1875 he placed his first bet and eight days later he had won two million old French Francs. This would be the equivalent of £400,000 today which in the 1870's was a huge sum of money. His secret method to beat the system was all to do with the cylinders of the Roulette wheel apparently. I tip my hat to anyone who takes on "the system" and beats it.

With a grin and a chuckle I left the Chapel graveyard and carried on along the main road till I turned up Burned Road and passed by the fine Upper Witchfield House from where a tunnel was reputed to have run to the nearby Windmill. This corn windmill was the last in the district to survive, and before falling into disrepair it remained as a local landmark until in 1960 when the top of the building was destroyed by a lightning strike before being finally demolished in 1964. Each of the four sails were seven feet in width and 60 feet in length and weighed one ton. In 1904 the sails were removed and a stream engine was introduced to provide power to grind the corn from the local farms. In 1914 the owner at the time Francis Barraclough closed the business and it remained unused until its final demise.

The actual site of the Windmill is now simply a piece of scrubland behind the remaining adjacent cottage but standing there I could use my imagination and conjure up visions of the massive lofty sails thundering as they whirled through their repetitive windy dance. Shaking my head to bring me back into the present we moved on past some modern boring bungalows on Stanage Lane until the passing scenery developed a more countryside feel to it.

Climbing a sizable grass covered spoil heap of a former coal pit, Lou and I came face to face with a most unusual sight at the point where Stanage Lane becomes Bracken Lane. Before us stood a large square stone gateway with a resting stone Lion perched upon the top. To each side was a smaller arched gateway and all three entrances were and locked. Not surprisingly this is known locally as The Lion Gate and once formed the Southern entrance to an estate known as Low House. John Hirst bought Low House in 1665 which was then known as Brightwater. Yarn was spun for a while on hand looms on premises adjoining Low House. Sometime after that Joseph Hirst and Henry Sagar Hirst formed Low House Brewery and subsequently named it The Lion Brewery. Joseph died in 1890 and in 1893 his Sons sold the whole estate to Bentleys Breweries.

Moving off from the Lion Gate we passed by the location of the long gone hamlet of Upper Bracken Beds. This was recorded as having being built in the 18th century possibly by Ayton and Elwell the bridge builders and founders, for their workers. Today only a small number of bumps and humps in the ground remain as evidence of this small hamlet. We moved on along Brackens Lane past more former small coal pits and joined Giles Hill Lane before passing by the 18th century farmhouse named Green Head. By this point the fields were open and expansive and the road was straight and true. Apart from the occasional farmstead we had not seen any built up areas or buildings of modern construction for perhaps three miles which pleased me greatly. In the middle distance I could see the farmstead and buildings of Long Lover and before long we were at the main Brighouse Road.

Lou and I were now approaching the open expanses of the Queensbury area, but this would no doubt end for a time as we entered the lower part of the village. Crossing over the Brighouse Road Lou and I walked at a steady pace down Jackson Hill Lane where we passed by a terrace of four 18th century cottages preceded by a small row of those tiny dwellings known as "Low Deckers" These common one room cottages in the South Bradford area were rented by labourers who worked in the local mining and quarrying business.

At the junction of Jackson Hill Lane and Paw Lane I knew that there used to be a tiny two cottage hamlet named Paw. Nothing now remains apart from a scrape in the ground surrounded by a small earth bank. But seen from above in Google Earth it is plainly visible as being the location of former dwellings. Sat on the banking it was here that Lou and I rested for a while and took out our dinner. As I munched away on my usual humble peasants fare of cheese and onion sandwiches my imagination once again grew wings and transported me back to the time when these dwellings were home to perhaps a simple Quarryman or Miner and his small family. What did they eat? How did they dress? Did they go to church in their Sunday best every week? Did they fear God or did the Father forsake his family and squander his wages on ale in the taverns of Queensbury? You know what they say about strong cheese.

After refuelling we moved off down Syke Lane and after creeping by a copper sat in his car in a layby eating his dinner, we passed by the 16th century mullioned window farmhouse of Collier Syke to turn off up Deanstones Lane towards the site of another former fever hospital at Long Lane. Built in 1893 in the days when infectious diseases were still a major problem, Long Lane Fever Hospital was a twenty bed facility built by the local health board. Constructed on land bought from Geo Ambler for £280 the first ten years saw 251 patients admitted (249 for Scarlet Fever, 1 for Diphtheria and 1 for Enteric Fever). Since the discovery of Sulphonamides in 1937, Penicillin in 1929 and the subsequent inoculation program the hospital closed in 1945. Today the site is occupied by an estate of new build houses.

Continuing along Deanstones Lane we reached the West End part of the village of Queensbury. It was here that I saw the house with the largest number of bricked up windows I think I can remember. On the gable end of this row of three early 18th century terrace houses are four large bricked up former windows. They were bricked up to avoid the dreaded "Window Tax". The window tax was a property tax based on the number of windows in a house. It was a significant social, cultural, and architectural force in England, France and Scotland during the 18th and 19th centuries. To avoid the tax some houses from the period can be seen to have bricked-up window-spaces (ready to be glazed or reglazed at a later date). In England and Wales it was introduced in 1696 and was repealed in 1851, 156 years after first being introduced.

We turned down towards Halifax and walked for a short distance until turning off up Fleet Lane and crossing over the old railway tunnel that took the line from Staines cutting on to Queensbury Station and moved on towards the far side of the village. We passed by another short row of the lovely one decker workers cottages and a succession of larger local vernacular style cottages on Fleet Lane before stopping for a few moments to admire the coursed

Sandstone detached cottage of Upper Fleet House. Now home to a dog and cat boarding kennel it was from that I had heard the cacophony of barking from over a mile away in Queensbury. Passing between Queensbury Park and the site of the former Mountain and Pineberry Quarry we joined the Brighouse and Denholme Road which would take us over towards the highest place in the Bradford area, Soil Hill.

Queensbury is known as the highest village in England and judging from the view from this point that title is well deserved. As Lou and I tramped along the main road I glanced over the drystone wall and I could clearly make out the far away shape of Idle Hill in the distance. The massive chimney of Listers Mill in Manningham was also visible as was Salts Mill in faraway Saltaire. The view was simply stunning from here as the fields and countryside just seemed to open up down in front of me. Lou and I continued walking and before long entered the small collection of former mill cottages and houses known as Mountain.

As the name suggests it is as high as a mountain and provides a fantastic vantage point overlooking the whole city of Bradford. It is said that on a clear day no less than three of England's National Parks can be seen from here. The Peak District to the south, The Yorkshire Dales to the north and in the very far distance The Hambleton Hills on the edge of the north Yorkshire moors. Phew took my breath away it surely did.

A little further on along Brighouse and Denholme Road we came to The Raggalds Inn. Located at the highest point in Mountain in stunning surroundings affording magnificent views across Calderdale, this infamous country pub and restaurant has achieved a degree of notoriety due to a double shooting and a murder in 1995. Original a staging post for the cloth trade at the end of the Industrial Revolution, the earliest record of its existence is in 1845. On the 24th April 1995 two masked men burst in and armed with a sawn off shotgun and a pistol, shot dead the landlord Michael Briggs and wounded a customer. Two local men were later convicted and sentenced to life terms plus 15 years for the killing. It was said that the murder was carried out on behalf of rivals of Mr Briggs. Strangely enough the name Raggald is a local term originating from Old Norse meaning villain or ruffian. I shivered and crossed myself as we moved on up Perseverance Road towards Soil Hill.

Newly sheared Sheep lay sleeping in the warm early summer sun in the fields around as Lou and I made our way past yet another row of humble sandstone former quarry workers cottages. I could clearly see Soil Hill as it started to rise up as it came into view. Perseverance Road turned into Ned Hill as we wound our way along the base of Soil Hill making for a track by Laverock Hall which would take us to the summit. I checked my trusty dog eared old map and saw that this track would lead us over the side of Soil Hill and onto the top where there was once a fireclay pit. Down on the other side there is still mining activity of some sort due to the trucks and wagons I could hear rumbling about in the distance. There was also once a pottery factory here which in the years preceding World War I employed 13 men making mixing bowls, flower pots and bread crocks. These items were highly prized and valued I understand. As Lou Parson and I reached the top of Soil Hill I noticed amongst the fields to the side of the track a ruined building and a number of strange oblong standing stones of some description.

So heaving Lou over the high drystone wall I followed her and crossed the open expanse of the field towards these weird looking stones. As I neared the stone circle I could make it out more clearly and it appeared to be a smaller version of Stonehenge. For a few seconds I had visions of white robed chanting Druids dancing around at midnight up here high above Bradford. Now I know that strange things can sometimes happen in Bradford but dancing Druids? I could see there was a small pond in the centre of the stones so maybe they bathed as well as chanted.

Any ideas I may have had about strange religious nuts at midnight were firmly put to bed when standing next to the stones I could see it was simply a pond surrounded by a stone fence, presumably to stop cows from falling in as there is an entrance on the left where I would expect a ramp to lead safely down to the water. The ruined building nearby appeared to be an old barn containing a number of rusty old silage clamps. We tramped back to the track and from there I could see down the far side of the hill. Heavy wagons were traversing the still active open cast mine. I could make out the cottages on the main road next to where a small narrow gauge railway used to run up into the quarry. We had to get across this open and busy landscape to continue on to Keelham and up to Wellheads in Thornton.

But before then I sat down to take a rest on a massive rock right up there on the summit of Soil Hill. I really wished that I had an ipod or something full to the brim with Mike Oldfield tunes as I could have spent hours sat there getting all mellow maaan. Looking to the West I could make out the former homes of the famous mill owning Foster family of Denholme, Waterloo House and White Shaw, and the long straight road leading to Oxenhope, Long Causeway. Even Thornton Moor reservoir was visible from my lofty seat. Thankfully the few men that were working down below paid us little attention as we walked down from the hill and across the mine workings, and no trucks ran us down so we reached the main road in one piece and continued on to Keelham.

Lou and I passed by the tiny school and the handful of former mill workers cottages in Keelham to take on the final short leg of this great walk. I was flagging by this time and instead of trekking on into Thornton as was my initial idea I decided to catch the bus back to Bradford at the top of this long gently rising road by the small settlement of Well Heads instead. It was 4PM and I was ready for a pint in The White Horse Inn. As I entered the front door I looked above and noticed a date stone with the year 1815 carved into it. I remembered todays date was June 18th and before I left home Sky News had been reporting that it was 200 years to the day since the battle of Waterloo.....1815.......funny that ?

Bolton Woods to Northcliffe Park Shipley

To me there is nothing quite like starting a walk right from the back door of my humble old cottage. So after consuming a hearty breakfast, a large mug of Earl Grey and sorting my two beautiful Jack Russell's out with their food Lou and I set out down the ancient packhorse trail of the lower half of Wood Lane. Today it is no more than a mere footpath that leads around the side of Bolton Woods quarry and down towards Canal Road. But in days of yore this track was part of the main trail from Idle Moor that the merchants and famers would take when transporting their goods into the markets of Bradford.

Passing by my favourite Blackberry bush I followed the well-worn path that I have grown to know so well over the fifteen years I have lived here. I often take the dogs into the quarry to marvel at the ever changing exposed seams of stone that date back millions of years. The Quarrymen appear to work one part of the quarry for a few weeks then move to another for a while. Although not as busy and industrious as in years gone by it is still worked on a limited scale to produce stone for small local projects. On occasion the blasting of rock can be heard breaking the silence of the early morning, and the chipping of the Stonemasons tools ring out as they work the blocks of stone. Sometimes in the summer I sit high above on the spoil heap and observe the local Territorial soldiers playing war games with their brightly coloured smoke flares filling the air with the smell of cordite.

But today Lou and I were passing by the quarry to walk down Hepolite Scar on the far side to make our way towards the old and historical settlement of Frizinghall. Hepolite Scar is the local name given the steep slope that rises up from Canal Road towards the top of the massive spoil heap of the quarry. Decades ago people would race their motorbikes up this slope in timed hill climbs and the name originates from a local factory that once made pistons and their rings for car and bike engines that were named "Hepolite". The tiny long since disappeared hamlet of Delf Hill used to sit nearby but today the site is taken up by a small junior school. Passing through a patch of moorland where I once had a marvellously simple but long remembered picnic with a lady who shall remain nameless (she was married) we made our way down onto the main road through the village of Bolton Woods.

Long established as a thriving industrial village due to its two mills, Bolton Woods is now a fairly quiet place where even the old blocks of council flats have now been demolished. Passing by the site of the also demolished Oswain Mill and over one of the remaining Bradford Canal bridges we were soon at the junction with Canal Road. I always stop here for a few minutes to observe the gentle rush of Bradford Beck as it weaves its way across its brick lined bed to make its way to join the River Aire at Shipley. Gazing down into the water I could see that it was in good condition. Not discoloured in any way and free of floating waste it is always a joy to see such an historic waterway in fine fettle.

The ever busy Canal Road is always a pain to cross and I was thankful for the recent pedestrian crossing that has been built. From there is it a short walk over the railway bridge and along Frizinghall Road towards the historical village of Frizinghall and one of my favourite pubs in the area The Black Swan. Situated next to a Grade II listed row of rendered Sandstone cottages, this mid to late 18th century pub is a great place in which to enjoy some fine summer evenings. The oak beams and numerous horse brass's inside give it the feeling of a time capsule and the ale is not bad either. The adjacent row of cottages named Swan Hill is possibly the oldest part of Frizinghall having being built in the early part of the 18th century with numbers 2-7 being Grade II listed.

Passing by the sports grounds of Bradford Grammar School and a row of early 19th century terrace houses we soon came to a small group of cottages in an area known as Carr Syke. These are named after the beck which runs through nearby Lister Park, under the lake and waterfall and then under the Grammar school. The local Toll house was situated near here in 1816.

Lister Park is situated about a mile outside the city centre on Manningham Lane. It is one of the city's largest parks and was donated to the City of Bradford by Samuel Cunliffe Lister, who built Lister's Mill. The park has been successfully renovated in recent years, the lake has been re-opened for boats and a Mughal Water Garden constructed. There are also tennis and basketball courts, bowling greens and a children's playground. Lister Park contains the Cartwright Hall art gallery, where permanent and temporary exhibitions of modern and traditional art can be seen. But today we were not to visit Lister Park and instead made our way up Emm Lane, and passing by The Turf public house headed towards Heaton. Here once again there is a Jowett connection as a previous landlord of The Turf, a Mr E Jowett shot and killed a rabid dog after it was seen "behaving in a strange condition" according to contemporary reports. Part of this pub collapsed in 1894 during alteration work, the landlord and 12 other men being injured as they lay buried in the ruins under the scaffolding and fallen masonry. The two most badly injured men were an apprentice named Holroyd and a stonemason named Redmond. They were both dug out of the ruins still alive but in an unconscious state.

We continued up the forbidding and steep Emm Lane heading past The University of Bradford School of Management and an assortment of fine late Victorian semi-detached and detached houses. Most of these houses are extremely grand and most have balconies and castellated turrets along with fine mature wooded grounds as befitting their status as dwellings of quite wealthy Bradfordians from the last century. Many were built in the "Arts and Craft" style in the years 1880-1909. Yorkshire stone is most commonly used in brick form at ground level with a course render. In some examples timber breaks up the render to give a mock Tudor effect. The windows and doors often incorporate attractive leaded and stained glass to great effect.

The wide leafy suburban road lined on each side with mature trees soon gave way to houses of a more humble nature as Lou and I approached Heaton village. The Yorkshire Ripper Peter Sutcliffe lived with his wife Sonia not far round the bend at 6 Garden Lane but we were not going that far and turned off down Quarry Street next to Heaton Cemetery. This small and superb Victorian graveyard contains over 1100 graves and was instituted in 1824. It is the final resting place of several thousand paupers and children who were buried in communal graves of which there are no records.

We strolled down Quarry Street in a jaunty manner, past 18th century cottages complete with the obligatory bricked up tax avoiding windows down towards Heaton Woods and the famous "Cat Steps". These steps were nicknamed so due to their step nature that "only a cat would choose to climb them". Heaton Woods is an ancient woodland situated on a steep sided gully and has been protected in recent years from any development. Today it is a valued local beauty spot where Deer still roam and Sparrow Hawks hunt the sky looking for prey below. At night Bats and Owls rule the quiet expanse of heavy, thick tree laden wood. Even though it was early afternoon and bright sunlight when we were there it was quite dark as the tops of the trees formed a great canopy above us to block out the sunlight. A menacing and brooding feeling pervaded the still air. Distant creatures could be heard scurrying amongst the undergrowth as we plodded down the sloping gully towards the floor of the valley. As we weaved our way down through the trees I noticed an old metal gatepost on the end of a fallen drystone wall. A gateway to where? There was no evidence of anything ever being here.

It puzzled me for a while but I dismissed it from my ever enquiring mind and carried on towards the sound of rushing water. I almost fell headlong into Red Beck as I slid down the banking after snagging my leg on a large exposed tree root. It was only my grip on Lou's lead that prevented me from entering the water. The name of the beck was obviously a nod to the fact that the water that emitted from beneath the track beside was coloured with an orangey red tint. This is caused by the water running through natural Ironstone rock and is widely prevalent in many of the local streams and small becks in the Bradford area.

Making our way through Royds Cliff Wood I could hear the sound of an approaching car. Dance music with heavy beats came grew louder as the car approached towards us along an as yet unseen road. I had no idea where we were at this point and I had never even considered that we were anywhere near a road. The loud music disturbed a group of large black birds in the nearby tree tops and startled, they flew away into the distance with huge wings flapping wildly. The knowledge that we were lost came to my mind and I thought it may be a good idea to make for the general direction of the car and its music.

I decided to follow the route of the beck and within a couple of minutes Lou and I were climbing up a small bank onto what I now know to be Shay Lane. I didn't want to return to civilisation just yet so I crossed over the road and dived headlong into another part of woodland still following the beck upstream. I know from past experience that there is often evidence of past human industrial activity alongside watercourses. Dams, goits, culverts and bridges often lie alongside streams and becks and these are likely to point to nearby ruins and such like which can be interesting to explore. So with this in mind Lou and I fought our way through Cliffe Wood and along through Weather Royds Wood in the general direction of nowhere in particular. It's not often that I ramble without any sense of purpose and direction so in fact this made for quite a nice change as it added to the feeling of seclusion and isolation that I was enjoying at this point.

This area of woodland had become very dense with holly bushes alongside the ever thickening stout trees and it was hard work to traverse through such an environment. So when we came across a tiny ancient pathway I was quite relieved and we followed this towards the distant sounds of golf balls being struck. I knew we had reached the end of the woods and civilisation of sorts but exactly where we were was a mystery.

The familiar sound of passing traffic was almost upon us as Lou and I surfaced onto Bingley Road. The trek through the woods had been hard going and even the dog was panting with the exertion from it all. I was sweating beyond belief and upon feeling the pangs of hunger decided that this would be a good time for a rest and to take some food. Fortunately there was a large expanse of what appeared to be a school playing field directly across the road so I crossed over the busy road, and leaping over the stone wall plonked myself against the base of a tree and sank to the ground.

Usually I simply eat what I need to keep going and carry on walking but this time the exertion of fighting through the woodlands had taken its toll on me and I rested for what seemed an age. I knew where we were now though and also know that we had to get going again as time was ticking along. So with that in mind I packed my gear up and climbed over the wall once again and continued downhill along Bingley Road in the direction of Shipley.

The road was long and straight as we passed by the site of a demolished cottage hospital and turned down High Bank Lane in the direction of Dungeon Wood. I had read some time before that there was reputedly the remains of a 17th century Dungeon in this wood hence the name, but I dismissed any thoughts of searching for it as I had enough at that point of wandering through unfamiliar woodland. It would have to wait for another day and another walk.

The road on High Bank Lane contains no pavement on which to walk so we had to take care and I reeled Lou right in tightly as the traffic was speeding past at high speed. I looked over to my left and took in the quite magnificent view over towards Baildon Moor. Our final destination of Shipley lay at the foot of the valley below but was unseen from here. Thankfully after a while a large expanse of grass opened up to the side of the road and we could walk on here till we reached NorthCliffe Golf Club. When we reached this point Lou and I turned off the road and started along a long grass field that runs between North Cliffe Wood and Old Spring Wood.

The information board at the entrance told me that it was a vast natural habitat for many varieties of wildlife and birds but all I saw were the occasional bags of dog crap hung from the bushes in the usual little black plastic bags. I cannot understand why people do this. They take the trouble to bend down and scoop up their dogs mess and bag it up then hang it on bushes and gates like offerings to some ancient local Gods. The field led us gently downhill towards North Cliffe Park and after passing by the pavilion and the Tennis Courts we emerged onto Bradford road by the main gates. Back in suburbia and civilisation it was but a short distance through the side streets to the familiar bus stop outside the Weatherspoon's pub The Sir Norman Rae. As I took my seat on the bus that would struggle in time honoured tradition up Carr Lane towards Wrose I realised that I had not spoken to one single person during the whole day. And you know what? It didn't bother me one tiny bit.

Everyone loves an atmospheric and historical old Victorian house. A simple statement with which to start this chapter but pretty accurate all the same. I certainly do even if the house is long gone and all that remains is a collection of moss covered skilfully carved blocks of stone in a dense patch of woodland. Often these magnificent residences from a past age have been well documented in print and in photographs but sometimes not and all that remains are the building plans. Sometimes even those people with first-hand knowledge of such places have followed the buildings into eternity leaving behind them only hear say and rumours. The focus of this walk around lower Baildon and Gilstead was three such fine late Victorian houses.

To most people today the names The Knoll, Ferniehurst and Milner Field mean very little, but to some they invoke images of Victorian splendour, innovation and even excess. The name Salt is recognisable to most local people though and it is this name that is wound around these three magnificent residences like a Serpent coiled around the staff of Hermes. Today I was to journey not far from home and visit the sites of all three of the Salt family's historic Victorian homes and to say I was excited was something of an understatement.

Lou and I caught the bus down into Shipley and after a short walk found ourselves in the centre of Saltaire, Sir Titus Salt's masterpiece of Victorian social engineering. This Victorian Model Village and World Heritage site is renowned the world over for its innovation and for Sir Titus Salt's vision and philanthropy. Salt built neat stone houses for his workers (much better than the slums of Bradford), wash-houses with tap water, bath-houses, a hospital and an institute for recreation and education, with a library, a reading room, a concert hall, billiard room, science laboratory and a gymnasium. The village had a school for the children of the workers, alms houses, allotments, a park and a boathouse. Because of this combination of houses, employment and social services the original town is often seen as an important development in the history of 19th century urban planning. Today the village has changed little and the relevant authorities have resisted any changes that would detract from the small conurbation that Sir Titus envisaged when he constructed it.

The warm early morning May sun warmed the aged flagstones as Lou and I walked down Victoria Road past neat rows of Salt's workers houses. They were indeed termed houses as the more humble cottages that Sir Titus Salt's workers had formally occupied in the inner city area of industrial Bradford were literally a world away. Passing by the magnificent Victoria Hall and its Wurlitzer theatre pipe organ and then the imposing presence of Salts flagship mill we entered the busy Roberts Park. Originally named Saltaire Park this space is an integral part of the Saltaire World Heritage site. Set in 14 acres and designed by William Gay it was opened by Sir Titus himself on the 25th July 1871. The development included the widening and deepening of the River Aire for boating and swimming purposes, and the construction of a boathouse on the southern bank of the river.

The park is divided by a long broad east-west promenade with east and west shelters at the ends. To the north of the promenade are serpentine paths and flower beds, and to the south a cricket ground and an open playing field. In the centre of the park is a semi-circular pavilion designed by architects Lockwood and Mawson which was constructed in 1870. In 1891 the park was purchased by Sir James Roberts and in 1903 he commissioned a bronze statue of Sir Titus and this was erected by the main promenade. In 1920 Roberts changed the name to Roberts Park as a memorial to his Son Bertram Foster Roberts when he gave the park to Bradford Council.

We passed by The Boathouse pub where early drinkers were enjoying themselves in the sun and walked across the iron bridge over the river Aire that links the mill and houses of Saltaire with Roberts Park. This bridge was constructed to replace the original bridge that was damaged during World War II by tanks making their way to Baildon Moor for training purposes. We left Roberts Park almost as soon as we had entered it, passing by one of the entrance lodges in the direction of Thompson Lane which would take us to the ancient hamlet of Baildon Green. This lodge again designed by Lockwood and Mawson is a Grade II listed building. Walking along Thompson Lane Lou and I skirted past the edge of a small council estate with its maisonettes and low rise blocks of flats. Across the lane is the expanse of Walker Wood and Midgeley Wood. Passing by a lovingly restored farmhouse and cottages at the junction with Green Lane, we took Green Road to pass an old clay pit to approach the historic hamlet of Baildon Green.

Baildon Green is located on a small south facing shoulder of lane elevated above the River Aire. The records of early buildings and the occupations of the earliest inhabitants suggest an economy based upon farming and textiles in the 17th and 18th centuries. The construction of Clough Mill by James Clough in the 19th century led to the expansion of the hamlet to house workers, as did the start of quarrying operations at Baildon Green and Baildon Bank. The larger population led to more facilities being provided including three places of worship along with their related schools. One of these, the former Methodist Chapel "The Church on the Green" survives today. A public house The Cricketers Arms was also constructed in 1899.The was preceded by an earlier public house of the same name that was originally situated across the road.

This establishment was also called The Smiling Mule. The licence of this pub was surrendered in 1897 and the building is now a private house. The settlement of Baildon Green went into decline in the early 20th century with the cessation of local quarrying and the decline of the textile industry. Happily today the hamlet retains much of his original character and obvious charm. Lou and I passed through the hamlet along Green Road and as is usual I resisted the urge for an early beer in The Cricketers Arms and pressed on past the quaint pond of Crutch Well. After a short distance we turned off along Bertram Drive and towards the site of the long gone house known as The Knoll.

Built for the first non Salt director of Salts Mill Charles Stead, The Knoll was a large Victorian mansion of Gothic design which was built in the late 1850's and early 1860's. It was decorated with crenellations and gargoyles and even possessed a tower. Formal gardens were laid out in the grounds with a carriage drive which led down to two lodges, one of which still survives today. Situated at the top of a hill it would have enjoyed magnificent views across the valley to Saltaire. There are surviving photographs of the house but today no building plans survive. The land on which it was constructed had belonged to the Ferrand family who sold it to Sir Titus Salt who then sold it to Charles Stead for £3400. Charles Stead was declared bankrupt in the 1890's and the house was then sold to Sir James Roberts for £10,000. When Sir James moved to nearby Milner Field his Son Bertram and his family moved into the Knoll. Members of the family continued to live in the house until after World War I. In the intervening years the house had various owners until being sold to Baildon Urban District Council for £8950. The Knoll was demolished in 1961 and the present day flats were built on the site in its place.

Although nothing of The Knoll remains today the carriage drive which runs downhill through Fairbank Wood still remains. This is easily accessible and I found it straight away and started to follow it along through the heavy wooded area. The tall thick trees formed a canopy which blocked out the late morning sun and the resulting lower temperature made me shiver. The air was quiet with only the distant bird calls breaking the silence. Lou scampered away into a dense Holly bush in pursuit of a Squirrel and with some difficulty I managed to pull her back on to the drive. Thin tracks of hard packed soil led off in all directions through the undergrowth. Despite the early hour I found the atmosphere slightly oppressive as the light seemed to fade away leaving me with only the ghost of the past as company. A small series of steps led up the bank to the site of one of the two estate lodges.

I stopped for a few minutes and sat on the crumbling moss covered wall of the former lodge to light a smoke. Lou rolled around in the soil at my feet in some droppings she had found. Jack Russell's do this from time to time it seems. I gazed down the carriage drive and could almost see in my mind's eye a small two seated Studebaker carriage driven by a pair of fine jet black Geldings racing up the drive towards me. Flashing by at high speed the occupants stared straight ahead focusing their attentions on the coming evenings opulent dinner party hosted by The Steads no doubt. They never even noticed the humble village boy sat silently on the wall smoking his roll up. The tobacco had burnt away down to my fingers and the resulting sharp pain brought me back to 2014 with somewhat of a jolt. I had much to see this day and had to move on so pulling myself to my feet I dragged Lou from the dirt and mounted the steps to once again reach the carriage drive and move downhill.

After only a couple of minutes we had arrived at the entrance gates by the second estate lodge. The gates themselves are not original but the gateposts are. A third stone post attached to the side once contained a small gate for pedestrian access. The two main gates were slightly askew and showed signs of great age and once again my vivid imagination made me wonder just who had passed through them over the years. Now back in the bright sunlight my chilled flesh started to tingle as it regained warmth. I was glad no ghosts had followed me down from the fine Victorian house which once sat at the top of the hill.

We made our way along Southdown road, past rows of 20th century contemporary houses onto Cliffe Terrace and towards the area where I knew

Edwards Salt's mansion Ferniehurst used to stand. As with The Knoll very little remains of this once fine Victorian mansion. There are no known photographs or building plans, however maps of the area do show the basic plan of the house and of the glasshouses and other buildings. Edward Salt married his first wife Mary Jane Susan Elgood on July 10th 1861 and it seems likely the house was built for her. The Salt family lived at the house until 1893 when upon restructuring of the family business at Salts Mill they left the area to live in Morecambe. Edward Salt died in 1903 and was buried in the churchyard at Bathampton.

Ferniehurst had 12 bedrooms, a tower and a billiard room with its own separate entrance. There were also outbuildings including a carriage house for six carriages, a separate laundry, a gardener's bothy, three vineries and a mushroom house. The house was surrounded by "pleasure grounds" and this was planted with forest trees, herbaceous and alpine plants plus shrubs and ferns of all descriptions. The house and estate was bought by George Camille Waud in 1896. His family owned and ran Britannia Mills in Bradford. His great interests were growing roses and breeding Hackney horses and he built a stud farm here to breed these horses.

In the 1920's Waud started selling off land from the estate and in the late 1930's the house and grounds were sold to a quarrying company. It is said they used stone from the house to build properties on nearby Rockcliffe Avenue. Baildon Council then bought the house in the 1940's and demolished it to create an urban area. Some stonewalling, railings and steps are all that remain of the house today. The lodge was on Baildon Road near the bottom of Rockcliffe Avenue and was only pulled down recently. The sad demise of yet another of the districts fine old Victorian mansions was complete.

We approached the estate grounds from the rear and walked up through slightly less dense woodland than that we had just left towards the only remaining building on the estate. Ferniehurst farm was in its day known as a "Model Farm". The surrounding fields were packed with cattle to provide meat and dairy products for the tiled fully functional dairy. A piggery contained beasts that were destined for the farms bacon curing room, and the farm even had poultry and Pigeon houses.

Today the farm is still in working order and as we passed up the carriage drive beside it the small of the countryside pervaded my twitching nostrils. Walking beneath and alongside a massive towering stone wall I reached the site of the former Hackney Horse stud farm. Two massive angry looking Bulls guarded the field like sentinels awaiting their dead master's return. We continued on towards the field that once contained the massive impressive glasshouses for Edward Salt's beloved Orchid collection. Salt had one of the foremost collections of Orchids in the country and his Odontoglossum house was considered a model of perfection.

We dropped down a steep path into part of the gardens now known as The Dell. This expanse of ground surrounded by trees and bushes contains the remains of some stone walls and steps. Amongst these is one massive high piece of wall that took Lou Parson two seconds to climb but took me about two minutes. From here I looked down into what the official Bradford Council blurb calls "an oppressive atmosphere". Strangely enough I found it to be much the opposite as the trees stood around the open ground to form an almost inpenatrative wall to keep the history safe within. I found the feeling comforting and sitting down, reached once again for my tobacco tin and my imagination.

I had no time to peel back the decades to a past time as two local yobs with an unleashed Staffordshire bull terrier came bounding in and broke the spell. Time to move on as I tend to avoid the usual inevitable confrontation that results from such meetings. We made our way down the short distance to the main entrance gate of the estate on Baildon Road. The gates came from Baildon Town Hall and are not the original Ferniehurst gates. After a short stroll down Baildon road we came to the end of Rockcliffe Avenue and the short track named Wauds Gates. This was the original location of the entrance and carriage drive to the Ferniehurst estate.

Setting off once again Lou and I continued to walk down Baildon Road and after passing the site of the demolished Lower Holme Mills walked along Otley Road to the junction with Green Lane. The site of Lower Holme Mills was owned for a period in the 19th century by Sir Titus Salt and it is reputed to have been the site originally intended for Salts Mill. This was of course constructed further west along the valley at Saltaire instead. Salt sold the site to C.F Taylor in 1862 who constructed a Mohair spinning and weaving mill on the land.

As is evident so far the Salt family and Sir Titus in particular have their footprints all over the area in which I had been walking and the road that I was now heading for was no different. During the 1860's Sir Titus Salt bought up huge tracts of land on the north side of the River Aire, but apart from creating

Roberts Park and laying down Coach Road he did little else with it. Coach Road would lead to his Son Edward's house Ferniehurst in the east and the house of one of his other Sons Titus Jnr at Milner Field to the west.

The inheritors of Salts Mill still owned this land after World War II and in 1952 Shipley Urban District Council bought the land and built the present day social housing to replace slums in Shipley, Windhill and other areas. Shipley Urban District Council's commitment was to blend their housing plans in with the natural environment by consciously resisting the "stack them high pack them cheap" thinking that was common in much council planning in the 1950's. Some of the residents who moved in to their social housing in the 1950's are still living there today as they have never wanted to leave this well designed estate. The houses on Coach Road and Higher Coach Road were constructed by a multi skilled labour force put together by the Council named The Shipley Direct Labour Force in the years between 1956 and 1962. According to records the total building costs for the whole estate were £386,515.

Carrying on along Higher Coach Road Lou and I came to the tiny hamlet of Trench. Surrounded on one side by the ancient Trench Wood this small 17th century settlement was original owned by Yeoman Clothiers of the Hudson family with the first record of inhibition being 1665. Trench House can be seen nestled nearby. It is a listed building which has a date stone initialled I H E 1697. This refers to an extension to the house, probably added by Jonathan Hudson who lived there until the 1720s. It is an excellent example of a yeoman's house. The front facade of the house is interesting as the builder deliberately moved away from the normal local style and incorporated classical elements. Close to the house is a listed barn, which used to have a date stone of 1669 with the initials SH over a door. Trench Wood itself is a dense semi natural woodland with Beech and Holly being just two of the wide varieties of native trees and bushes to be found there. We turned off Higher Coach Road at this point to follow a small well-worn footpath across Trench Meadow to enter Trench Wood itself.

Once again the wood was rather gloomy due to the densely packed trees and after passing a number of massive Gritstone rocks that may well have been deposited there by an Ice age glacier we reached a marvellously serene and remote mill pond. This was the pond and dam for the dye house at Salts Mill and was created in 1911 and old post cards show this area as Crag Hebble.

In the Victorian and Edwardian eras this and the nearby Shipley Glen was a very popular picnic area for the millworkers of Shipley and Bradford.

Here, close to the pond in the lower part of the wood, is the remains of Sam Wilson's Toboggan Run which was one of the many attractions associated with Shipley Glen in late Victorian times.
The riders were carried in small cars from the top of the edge of Brackenhall Green down to this area. On Whit Sunday 1900 one of the cars on the upward side fouled the steel cable which lifted it back up to the top. This resulted in several injuries and Sam Wilson immediately closed it, never to reopen it. So ended 'The Largest, Wildest and Steepest Toboggan Slide Ever Erected in the World'. I was delighted to see nearby what is known locally as the Bird Cage. This is an elaborate "Kissing Gate" built in 1872 as part of the development of Milner Field house and estate.

Lou and I found the track that is known as Sparable Lane and followed this for a while through Delph Wood and across Little Beck until it tuned northwards to skirt alongside what was once the Glasshouse and kitchen garden area of Titus Salt Junior's lavish Victorian mansion of Milner Field. Walled kitchen gardens were found in many of Britain's large country houses of the period and those of Milner Field were innovative and lavish in the extreme. The kitchen gardens were laid out in well arranged plots to provide all manner of vegetables for consumption by the residents of the nearby house. In front of the walled garden there were ten greenhouses, thirty four feet long and eighteen feet wide. Laying north to south to take full advantage of the sun it was all well planned by the leading Horticulturalists of the day. Potting sheds were located at the end of each Greenhouse each being fitted with its own water cistern. Apple and Pear trees grew all around the area again to provide fruit for Milner Field's inhabitants. Pineapples were also cultivated here and these exotic fruits were unknown to all but the most affluent of the landed gentry and royalty at this time. A Mushroom house was built near to the boilers. These were sown on soil heaped over damp horse manure.

Talking of horses it was my intention to cross the central field to try and find the remains of a base from a fountain that once stood there. Right in the middle of this small field stood a very dodgy and angry looking horse. He was staring right at us and was strangely nodding his head up and down as if he was urging us on to "ave a go" and test him. Even though I have worked with horses at Roleystone Sanctuary in the past I have learnt to treat them with respect so I wisely thought to give this beast a wide berth and stay on the footpath outside his domain. So I leaped down from the wall and urged Lou on down the path and walked towards the trees where we could enter the site of the long gone but not forgotten magnificent house of Milner Field.

The house of Milner Field was built on the site of an Elizabethan mansion bearing the same name that Sir Titus Salt had bought in 1869 for £21000 from an Admiral Dunscombe. He immediately demolished the house and passed ownership of the land to his youngest Son Titus Salt Junior who proceeded to commission the building of a new house. The original Elizabethan Milner Field house was built by John Oldfield in 1603 and Salt Jnr retained the commemorative stone bearing this date and the monograms of Oldfield and his wife and incorporated them in his new mansion. The grand new version of the Milner Field house was constructed on the sunny northern bank of the River Aire about one mile from Saltaire (but well-hidden amongst trees and gardens) and was amongst the most grand and lavish of any Victorian mansions of its time. When first built it was a wonder of contemporary Victorian living. Sadly, little remains today except an archive of wonderful photographs of both the interior and exterior, which give a fascinating insight into the lifestyle of well-to-do Victorians such as the Salts.

Work began in 1869 to the plans of Architect Thomas Harris in the (then fashionable) neo-Gothic style, with a nod in the direction of the Arts and Crafts movement. The material used in the construction was "the grey local stone, the outer walls being lined with brick so as to form hollow walls and thereby prevent the possibility of dampness" The roofs were covered with Whitland Abbey green slates bought and transported from Wales. After leaving Saltaire via what is now Victoria Road and originally crossing a stone bridge, Milner Field could be reached by a carriage drive along a private road westward below Shipley Glen, past Trench Farm and Fell Wood, before reaching South Lodge.

This lodge (also known as Bottom Lodge) was the start of an uphill climb to Milner Field using a long tree lined approach road through thick woodland. To the left of this road lay a small lake and fishpond with an island and rustic wooden bridge, a boathouse and several rowing boats. Eventually the road turned left to approach the entrance-way to the house. Milner Field was built facing almost due north and south, the entrance being on the north (rear) side of the building through an arched gateway into a spacious enclosed courtyard.

To catch the sun, the principal rooms of the house faced south and opened onto a wide terrace with steps leading down to the park.

It had its own water and electricity supplies, sewage system and filter beds, water-cooled storage rooms (the forerunner of refrigerators) and was connected by telephone to the mill in Saltaire. It had splendid facilities to cater for the family's recreational needs - a huge billiard room with pre-Raphaelite stained glass and murals, a magnificent library, a music room with a massive purpose-built pipe organ, and stables with buildings to accommodate horse draw carriages. It also had landscaped gardens and a large 'winter garden' conservatory connected to the main house via an Orangery.

Milner Field

The Salts entertained lavishly using the nine bedrooms to accommodate their guests and were even visited twice by royalty during their time at Milner Field. Titus Jnr died prematurely of heart disease in the Billiard room on the afternoon of Saturday 19th November 1887. After the death of Titus Salt Jnr, Catherine his wife and George, one of his sons continued to live at the house until 1903. However in the intervening period and partly because of a trade slump Catherine was forced to sell the business to a syndicate of four Bradford business men, including James Roberts who within nine months became the Managing Director of Salts Mill. Roberts moved into Milner Field in 1903. He and the next two residents of the house, Ernest Gates and A.R (Teddy) Hollins (a later Managing Director of Salts Co who died unexpectedly in 1929) all suffered a series of personal tragedies. This led many people to believe that the house was jinxed.

The house was put up for sale in 1930, but given the series of tragic events affecting all the owners and tenants, it is not surprising that the mansion subsequently failed to sell. Over the years nature reclaimed the grounds and the building fell into disrepair, was stripped of its contents and then of its roof, and before long the site began to be robbed of its stone. During the Second World War it was used for grenade practice by the local Home Guard. Whilst the exact date of demolition of the house is not known local legend suggests a date between 1950 and 1959.

I had read enough about Milner Field and its history before I visited the site to be well aware of its supposed jinx. So with this in mind and considering the area was almost as dark as it would be at midnight due to the heavy tree canopy, I swallowed heavily and approached through the trees with some trepidation and unease. Even the dog seemed reluctant to enter the inky blackness. She was wired and alert over something although I had heard nothing. The air was eerily still so what had spooked her? Maybe she had sensed something that I could not? I dismissed such nonsense from my hardened local historian mind and trod carefully along a small path towards the ruins that now loomed up in front of me.

I passed through what remained of the ivy covered main entrance arch and immediately recognised part of one of the stone gateposts from the original house laid in the undergrowth. Turning around I could plainly see the large flat tree covered area that was once the Croquet lawn. Large piles of still superb moss and lichen covered ornately cut stone lay all around a few feet away. I identified the mosaic tiled floor of the Conservatory away to the side. Pushing back some bushes I made my way there to stand upon the ground where Royalty once drank fine aged Scottish Whiskey and played cards with Salt and his wife. The remains of the Orangery which connected the Conservatory to the main house were immediately evident as was the footprint of the Billiard Room where Titus Salt Jnr breathed his last.

I mounted what remained of the wall here to stand upon the top and gaze down upon him writhing in agony as his undiagnosed heart disease took him away to meet his maker. My vivid and lucid imagination was in overdrive by this point and images driven by the photographs I had seen flashed through my mind. Did they carry his body through to the house along this passageway?

Was it this one over there? Did they carry him out through the French doors in the Conservatory? Lou and I were totally alone amongst the ruins but I felt as though someone or something was there watching us.

We scampered over the ruins towards the area of the kitchens. Here I could see the brick lined walls and archways of the cellars and store rooms. At one time they will have been filled to the brim with bottles of expensive French wine and fine food from every corner of the world. Now they were stuffed full of rubble and old beer cans. Stumbling over the piles of stone and rubble I found myself near to the south facing front terrace wall close by what was once an area of manicured lawns, small bushes and trees. It was here I felt a distinct shiver running down my spine. Like someone has just walked over my grave as my old Grandma Jackson would have said. But there was no wind nor breeze to cause such an unearthly feeling. Maybe the reports of ghostly happenings here at Milner Field did indeed have some substance and were not just the ramblings of local folk with too much beer in their systems.

I paused here to take yet another photograph and what resulted has since been seen by many people who could indeed see strange figures amongst the brickwork of the ruins. Many people myself included can clearly see the figure of Titus Salt and a group of Edwardian woman. Suddenly almost as soon as the shutter had closed something stirred inside a nearby holly bush and that was enough for me. Picking Lou parson up roughly by her harness I ran like the devil himself was chasing me.

Without even pausing to look behind I kept running and stumbling through the trees till the ruins receded into the distance and we came to the huge wall that surrounded the estate and safety. With no thought to the passing traffic on Primrose lane I launched Lou over the wall and then myself and landed with a bump on the pavement. I was sweating like a man on the gallows and could hardly breathe but at least we had escaped from whatever it was in that bush. This local historian stuff is supposed to be fun and enjoyable but I'd never been so scared in all my life.

I have visited Milner Field on a couple of occasions since and did not find it as haunting and spooky as I did today. Perhaps that is due to me knowing what to expect and the suppression of my usual rampant imagination who knows? After regaining my usual composure and dusting myself off I calmed Lou down and headed along Primrose Lane towards the canal. I turned off down a footpath at the side of a quaint row of 18th century weaver's cottages, and within a few minutes I was stood in the bright sunlight on Dowley Gap Bridge watching a canal boat make its slow unrushed way towards Shipley. Not a ghost or ghoul in sight for a change. Apart from the occasional unleashed dog and its uncivilised owner a walk along the canal is something of a joy. The towpath is flat and I can rack up the miles with little trouble. So the walk back from here to Shipley was not going to be a problem and we passed Coppy Bull Wood and Hirst Locks in little time.

At Saltaire the canal runs between the two massive gargantuan buildings of Salt's Mill on one side and the block of apartments on the other. A swan flapped its huge wings as it ran along the water and took off from the surface. The resulting noise reverberated from the stone walls of the buildings like a Lancaster bomber had taken off not a humble swan. Lou and I were soon in Shipley and nestled at the rear of the 633 bus once again groaning its way up Carr lane. I glanced back over my shoulder as Baildon Bank came into view and silently gave a nod of thanks to the Salt family for providing the area with such a fine legacy but also Lou and I with a day we will remember for a long time.

Thackley Corner to High Esholt

When I was a child growing up in Guiseley we first lived on Victoria Road and then moved to the Silverdale estate near to the ancient Esholt Woods. From the age of twelve or so my friends and I rooted around the woods doing what young boys do. We used to try and catch Rabbits in a field near Springs Wood at Esholt Junction, and played near the railway line taking our lives in our hands. Our gang used to ride around the tracks on an old battered Lambretta 150cc Scooter that one of us had got his sweaty pubescent hands on. When it was my turn to keep it at our house on the estate nearby such an idea was met with anger and discouragement from my Mum. As was most things I did but that's another story and not for here. We were aware of all kind of stories of previous events in the woods. A wartime army camp here, a long ago murder there, that kind of thing. But the one that sticks in my memory over four decades later is a story of a downed Spitfire. The story was that it had got into trouble for some unknown reason over the woods and crash landed nose first in a bog deep in the middle of nowhere. Naturally my friends and I searched endlessly for this plane but sadly never found anything and over the subsequent years the idea was forgotten about.

This was until late June 2015 when a member of Banter about Bradford started posting a series of old photographs of Esholt village on the group Facebook page. This stirred my memory to regress some four decades and transport me back to Esholt Woods as a young boy and the search for the Spitfire. My adult mind told me it was a load of nonsense but my imagination spoke to me and said "Hey, you never know". It was an excuse for a good walk anyway so consulted the old maps and made my plans.

No buses were needed as Lou and I once again set off the following day. We strolled down past the former Jowett car factory and the site of an even older quarry at Five Lane Ends towards the historic village of Idle and Lou's birthplace. The massive Morrison's Supermarket now occupies this site and when I visit there I always make a point of pursuing the large photographs inside of the Jowett cars being assembled. After a short distance I turned off the main road along Idlecroft Road to follow the route of the old G.N.R railway line to where Idle station once stood. The old Oddfellows public house stands nearby and we turned up hill at the side of the pub along High Street. Passing by a lovely collection of early 18th century weavers cottages we soon made Town Lane heading towards Thackley Corner.

At the junction of Town Lane and Leeds Road stands an old open air gents urinal. A strange little place it is no more than a slit in the wall behind which stands a trough. It has not been used for decades officially but judging by the smell it continues to be used by blokes when they leave the nearby Great Northern pub I assume. This I know as I could smell it from twenty feet away as I crossed over and walked down Thackley Road. Using the road bridge I passed over the long gone railway line and carried on towards Ainsbury Avenue which winds down the edge of the ancient Buck Wood to the canal. There is reputed to be a wartime bunker set in the banking along here where the Police would explode in safety any ordnance they came across, but in June the vegetation is so thick that any idea of having a quick attempt at finding it was dismissed and we pressed on.

Buck Wood was quiet and still as we plodded downhill along the wide avenue. Only the distant birdcalls broke the lunchtime silence as Lou and I passed by Field Wood and then Hollins Wood. At this point there is no mistaking that Esholt sewage works are nearby as even if the breeze blows downwards to hell it still pervades your nostrils like a fart in a sleeping bag. But thankfully we were about to cross the canal at the turn bridge and follow the towpath towards Apperley Bridge. It would be nice to go straight ahead through the plant at the bridge but it's always locked up tight so there is no choice but to walk the long way around to reach the small antique footbridge across the river Aire.

Dodging the manic cyclists along the towpath Lou and I were soon at the next turn bridge that once gave access to a small farm on the far bank named Rawcliffe. This bridge would have linked the farm to the track to Apperley Bridge before it was demolished. Passing by the site of another small demolished farm named Crow Croft we came to Thackley Canal Bridge and paused for a moment at the tiny garden to the side of the towpath that someone has made for their dead child. It's always neat and tidy which is nice to see. It was just as well that I was about to leave the towpath and cross one of Bottom Farm's fields as I could see a large giddy unrestrained Labrador bounding along towards us. As is usual the "owner" was fifty yards behind just strolling along but in an instant we were through the fence and into the fields.

I pirouetted gracefully like a ballet dancer underneath the electric fence to reach the second field and making for the twin bridges underneath the railway headed towards a massive open field carpeted with yellow flowers. It was here that I saw the Labrador approaching us once again. The "owner" must have come through a gap in the fence that I had missed prior to my own exit from the towpath but fortunately the grass was tall and the errant dog didn't see us as we passed by. At the far side of the field is the most fantastic iron suspension footbridge that gives access across the river Aire to the former Esholt estate beyond. Guarded at each end by twin iron pillars surmounted with crowns a larger version would not look out of place spanning a great river. I have never been able to find any information as to its history but I like to think it was designed and built by someone historic like Isambard Kingdom Brunel.

The track alongside the river was heavily overgrown and was spooking Lou so I had to urge her along till we reached the sewage plant and its stirring tanks of sludge. I tried not to think of what exactly was being stirred by the rotating arms and turned my thoughts to finer things like downed Spitfires. It was upon entering the main road through the estate named The Avenue that my mind tuned to thoughts of a lad who had been in my class at school some forty years before. Timothy Alderman was a quiet and studious pupil at Guiseley School, in fact he was what we used to term a "swot".

Upon leaving school he had been working at The Blue Barn in Pool in Wharfedale and was erroneously accused of stealing money from the till. The resulting shame brought him down to Esholt sewage works where he laid his head under one of the large stone wheels that allowed the machinery to travel along the beds. Even though he was never one of my close friends I still said a silent prayer in his memory as I stood at the exact point where he met his maker all those years before. Regaining my usual composure we moved on to pass by the office units of Home farm and before long reached Gill Lane on the edge of the woods. Gill Lane was the old packhorse trail which the merchants would use to transport their goods from Esholt to Nether Yeadon and beyond.

But we were not going in that direction so we only climbed the slight incline for a few hundred yards before turning off to follow the line of the railway up towards Spring Woods where as young boys we used to search for the downed Spitfire.

Back in my youth neither I nor any of my friends had any idea of the historic past of the woods as things like mills and such like were only for scruffy old men to reminisce about. As far as we were concerned nothing happened in the woods apart from stories told to us by strange local characters and what we could conjure up from our own imaginations. Spitfires and murders were interesting whereas mills and becks were not. But now I had become a strange old local character myself the urge to find the remains of Waterloo Scribbling Mill and Guiseley Beck that served it seemed to make more sense than looking for a mythical Spitfire that frankly was probably no more than local folklore.

So with that in mind Lou Parson and I turned off up Springs Road towards where my map had indicated the presence of a lodge. And where there was once a lodge they would usually be a mill or a house of some description. I quickly located Guiseley Beck as the sound of the water rushing over the weir was a dead giveaway. It runs through the trees along the bottom of a gully to the side of the ancient Springs Road. As I stood there taking photos of the beck I heard a sound in the bushes behind me. Spinning around I saw two old men coming out of the trees. They looked rather sheepish and one was buttoning up his shirt so I guessed they had not been checking out the points of the nearby railway line. I shook my head and tutted before moving off through the wood leaving them behind.

A little further along Springs Road I once again looked down into the gully and could clearly see a natural basin alongside the beck. Even though it was now filled with trees I could make out the shape of the former mill pond. Every mill needed a water source and a pond in which to store the water for further use when needed. Waterloo Mill will have been no different and I knew I was close to the area where it was once situated.

The wood at this point had thinned out somewhat and was not nearly as dense as the woods I had previously been used to during my walks. There was plenty of light and this gave it a pastoral ambience rather than the dank and dark broodiness of Milner Field for example. Lou pulled sharply at her lead as she tried to give chase to a Squirrel and with some effort I managed to reel her in and the Squirrel fled up a nearby tree to safety. We moved through the wood in silence marvelling at the cobble stones still evident on the road. How many horse driven carts had travelled over these stones to and from the mill? Who were the people that drove them? Where and how did they live?

Questions filled my mind as we tramped along Springs Road towards the giant stone gateposts that I had seen a little further on.

The stone gateposts stood at the entrance to a track that led off into the woods. Waterloo Mill would surely have been situated down here beside the dam of Guiseley beck. This mill belonged to Esholt Estate and the old Ordnance Survey maps show it as a "Scribbling" mill. Scribbling was the process of preparing the raw fleece for spinning and includes the separation or "carding" of the wool fibres. This was traditionally done by children at home but upon the advent of mills it was carried out in a more mechanised manner.

The image of the heavy laden carts piled high with dirty foul smelling fleeces lumbering down the road I was stood on was hard not to imagine. Any thoughts of following this track through the woods were dashed by the sound of a man shouting some distance away across the beck. Drawing my attention he came into view through the trees although he had not yet seen us. He had with him five large and unleased dogs. They looked like hunting dogs of some kind, perhaps Irish Wolfhounds I could not tell for sure. Luckily none of them were coming in our direction but as always I was taking no chances. Lou or indeed I would stand little chance if we were pounced upon by such a number of dogs with such an obvious pack mentality.

So clicking the shutter on my camera one final time we moved swiftly along the road in the opposite direction from the hounds of hell. I have been in so many situations on my travels where some stupid unrestrained dog is leaping up all around us that I never leave anything to chance now. The "owner" is always fifty feet away waving at us and shouting that its "alright he only wants to play blah blah blah". It's not "alright" and I will take a kicking if I have to but I won't stand around smiling whilst this goes on. So I have learnt to look ahead and see any situation before it develops.

After only a few hundred yards Lou and I crossed under an old stone railway bridge that spanned the road and I came upon I field I recognised from my boyhood days. It was here alongside the railway line where aged eleven I had searched for Mushrooms with my elder Brother in Law Graham McGee. He had woken me up one bright and sunny morning at about 4am to go with him into the woods to look amongst the cowpats in the woods. I can't remember if we did pick any that morning but the memory stays with us both to this day despite the four decades that have passed since.

We were now right on top of the site of the famous Esholt rail crash. At 3.30am on June 9th 1892 two trains collided only a few feet from where Lou and I were sat. The crash left five people dead and twenty six injured. The subsequent inquiry concluded the primary cause of the crash to be the obstruction of a signal by dense vegetation. A Leeds to Ilkley train arrived at the junction as it was being crossed by an Ilkley to Bradford train. The Ilkley bound train ploughed into the last six carriages of the Bradford bound train overturning the last three carriages. As I sat in the grass in the warm afternoon sun I closed my eyes and could almost hear the screams of the injured from 123 years before. Its times like this that I sometimes wish my imagination was not as lucid as it is.

As I sat in the grass munching my cheese and onion sandwiches I realised that I was firmly in Guiseley and beyond the Bradford boundary. I always like to post a short review of my walks and the photos on the Banter about Bradford Facebook group page and the rules are that only matters concerning Bradford are allowed. You even have to print the word "Leeds" as L***s, that kind of thing. So no doubt I would incur the wrath of the Moderators and I could almost hear Michael Murphy's beard twitching from here. So with that image in mind I thought it prudent to make my way across the fields to Sodhall Hill and thence to Old Hollins Hill where I could make my way to Esholt village.

My Uncle Neville used to live at the top of Old Hollins Hill and I didn't even know if he was still alive, but I thought of him for the first time in years as I passed near to his house. As a kid he would take me on occasion to watch Bradford Northern when Rugby was Rugby and The Bulls were T'Northen. Happy days Uncle Neville thank you. The road of Old Hollins Hill winds steeply downhill past the disused Hollins Hill Quarry towards a fine Victorian Viaduct on the edge of the village. Many years ago I stood underneath this magnificent structure and watched a bloke fall from his motorbike and slide some fifty yards down the road on his back. Protected by his leathers he simply stood up, dusted himself down and remounted his trusty steed to ride off.

Station Road took Lou and me into the village which is correctly named as Upper Esholt. All was still and quiet in the late afternoon sun as we stood in the centre of this quintessential English country village. With its tiny village shop, close cosy cottages and pub it is little wonder that it is renowned the world over for its charm. We turned along Chapel Lane passing by Esholt Old Hall. Originally belonging to the De Warde family the medieval Manor house is the oldest in the village. Now Grade II listed this stone built jewel once even had a moat. The building dates back at least as far as the sixteenth century and some of its timber frame construction, with stud partitioning and altered king post roof trusses, has survived. This section may well incorporate part of the medieval hall that stood on the site. The building is now an irregular structure, consisting of two storeys that were rebuilt by the Sherbourne family in the late sixteenth century and a taller two storey and attic portion under one large gable that was built in the mid seventeenth century by the Calverley family. The historical development of the building contributes greatly to its interest, demonstrating the changes in tastes and building techniques as the centuries proceeded.

The building is built of large blocks of coursed gritstone and has a stone slate roof with saddle stones to the gables. The attributes of the building are now mixed. The windows, for example, vary from the five light and four light chamfered mullioned windows with drip moulds on the mid seventeenth century section, to the earlier square mullioned type. The tall chimney stacks that stand above the roofline contribute greatly to its stature and the clapper boarding of the gable wall is particularly unusual. Internally, too, the building has retained some rare and interesting features, such as the coffered oak ceiling of the parlour.

Many of the village's fine early 18th century workers cottages were used in the filming of the famous soap opera Emmerdale Farm or Emmerdale as it is known today. As we left the village behind the cottages gave way to open fields containing horses grazing in the warm sun. We passed by the late Georgian property named Home House then I paused for a few moments at the bottom of Cunliffe Lane to admire the terrace houses of Bunkers Hill. These houses were known as Demdyke Row in Emmerdale. Here at the end of Cunliffe Lane there was once a Tannery served by forty stone pits and three springs to provide water for the tanning process.

We continued along the narrow and winding Esholt Lane past the site of the long gone Upper Esholt Mill towards the final part of our walk. Following the path of the nearby river Aire alongside us we came to the tiny settlement of Tarn with its 18th century vernacular style workers cottages and Tarn Grange as its centre. This marvellous property contains a stone dated 1827. Opposite standing in splendid isolation amongst the fields is Bean House.

I could hear the cars rushing by on nearby Otley Road and sadly I knew this walk was at an end. Sitting in the bus shelter waiting for the bus that would take us back to Shipley, I looked down at Lou as she jumped up at me and licked my chin just as she had done the first time we met when she was 10 days old. I simply could not imagine a better companion to accompany me on these walks than this little dog so full of life and spirit. I picked her up and sitting her on my lap my thoughts went back over the day's events. I had revisited many memories and places from my distant past this day but one thought did occur to me. I never did find that bloody Spitfire.

Hodgson's Fold to Walnut Farm via Peel Park

Everyone loves a time bubble if they can find one. A place where time stands still and all your cares and woes simply drift away leaving you in a state of suspended animation almost. A place where there are no modern inconveniences, no take aways, shops or music blaring out. A place where modern life simply does not exist to a certain extent. On my travels around the Bradford area I have found quite a few spots that could almost fit the bill. I use the word "almost" as they are near enough but not quite perfect to create that mythical feeling of disassociation with 21st century life that I crave sometimes. It just happens that I know of a place that does and it is only five minutes walk from home.

I knew this walk would not be a long drawn out slog through deep dark woods, or a hike over barren windswept moorland. I needed no bus fares nor packed up food to give me sustenance along the way. I needed my black flat historians cap, my boots and my dog nothing more. As usual the magnificent Lou Parson was ready at the back door with a wagging tail and an excited yelp. And so with that we were off once again to turn back time and dream of people long deceased. Leaving our cottage we set off in the bright late morning July sun downhill towards Kings Road. Here we entered the site of the long demolished abut somewhat grand Bolton Lodge which today is covered by a new build estate of houses.

Bolton Lodge was a fair sized gothic style mansion built by Wm. Stead in the 1850`s on land adjoining Wood Lane Farm. The site had, before this, been a public garden kept by John Ackroyd, a local Wesleyan preacher, whose house had also stood on the site. There was an ornate cast iron lamp post by the kitchen door which stood in a rockery. The house stood on a terrace of level ground and had steps down to the gently sloping grounds surrounded by a perimeter wall with large trees. The outline of the Lodge grounds is still clearly defined by mature Sycamore trees, and it was through these trees that we now walked to cross Kings Road on the way to surmount Old Hill.

Climbing up the steep steps towards Old Hill Lou scared the hell out of a group of kids from Hanson School. They ran off giggling and shouting but I think Lou was more scared of them than they were of her. We joined the footpath that runs along the top of Old Hill along the side of the present

Hanson School playing fields. It is an ancient track that merchants once trod along their way across from Bolton on the other side of the hill. After perhaps a thousand yards the path forks down to the right into an estate and left towards my time bubble. It is quite an innocuous start as the path skirts alongside the huge side of an 18th century house on one side and a grass bank on the other and after thirty yards or so I came to a stone stile at the footpaths end.

This is known as a Kissing Gate and the word has evolved from the ancient word "Kisting". These stones are arranged in such a way as to form a solid wall, and when looked at from near ground level by cattle and sheep it would appear to form a solid obstacle. Possessing only two dimensional sight this tricks the animals into believing there is no way through, whilst humans with their three dimensional sight can see the opening. So after squeezing through the narrow gap Lou and I entered the marvellous and evocative place that is Hodgson's Fold. From here on I will refer to it as Hodgson's Fold with an "S" as that is the way it is spelt on all the old maps. Bradford Council don't use it on their blurb but what do they know?

The diminutive former agricultural hamlet of Hodgson Fold is located in the neighbourhood of Bolton, which is located approximately two miles to the northeast of Bradford city centre. Hodgson Fold was one of a number of tiny hamlets located in this ancient township and mentioned in the Domesday Survey it is thought to have Anglo-Saxon origins.

Little is known of the form or size of Hodgson Fold until the first reliable maps of the 18th century were created. However, documentary evidence suggests that a settlement developed at Hodgson Fold around the mid-17th century when several buildings, including a house dated 1652, were constructed. It seems likely that John Hodgson, whose initials are inscribed over the door of the dated house, gave his name to the hamlet. The Hodgson family continued to live in the Fold for the next three hundred years. The township of Bolton was renowned locally for its beef and dairy produce, which supplied the surrounding towns and villages. Records show that as well as farmers and farm hands, a number of worsted and cloth weavers lived in Hodgson Fold in the late 18th century. Historical records indicate that they worked from the upper rooms of the cottages that were demolished in the late 19th century.

By the late 18th century, records show a diversification in the occupations of the residents of Hodgson Fold, with a move away from agriculture. Several members of the Hodgson family became butchers by profession. A number of worsted and cloth weavers also lived in the hamlet. It is reputed that the upper rooms of several cottages were used for weaving by Messrs Ackroyd and Lightfoot. This venture into small-scale textile manufacture was common in many agricultural areas during the late 18th century. However, once the production of textiles moved into the mills, hand weaving and spinning became swiftly uneconomical. It is likely that the main source of employment returned to agriculture during the 19th century as the demand for fresh dairy and beef produce increased in the growing town of Bradford.

Until middle of the 19th century the land at Hodgson Fold remained in the ownership of the Hodgson family. The Ordnance Survey map of 1852 shows the Fold at the end of a long narrow lane and surrounded by fields. The form and size of the hamlet is not much different to that of today, though the later Victorian developments had yet to be built. In 1854, following the death of the principal land owner, John Hodgson, his substantial estate was split between his three offspring – John Hodgson Jnr, Mrs J. Atkinson-Jowett and Mrs Crowther. Upon his wife's inheritance James Atkinson- Jowett took up residence in the hamlet. A large Italianate residence called Grove House was built to the northeast of Hodgson Fold and the old cottages along the lane demolished to make way for a pair of villa houses c. 1870. A formal carriageway was laid linking Grove House to Myers Lane.

By 1891 James Hodgson Jowett-Atkinson was the largest landowner in Bolton and one of most affluent men in Bradford. After the Second World War there was much residential development around the township of Bolton. Many of the tiny rural hamlets that made up the township were surrounded or enveloped by these new housing estates. Hodgson Fold was not an exception to this and now stands amidst the Ashbourne and Grove House estates.

I stood there in the centre of this tiny hamlet and took in a series of deep breaths. There are three unrivalled aromas in life, newly cut grass, Coffee and freshly baked bread. My nostrils twitched then flared upon sensing grass and bread. Somewhere in one of the small cottages a little old lady in an apron was baking bread on her old coal blacked wood fired oven perhaps. I looked around for the source in the tiny square we stood in. Although it was only small the cottages seemed to step back to create a feeling of endless openness.

Intoxicated by the unworldly aroma of the baking bread I walked through the tiny passage way between two cottages at the bottom of the courtyard. Here the humble dwellings are close enough for the residents to shake hands across the cobbled pathway.

I turned and once again stopped to admire the initials JH carved in the stone above the doorway of his first house in Hodgson's Fold. To my right ivy grew and fingered its way around the mullioned windows of yet another timeless cottage. Here before me was an open door and the heavenly smell of yeast and bread wafted out along the street as if to entice passing weary travellers to come and rest ye a while and feast. The baker was not an aged old women in a pinny but a shaven headed Grant Mitchell type on his day off from the office. I wasn't going to let a mere detail like that break the spell though and nodded at him as we passed along to turn up the side and enter another tiny track alongside his cottage.

Hodgson's Fold is so small you can walk around it in about thirty seconds so you have to do it twice and then once more again. Round and round I went, my head spinning with images of old farmers in flat caps and heavy boots, the small of newly cut grass forcing my imagination into overdrive. In my head I was back in the 18th century, I was feeling it, living it and loving it. This is what being a hardened local historian is all about I said out loud to the dog. She looked up at me with her large bright eyes and didn't disagree.

There is a well-tended patch of garden to the rear of the centre of the tiny courtyard. To which cottage it belongs I know not and perhaps it is a communal space. It sits behind a stout drystone wall and is entered by a small metal gate. I always sit on the step by the gate and from there I can survey all that is in front of me. The marvellous cottage "Fieldhead" stands opposite and is flanked on one side by the rear of a converted Grade II listed barn and by the gabled front of the 17th century cottage of number fourteen on the other. Built from yellowy hued sandstone and with a stone slate roof, Fieldhead sits well amongst the group and is my favourite of all the dwellings here. Sitting on the step I pulled out my tobacco tin and in a few seconds the smoke was drifting lazily up towards the tree branches above me joining my mind on its trip back through time.

I sat there for what seemed an age, Lou laid quietly at my feet like she understood the reverence of the place and respected it. It was dinnertime at the junior school on Myers Lane and the distant excited shouts of the children filled the air. The sounds didn't detract from the ambiance but merely added to it in a strange almost innocent kind of way. Nothing was going to break the spell and spoil the moment. The children playing tig in the school yard have little idea of what life will chuck at them in the coming years and should value their formative years whilst they can.

Sat there on that step with my own personal Jesus of Hodgson's Fold before me, all that had been thrown at me over the years simply ebbed away and meant nothing. That is the added beauty of having your own time bubble. If I didn't shift myself I would become part of the place so I jumped to my feet and urging Lou on we departed for Myers Lane and onwards to Bolton Outlanes.

Myers Lane was named after the local Myers family but before that it was called Owl Lane. The Myers built houses on the lane and were occupied as Cartwrights and Cow Doctors. One family member Joseph Myers (known as Dozy Doll) was employed as the local "Pinder". A Pinder was a man who would round up the local straying cattle and sheep and place them in the local pinfold to await collection by their owners. This local pinfold was the exact place I had been sitting in at Hodgson's Fold.

Walking along I glanced up at the green playing fields that slope up the hillside towards Hanson school, which sits on top of the hill overlooking Hodgson Fold. The school, which was built during the 1970s, was constructed on the site of Grove House, the Victorian villa built for James Atkinson-Jowett in 1860. The lodge for the house is still stands at the end of Grove House Road and gives some idea of what Grave House would have looked like before it was demolished in the 1950's. We passed by the lodge as we walked steadily up the slight incline towards the Swing Gate public house.

Standing in the car park of the pub I marvelled at Bolton's oldest building, the superb Ivy Hall. Built in 1616 and owned at one time by John Bailey it has a large buttressed chimney with steps on the inside for sweeps to use whilst cleaning it. Bailey also owned the Tollbooth and prison which once stood at the junction of Ivegate and Kirkgate in Bradford. A local legend states that a tunnel once led from here to Bolling Hall. Why Ivy Hall stands side by side with the rear of William Morrison's first Supermarket is anyone's guess!

Passing through Bolton Junction next to the now sadly disappeared pub The Junction, Lou and I walked along Idle Road for a while. This long straight road would take us all the way to our next port of call and past my former home at number thirty. I moved from there to my present house sixteen years ago but have fond memories of living at this house. Boy did I have some good times one way or another in that little front back to back house but that's all for another book and not for this one. We passed my old local pub The Malt kiln and I smiled at the recollection of watching Dean Windass on Sky Tv shaking the Kop at Anfield by scoring for Bradford City in The Premier League. We turned down Otley road to approach one of England's greatest Victorian Cemeteries. Rivalled only by Highgate Cemetery in London, Undercliffe Cemetery is an absolute marvel of Victorian Funerailia and a visit there is always a joy.

The cemetery stands atop a hillside overlooking the city and contains some very impressive Victorian monuments in a variety of styles. It is a notable example of a Victorian cemetery where a number of rich and prominent local residents have been buried, notably mill owners and former mayors. Undercliffe Cemetery is Grade II listed by English Heritage in their Register of Parks and Gardens of Special Historic Interest in England. In the early 1800s Bradford's textile industry underwent rapid growth and with it Bradford's population, consequently there was pressure on housing then on burial ground space and this eventually became a health hazard.

As a result many of the existing cemeteries were closed by order of Bradford Council. Partly in response to this situation the 'Bradford Cemetery Company' was set up and provisionally registered in 1849. Membership of the company included local notables Henry Brown, Robert Milligan, William Rand, Edward Ripley and Sir Titus Salt. The land used for the cemetery had previously been agricultural land with a farmhouse on part of the Undercliffe Estate owned by the Hustler family. The plot was purchased in 1851 by John Horsfall for £3,400 and he founded The Bradford Cemetery Company in 1852. The cemetery was designed and laid out over the years 1851–1854 by park and cemetery designer William Gay (1814–1893) and architect John Dale for the sum of £12,000 for landscaping, planting and building involving the construction in 1854 of two chapels on the main promenade.

The cemetery is at a height of 210 m above sea level with an area of 26 acres accommodating some 124,000 burials and about 23,000 marked graves. A major feature of the cemetery is the long east west promenade with the western end having excellent views over Bradford. Also at the western end is a small bandstand. Most of the western half of the site is consecrated for

Anglican burials while the eastern half is set aside for non-conformist burials such as Baptist, Methodist, and Quaker. The Quaker graves are characterised by their identical horizontal ground level memorial stones. The northern area of the cemetery was set aside for the un-baptised and those who had been excommunicated or committed suicide. Communal graves known as 'company plots' are to be found on the southern side of the site where up to thirty coffins at a time were interred in one grave.

I have always found this place to be inspiring and not at all sombre and sad. The monuments are awesomely thought provoking even if one or two are now in need of repair. Earlier this year I was approached to do some volunteer work involving litter picking and the like and although I was enthusiastic I simply had no time as there was a book that I needed to write. Three graves in this cemetery in particular have always interested me and I always search these out and pay them a little visit.

Alfred Angas Scott (1875-1923) was a British motorcycle designer, inventor and founder of the Scott Motorcycle Company. A prolific inventor, he took out over 50 patents between 1897 and 1920, mostly concerning two-stroke engines and road vehicles. Scott was a keen potholer and the second president of the Gritstone club. In July 1923 Scott travelled back to Bradford in his open Scott Sociable wearing wet potholing clothes and contracted pneumonia from which he died.

Alfred Scott's first motorcycle was developed from his own two horsepower twin-cylinder engine design which he hand built and fitted to the steering head of a bicycle. These engines were used to power equipment such as lathes and light machinery and Scott had been involved in the manufacture of 'Premier' pedal cycles. He developed this prototype into a motorcycle and six were produced under contract by friends with a car company called Jowett in Bradford. Scott patented an early form of calliper brakes in 1897, and designed a fully triangulated frame, rotary induction valves, and used unit construction for his motorcycle engine. Scott started making boat engines in 1900. He patented his first engine in 1904 and started motorcycle production in 1908 with a vertical two-stroke 450 cc twin, with patented triangulated frame, chain drive, neutral-finder, kick starter and two-speed gearbox. His patented two-stroke engine designs are still the basis of modern two-stroke engines and features such as the first kick start, monoshock suspension, efficient radiators, rotary inlet valves, drip-feed lubricators and centre stands also remain today.

Stafford Heginbotham was a local businessman and the Chairman of Bradford City Football Club at the time of the fire in 1985. In 1971, Heginbotham set-up the Bradford-based company Tebro Toys. Six years later the Bradford Telegraph & Argus had quoted Heginbotham as saying "I have just been unlucky" after the business suffered two major fires in succession. Heginbotham became chairman of Bradford City football club, where he was a popular figure, the current official mascot for Bradford City A.F.C. was introduced by Heginbotham in 1966, the 'City Gent' character being modelled on him. He was credited with saying that 'Football is the Opera of the people". In 1995, following a heart transplant operation at St George's Hospital in Tooting, Heginbotham died. He was His funeral was held at Bradford Cathedral in early May 1995 and he was interred at the west end of the east-west promenade at overlooking Valley Parade.

The last of the three graves is one that I have searched for in vain over perhaps twenty years. I never gave up though and today when talking to the man who offered me the volunteering job I was taken right to it. It stands in a quite neglected area where trees grow wild and thick and bushes are all around. I have walked past it many times without even knowing it was there and would most likely have spent another twenty years searching for it if this old man had not shown me the exact spot. So at last I knelt before the final resting point of a true English hero. A man like they don't make any more who braved the Russian cannons at Sebastopol and lived to tell the tale. In fact he lived to own and run a humble beer and lodging house at 147 Wapping Road not far from the cemetery but that does not detract from his obvious bravery in The Crimean War.

Matthew Hughes VC (1822 – 9 January 1882) was an English recipient of the Victoria Cross, the highest and most prestigious award for gallantry in the face of the enemy that can be awarded to British and Commonwealth forces. Hughes was approximately 33 years old and a private in 7th Regiment of Foot (now The Royal Regiment of Fusiliers), British Army when, during the Crimean War, he performed the acts that saw him recommended for the VC. The full citation was in the first set of awards of the VC published in the London Gazette on 24 February 1857, and read:

"War Office, 24th February, 1857. The Queen has been graciously pleased to signify Her intention to confer the Decoration of the Victoria Cross on the undermentioned Officers and Men of Her Majesty's Navy and Marines, and

Officers, Non-commissioned Officers, and Men of Her Majesty's Army, who have been recommended to Her Majesty for that Decoration, in accordance with the rules laid down in Her Majesty's Warrant of the 29th of January, 1856 on account of acts of bravery performed by them before the Enemy during the late War, as recorded against their several names, viz. :—7th Regiment No. 1879 Private Mathew Hughes

Private Mathew Hughes, 7th Royal Fusiliers, was noticed by Colonel Campbell, 90th Light Infantry, on the 7th June, 1855, at the storming of the Quarries, for twice going for ammunition, under a heavy fire, across the open ground; he also went to the front, and brought in Private John Hampton, who was lying severely wounded; and on the 18th June, 1855, he volunteered to bring in Lieutenant Hobson, 7th Royal Fusiliers, who was lying severely wounded, and, in the act of doing so, was severely wounded himself".

Queen Victoria presented Hughes with his VC IN Hyde Park on the 26th June 1857. The English hero Matthew Hughes VC died at Wapping in Bradford aged 60 on 9th June 1882

Sat in the grass at the side of one so brave I felt humble. I was alongside the mortal remains of a man who was far braver than I or indeed most men could ever hope to be. He had with his own eyes witnessed and partaken in events that we today cannot even begin to comprehend. I was so pleased to have at last found his final resting place and felt honoured for having done so. Rest in peace brave old soldier your stint is done.

With that I stood bolt upright and remembering how to salute correctly from my own Army days many years before, did exactly that. I turned away and bid Matthew Hughes farewell, and urging Lou Parson on walked the short distance to the Otley road exit and left the cemetery. We were now heading for the famous Peel Park but not before noticing a strange set of two stone steps at the side of the pavement further down. A rather bizarre place to have the mounting steps for an 18th century carriage I thought as we moved on past the former swimming baths that is now Otley Road Community Centre. I knew I had to be on maximum errant dog alert from now on as I had a troublesome experience some years before in Peel Park with another large spitting dog and certainly didn't want to repeat it. So reeling Lou all the way in we entered Bradford's first public park.

Peel Park is a 56 acre urban public park in the Bolton and Undercliffe area of Bradford, England, located about 0.75 miles north-east of the city centre. A public meeting took place in St George's Hall, Bradford on 13 August 1850 to discuss the creation of a park as a memorial to Sir Robert Peel who had died that year. Together with a government donation of £1,500, funding was raised from Sir Robert Milligan, Sir Titus Salt, Forbes and Company and by numerous other private subscriptions to purchase 64 acres of land that was subsequently named Peel Park Estate, and some 56 acres of this land was developed as Peel Park. The park was opened in 1853 and a series of galas were held in the park to raise funds to pay off the remaining debt for the purchase of the land and its layout as a park—this took some 12 years. In 1870 the park was conveyed to the Municipal Borough of Bradford, and is now owned by the City of Bradford.

In 1902 an ornamental bandstand was erected midway along The Terrace and today this location is occupied by the statue of Sir Robert Peel. Another lost feature is the two cannons captured by the British in the Crimean War. The park had a total of four drinking fountains but two have subsequently been lost. The park had its own plant nursery south of the north western entrance at Bolton Road with computer controlled greenhouses but this property was sold off for commercial use reducing the park's area. In 1997 Bradford City's centenary year, 100 trees were planted in the park and this is commemorated by a stone plaque on a boulder near the southern entrance.

The southern Cliffe Road entrance has ornate gates and a lodge (1861) but larger and more impressive are the main gates and lodge (1862) at the northern Bolton Road entrance. There are two grade II listed two-storey Italianate lodges, one at the park gates on Bolton Road and a smaller lodge to a similar design at the Cliffe Road entrance. The main linear path through the park is The Terrace extending east west on which can be found a number of statues. One such is a statue of Sir Robert Peel made in 1855 and dressed in a mid-19th century frock coat and mounted on a cylindrical ashlar sandstone plinth. At the western end of The Terrace is the Viewing Platform (1853–93) giving views over the Bradford valley and Manningham. The platform was largely rebuilt in 1990 due to its poor condition. A cast iron bridge (1857) takes the eastern end of The Terrace over the carriage drive. The cast iron bridge beams are embossed with the words "RAILWAY-FOUNDRY. BRADFORD. 1857. Close to the Bolton Road entrance, adjacent to formal gardens is a 'distorted figure-of-eight' shaped lake with two islands and a variety of water fowl. The island in the east of the lake is so large relatively that the lake takes on a serpentine appearance.

With my eyes peeled and my internal anti large dog radar up and running Lou and I strolled along the wide winding path down towards the Bolton Road lodge. All of a sudden my radar compelled me to spin around as it had picked up the far away distinct yapping of Jack Russell's. There were three of them and they were flying along the path behind heading right for us. As usual the "owner" was fifty yards behind struggling to keep up. "Oh hell this is going to be fun" I exclaimed out loud. Four Jack Russell's together in a park is either going to be a love fest or a blood bath. But I have owned these feisty little buggers for twenty years and in a spit second my instinct told me not to worry and that everything would be alright. Not for the first time I listened to it and was rewarded with the most wonderful sight of four little balls of terror spinning around and chasing each other. This hearty and fearless breed of dog sometimes has an affinity with those of their own breed. Lou was in her element playing tag with her compatriots and the crescendo of yapping which would drive most people mental was but music to my ears.

The breathless panting little bald headed man eventually caught up and was really apologetic but I was having none of it as I was so thrilled to see Lou having so much fun. We both just stood and watched as these four tiny dogs danced the hookie coo with each other. After a while the dogs ran out of steam and calmed down and we all walked on along the path. He told me the tale of an old male Jack he used to have that one day stuck his tongue in an empty dog food tin to try and scrape out the last tiny morsels of food within. His tongue was sliced right down the middle by the sharpe edge of the open lid. He said the dog had a tongue like a lizard for the next thirteen years but it didn't bother him one little bit. Aye that I can believe as the Jack Russell is as hard and tough as they come and they have more courage than even most men I know.

We reached the lodge at the Bolton Road exit of the park and baldie head bid us farewell to continue his walk around the park. Crossing over Bolton Road we walked along Bolton Lane passing by the ancient hamlet of Low Fold towards the even more ancient Walnut Farm. This beautiful farmhouse and cottage has stood in its present location for centuries and has at times been known as Bartlett House, Bolton Banks Farm, Bolton Fold and Walnut Tree Farm. In 1651 it was in the possession of John Jowett of Ye Olde Kirkgate

Bradford. On the gable of the house are the initials B.E.B and the date 1736. These represent the names of Benjamin Bartlett and his wife Elizabeth who built the new house as a summer residence. A Walnut tree was planted here in the 1700's and by 1812 the tree was fully matured and according to records produced 100's of Walnuts each season.

Built in 1736 by Benjamin Bartlett the Bradford apothecary, this two storey farmhouse and lower adjoining cottage is built from irregular coursed sandstone with Gritstone and flush quoins and stone slate roofs. The gable ends of the farmhouse have parapet copings rising from shaped kneelers, four light chamfered mullions and a central mullioned transomed stair light. The famous executioner James Berry died here at Walnut farm on 21st October 1913 aged 61. He was the executioner who failed to hang John Babbacombe Lee – "The Man They Couldn't Hang" – in 1885. The trap door repeatedly failed to open and Lee's sentence was commuted.

From Walnut Farm it is but a short walk back up Kings Road to my cottage on the top of the hill. But the twenty first century defiantly made its presence known to me when a white BMW with blacked out windows and dance music blaring out came speeding up through Brow Wood and nearly ran us over. It damn near burst my bubble.

Baildon to Menston Village

Although just a few weeks before I had explored the lower part of Baildon extensively when discovering the delights of the Salt houses, I had not touched the main part of the village that lies further up the hill towards the moors. So to remedy that Lou and I set off from Shipley on the local bus that would drop us both by strangely named Potted Meat Stick in the centre of this old and well known village.

The Potted Meat Stick or to give it the correct name of The Ferrand Memorial Fountain was first placed in the centre of Baildon in 1862. According to contemporary news reports, the monument stood in the middle of Baildon for about a century but the road needed reorganisation and development and at that time, the council thought that it would cost about £ 150 to destroy the monument but £ 400 to move it. Eventually it was agreed that the fountain would be removed and replaced as soon as funds would permit. Alas this never happened and about twenty years later it was found damaged and in pieces on waste land on the other side of Bradford. The Bradford Council paid to have the monument re-erected in October 1986, not far from the original site. The nick name of "Potted Meat Stick" is believed to come from the colour of the pink granite part of the column.

I gazed at this phallic symbol of granite for a few moments before moving off in the direction of the moors that began on the north edge of the village. My life long sweet tooth was throbbing as we passed Robinson's old traditional sweet shop as I usually find that places like this have a veritable treasure chest of long forgotten sweets for sale. I resisted the temptation on this occasion as we had a long walk ahead of us and had to make head way on our journey across the moors to Menston. Walking past the street side rows of former mill workers cottages Lou and I took the foot gate at the side of the deep cattle grid just up the road. The noise that the traffic makes as it passes over the grid must surely annoy the nearby householders as it is an almost constant thud thud thud. From here the moors would not end until we had passed over Hawksworth Moor and dropped down to Menston village. So we took the footpath through the bracken that lines the side of Hawksworth Road and skirted along the side of the disused Low Eaves Delph.

Baildon Moor is an ancient place with a long and important history of pre-Industrial Revolution quarrying and coal mining. The stone that was heaved from the ground and over the moors was used in many of the local buildings and even some further afield. The coal was used to heat the humble cottages in the village and later on to create steam to power the local mills. The simple path took us past Whitehouse on the edge of the moor. The white washed building was built in 1730 and was used as a tea room for the moor walkers at one point in the past.

Our path took us closer to the main road from here as we approached the tiny hamlet of Low Hill and its magnificent former Methodist Chapel. Originally thirteen cottages stood here but now only four remain plus the Chapel which is also now a private residence. . The maximum population of Low Hill was 96 in 1861, reduced to 26 by the 1891 census. The cottages were built by the Lord of the Manor Abraham Maud of Rylstone near Skipton. They were built to house miners who worked the small coal pits across the moor and most of them were demolished in the slum clearances in the 1960's. The remaining cottages only received mains electricity in 1980. The Methodist chapel cost £500 to build in 1874 and people from Low Hill, Moorside, Low Springs and Sconce would worship here. In its heyday it held very popular fund raising concerts and was noted for the large attendances at open air services. As the population fell, so did attendances, until the congregation was less than ten. The chapel closed in 1917 and was sold for £320, becoming a tea room for some time in the 1930's.

I continued along the roadside footpath towards another tiny hamlet named Low Springs which is officially in Hawksworth and therefore part of the dreaded Leeds district. I shuddered at the image of Michael Murphy's beard once again twitching at the very thought of my transgression and chuckled out loud and carried on. I had to be careful now as the path had ended and we had to walk on the road. The traffic sped by at an alarming speed considering the narrowness of the road as we passed by the end of Scone Lane and followed the winding country road uphill towards Potter Brow Bridge. I glanced up and looking over to my right could see Idle Hill rising majestically in the distance. It appeared to be so far away even though it was not and it is visible from just about everywhere I have travelled over the Bradford district.

The road snaked around between Honey Joan Wood and Honey Joan Hill and before long we were alongside the site of the former Hawksworth Mill. This substantial 15th century former corn mill was served by water from nearby

Jum Beck. The water stored in the millpond powered the mill's waterwheel which in turn provided motive power to its basic machinery. This beck still runs into Gill Beck in the valley between Hawksworth and Baildon and then runs in the river Aire. The mill was burned down by Luddites coming back from breaking frames in Guiseley.

We continued along the road till we arrived at the entrance track to Intake farm. I thought this looked like a great spot to stop for some dinner as it afforded a great view back down the road to the mill. As I sat there on the grass munching away my thoughts once again went back through the centuries and conjoured up images of simply country folk bringing their harvests to the mill to be ground and milled. The basic carts would have laboured their way along the winding country road with the beasts huffing and sweating with the effort of it all. The miller will take his share of the corn as reward for his own efforts and another season and another year would be over.

After my refreshment Lou and I carried on for a short distance before arriving at Four Lane Ends. This is the area where Mill lane, Goose lane, Old lane and Hillings Lane all meet. We carried on straight ahead to take Hillings Lane then turned off along Odda Lane. This took me past the 150 year old Sandstone quarry named Odda Delph towards another demolished Wesleyan Methodist Chapel. Built in 1837 on land leased for one hundred years from Francis Hawksworth Fawkes, this Chapel was torn down in 1902 when a new one was constructed further down. The site was used to extend the graveyard which can still be seen along the side of the road.

This new Chapel built in 1903 at a scost of £940 had seating for 120 people. Designed by the Bradford firm of Walker and Collinson, the opening service was conducted outside due to the number of people present. Now at the junction of Main Street and Old Lane I turned along Old Lane and passing by Hillside House and its adjacent former village Pinfold headed towards Goose Lane and Jum Bridge. All along this road the drystone walls were low and the fields with their grazing cattle and sheep just seemed to open up all the way back to the high moorland of Baildon. In the distance the bracken and heather covered land swept upwards till it reached the summit of Baildon Moor. Between here and there the pastoral fields rolled on for what seemed forever. This road I was now travelling along was once a continuation of Old lane but has subsequently been renamed as Goose Lane.

Still having to take great care on the narrow country lane we approached the massive Reva Reservoir. Constructed on an area known as Whin Hills and completed in 1874, this 1.2 kilometre long body of water is home to a sailing and canoe center as well as providing water for the city of Bradford a few miles in the distance. Many varieties of birdlife can be seen here and it is in fact a popular spot for the areas Ornithologists.

With great care we crossed over Bingley Road at Intake Gate to start the trek over Hawksworth Moor towards my birthplace, the village of Menston. Naturally I had done my usual research before setting off on this ramble and had noticed there was an area marked on the old Ordnace Survey maps as an area of "Quick Sands". This ran alongside the beaten footpath Lou and I were now on and thinking back to the dream I had the night before I focused my thoughts on stepping very carefully indeed. In my dream the night before I saw a solitary black historians cap laid on the top of a puddle of a mud like substance. The owner was nowhere to be seen and I awoke with a heavy sinking feeling.

A startled Pheasant rose from the gorse alongside the track and Lou tried to give chase. Not having wings it was a bit of a none starter but that mere detail didn't stop her trying and she pulled me along for some yards before I regained my feet and reeled her in. It was here I noticed what is known as a Catchwater. This is a concrete lined ditch with some associated pipes and a sluicegate at the end. Its purpose is to literally catch the water as it runs off the moor from its numerous small streams around the area of Black Beck and White Flush.

The moor was flat and expansive with only drystone walls to break the land. Away to my right Reva Hill rose up as if to stand guard over the nothingness that surrounded me. At 900 metres above sea level it must have been a valued place for the pre-historic humans who once roamed the area. On the far horizon I could just about make out the famed golf balls of the communications intercept and missile warning site of RAF Menwith Hill. Between there and Reva Hill can be seen Otley Chevin. This whole area is littered with Limestone Bolder pits, tiny Delphs and age old marker stones. Centuries ago it would have been a hive of human activity but now is inhabited only by walkers, Pheasants and the men who shoot them. Thinking of shooting I remember as a boy hearing tales of a rifle range somewhere up here on the moors. I must have missed it as I turned off to the right and started to make my way over Stocks Hill towards Menston. When I checked the maps upon my return home I saw the rifle range was indeed only a short distance infront of me before I turned off the moor. The range is marked with "Danger" on all the old maps but now appears to be disused and neglected.

Walking with Lou ahead of me the moor descended gently down towards the captive fields and their scattered flocks of hardy sheep. In the distance I saw a place I remembered from my childhood. The now removed steel roof glittered in the sun no more but the stone outline of the surrounding walls told me that I was approaching my place of birth. This place behind its shroud of trees used to enthrall me as a child. I knew it contained water within its walls but it had a roof? Driving past my Father would tell me it was full of deep water and was a forbidden place. That only lent to its mystery but I was scared to actually ever go anywhere near it never mind inside behind the gates and trees that surrounded it. But now as an adult I could see it in all its naked glory below me as I descended from the moors above.

Hawksworth Moor Service Reservoir has lain derilict since the Yorkshire Water restructuring in 1995. Excavation of the site began in May 1903 and the construction was completed in August 1904. The roof has now been torn off but the surrounding stone walls are in great condition considering they have been under water for many decades. Permission has been granted for its conversion to a six bedroom house complete with a cinema, gym, sauna and steamroom. I stood atop the great stone wall and looked down side to see what looked like a complete building site below. It was that huge there were portacabins and excavators inside. Giant piles of sand stood all around. As I stood there I tried to imagine the massive body of still water it once contained. My mind boggled at the sheer thought of the many millions of gallons it would have contained when in use. Whoever has commisioned the building of his house within this structure must be a very wealthy man indeed I thought.

I had to get down somehow from this high wall so with some degree of difficulty I managed to extend Lou Parsons lead and lower her down the side into a small gully. Climbing down myself I joined her on the bank of Dry Beck. This beck forms the boundary between Menston and Burley Woodhead. From here it was only a few yards to Moor Road from where we could make our way towards the hamlet of Burley Woodhead and hopefully find some remains of a former Bleachworks that I had read about the night before. Although it was not a great distance it took Lou and I ages to walk slowly along the narrow busy country road. We had to stop every few yards to let the traffic past us. I was glad that Lou had appreaciated the gravity of the situation and refrained from her usual manic pulling. This was no time for such behaviour I told her. She understood and began to act civilised for a change.

We passed centuries old weatherbeaten quarry workers cottages. Situated right on the roadside their presence afforded no respite as there were no bushes to sink into to let the cars past. Eventually after what seemed an age we reached the small track that my map had told me would lead us down into a tiny collection of cottages. These were once the homes of the workers at Rombalds Moor Bleachworks Mill. Built in the 1850's and once owned by Joseph Gill, this mill was operational until 1927.

The workers would bleach the yarns from local Linen mills in a collection of buildings surrounding a series of millponds. By 1918 the manufacture of Linen yarn had declined and Gill and Son turned to the treatment of Cotton rag. The 1871 census shows James McKinley as the manager, and by 1900 it employed forty people. It was closed after local landowners protested about pollution in the local waterways. The millponds silted up and nature returned. Today only the mill cottage survives.

Upon reaching the end of the settlement of cottages we entered a field through a stone stile. Here we came face to face with an angry looking Ram. He was guarding his females as a good Ram should and seemed to take great exception to our presence. He stood only four feet from me and launched himself head first towards in his attack. With a swivel of my hips that Elvis would have been proud of the Ram went sailing on by only to turn round and attack again.

I had no intention of standing their like a Flamenco dancer with my hands in the air so we were gone over the nearby fence into the woods in an instant. Vegetation coiled around my ankles as I tramped along the side of the beck that ran through the wood. The Ram followed us down his field on the other side of the fence. He never took his eye off us till the field ended and he could follow no more. With some relief I looked up and could see a stone chimney standing proud in the wood only a few feet away. To the side were remains of a wall and a weir along the beck. It had all been covered by decades of plant growth and if you didn't know what was once there it would just be a collection of old stones. But I did know and I was happy that I had found at least some remains of the former Bleachworks.

Although the trees were sparse the vegetation was not and it sapped my strength as I waded through it towards the open fields that lay beyond. From here I could hear the occasional train as it ran along the distant line towards Menston Station. I knew we could catch a train from here back to Shipley so Lou and I headed in the direction of the line. With only a series of wire fences to cross we soon made the private road which runs alongside the railway line. Clarence drive is lined by massive detatched houses owned no doubt by people of some wealth. One such man mowing his front lawn shot me a look of disapproval that told me he didn't think I should be there. I shot him one back that told him that I'd wander just where I liked private road or not.

In the space of a few minutes we were sitting at the station waiting for the next Bradford bound train. A middle aged couple sat on the bench next to me engaged me in conversation. They asked where I had been and after I had told them of our adventures the man said "Oh why don't you write a guide or something?" You know what that's not a bad idea said I as the train pulled up.

Drighlington to Black Carr Woods via Tong

The First English Civil War touched the West Yorkshire area quite substantially. The towns of both Leeds and Bradford were involved in sieges and various skirmishes involving the Royalists and Parliamentarians. I use the word town as both Leeds and Bradford were not cities at this time. But the only battle of note inside the official Bradford area was on 30th June 1643 at Adwalton moor on the edge of Drighlington. In fact it was the only battle of any age that Iam aware of so it made for a great start to what was to be my longest walk of any that I have done on my travels.

Prior to this walk I had never even heard of this area never mind been there so I had to do more than my usual preparation. I didn't even know which buses to catch to get there but as usual the Internet and Google was my friend. The second bus of this overcast June morning dumped Lou and I outside the Railway public house on Moorside Road right beside the battlefield. The pub car park stands on the site of the long gone Drighlington and Adwalton railway station. This tiny station was opened on the 20th August 1856 and closed on the 30th December 1961. Today nothing remains of the station.

The site of the battle of Adwalton Moor is on high ground on the edge of the village of Adwalton, now commonly considered to be part of Drighlington. The Earl of Newcastle, the Royalist Commander, was marching on Bradford (which was Parliamentarian in sympathy) with 10,000 men. Fairfax, the Parliamentary commander, had 3,000-4,000 men in Bradford. However, despite his inferior numbers, Fairfax came out to intercept the Royalist army as Bradford was ill-prepared to resist a siege. The battle was of medium term significance, and victory consolidated the Royalist control of Yorkshire. The Parliamentarians achieved initial success, but once they were out on the open moor there was a sudden change of fortune. The Royalists' pikemen pushed the Parliamentarians back, their cavalry turning retreat into flight. The Royalists had won. The victory at Adwalton Moor gave the Royalists control of the North for the remainder of the year. It was second only in significance to Marston Moor in the history of the Civil Wars in the North. The landscape of 1643 was one of hedge-lined fields on the lower slopes and moorland with coal pits higher up. The expansion of housing and roads over the last 150 years has dramatically altered the character of the battlefield.

Lou and I walked the few yards towards the edge of the moor and mounted the small ridge that runs almost the whole length of the east side of the battlefield area. From here I could survey the whole battlefield site. Armed with my prior research and my usual vivid imagination it was easy to conjure up a picture of what the day's events during those three hours may have looked like. Although the air was still and silent I could almost hear the scared and excited shouts of the Parliamentarian foot soldiers as they rushed The Royalist lines on the exact spot I was stood on. The smoke from the few cannons available that day swirled all around to envelope the battlefield. The metallic clashing of the steel weapons and nervous whinnying of the horses only added to the confusion. Thousands of men were fighting for the beliefs,their families and their very lives. The screams of the injured and the dying filled the air, cursing their King and all he stood for as they met their God. Lead musket balls flew through the air before tearing through human flesh and bones, the earth stained with blood and covered with shattered bodies.

Confusion reigned all around as The Royalist Cavalry chased the Parliamentarians from the battlefield in the rout. Scrambling through hedges and falling into ditches they did their best to survive the onslaught but the Cavalry was persistent and hunted them down with no mercy to complete the victory. This now silent patch of open common was once a killing field and it came alive in front of me. I was a detached and silent observer of the deaths of many good men who perished that day and it is a sensation that I will never forget.

Today the former battlefield is visited by dog walkers and the odd person with too much time on his hands and too much imagination. Odd is perhaps a fitting word to use. I consciously broke the spell as we had to move on because we had a lot to see and a long way to go. So moving through the open moorland Lou and I made for Whitehall Road which would take us to the nearby area of Drighlington. As I passed through the crossroads I noticed up ahead an unusual church spire. What attracted my attention was the fact that the spire had the shape of a square battlement rather than the shape of a normal spire. When I reached the churchyard I paused for a few moments to admire the church of St. Paul. Constructed over two years from 1876-78 this grade II listed building of hammer dressed stone with a Welsh blue slated roof stands proud indeed even with its strange steeple.

Turning up Back Lane we walked for a short distance before coming to the quite magnificent Lumb Hall. Originally built in 1640, this Grade I listed house was home to the Yeoman Clothiers of the Brookes family. One of a group of small mansions built in the "Halifax" style in the period between 1630-1660, it is I believe the only remaining house in the area which dates back to before the nearby Battle of Adwalton. This fine house of Well-coursed gritstone and stone slate roof has many mullioned and transomed windows and coped gables. Above the front porch is a "Wheel Window" familiar to all the houses in the Halifax style. It is also reputed to have a ghost called Charlie who appears in Civil War attire and wanders around the ground floor.

Back Lane led me to a small public footpath through yet another golf course towards the ancient village of Tong across the valley. Dodging the flying golf balls we entered a small wooded plantation named Doles Wood and crossed the site of a former tiny Colliery of the same name. This coat pit was operational from 1863 to 1887 then reopened in 1908 for a short time. On the 2nd of March 1865 it was rocked by an explosion that took the lives of three local men.

I crossed Ringshaw Beck via a small ancient flagstone Clapper footbridge which took me to a series of open fields. The view back across the valley to Drighlington was superb from here so I decided to stop for a while and have my dinner. The hot late June sun was high in the sky as Lou and I sat amongst the cow pats and enjoyed the customary cheese and onion feast I had prepared that morning. A large bright orange Butterfly hovered close by and seemed to taunt Lou to chase it. It intelligently stayed just out of her reach as Lou danced around on her hind legs trying her upmost to catch it. I watched this performance with delight and no small wonder at Lou Parson's acrobatic abilities.

Remembering that the lovely village of Tong was only a short distance up the valley side I gathered myself together and set off once again. We were only to pass through the village on our journey across the fields, becks and woods of outer Pudsey. I turned up Keeper Lane at the side of what used to be the village Pinfold and from here I looked over to the small Cricket ground by the side of The Greyhound pub. This is said by many to be the most picturesque Cricket ground anywhere around the Bradford area, and with its small quaint pavilion I would have to agree. The sound of leather against Willow whilst supping a pint of well brewed local ale takes some beating. The Greyhound, a former coaching inn famous for its collection of Toby jugs, replaced the original village pub at number five Tong Lane when it was built in 1840. The Pinfold which measures twenty feet square stands next to what was once the village Smithy and Wheelwrights shop. Here I noticed a water hand pump adorned with a Lions head spout.

Lou and I strolled along Keeper Lane which after a short distance becomes a narrow bridleway closely bounded by drystone walls. This ancient right of way snakes its way down past the grounds of Tong Hall before crossing Pudsey Beck and rising again up towards Bankhouse and Fulneck.

We passed East View Croft with its long barn with two arched entrances and arrived at The Manor House. The superb grade II listed residence originally built in 1629 with an added 17th century eastern wing stands behind stout iron gates. Sir George Tempest lived here for a while when his usual residence of Tong hall was being rebuilt. For some reason the gates were open and I could see a most delightful lake standing in front of the house. Situated in mature lawned gardens surrounded by trees that swept low to kiss the water it looked simply superb and idyllic. Between the house and the lake is a kind of terrace fronted by small stone pillars that sweep down to the water's edge. I had to go in closer and take a few photos of this lake it impressed me that much. The only sign of life was a man mowing a part of the lawn some distance away so I sneaked up the gravel driveway and diving amongst the nearby trees found myself at the water's edge. The gardener carried on mowing oblivious that a member of the working class had dared to loiter on his immaculate hallowed ground.

Lou and I scampered back onto Keeper Lane and taking to the rough cobbles walked down this heavy tree lined ancient packhorse trail towards the bottom of the valley. As I tramped downwards past centuries old trees my mind once again drifted away. In my mind's eye I could see simple country folk leading their horses down this very track centuries before. The saddles piled high upon the plodding beasts as they wound their way towards the crossing point of the beck below. I saw a Shepherd dressed in his simple white smock and dirty toil stained breeches driving his sheep to market in Bankhouse. Perhaps even to slaughter or maybe both.

After passing by an old disused quarry on the edge of Acre Wood I came to the point at the bottom of the valley where Pudsey Beck is joined by Holme Beck. The trees are sparse here allowing much sunlight to bathe this small area. This gives it a peaceful and pastoral feeling that made me want to stay awhile beside the trickling waters of these age old becks. But I knew that the bridleway climbed steeply up towards Bankhouse and I would need to rest there so with something of a heavy heart Lou and I continued on.

The occasional cobbles were hard on my feet as we climbed up the valley side. I reeled Lou all the way in so she could pull me up to conserve my strength. The trail seemed to go on forever and I was having to pull in deep breaths as I staggered along. The farmers and shepherds of centuries past would not have spent a lifetime smoking so would no doubt have sprinted up here with little effort. I had to keep stopping every twenty or so yards to fill my lungs with air. Massive exposed tree stumps in the tall surrounding earth banking laughed at me with distain at my obvious struggle to climb the valley side. After an almost superhuman effort we reached Bankhouse and I slumped to the ground in a sweating heap gasping like goldfish out of water.

We were not far from the Moravian settlement of Fulneck. First established in 1744 when Protestants from Moravia came here after fleeing forced Catholicism back home. It is named after Fulneck, the German name of a town in Northern Moravia, Czech Republic. Members of the Moravian Church settled at Fulneck in 1744. They were descendants of old Bohemian/Czech Unity of the Brethren (extinct after 1620 due to forcible re-Catholization imposed on the Czech lands by Habsburg emperors), which in 1722 had found refuge in Saxony on the estate of Nicolaus Ludwig Count von Zinzendorf. Within the next few years after settling, housing as well as a school and a chapel were built. The chapel building was completed in 1748. In 1753 and 1755 the Boys' and Girls' Schools were opened.

Many of the 18th-century stone houses in the village are listed buildings. Cricketer Sir Leonard Hutton, who played for Yorkshire and England was born in Fulneck. Hutton still holds the record for the highest innings (364) by an Englishman in a test match. H. H. Asquith, Prime Minister of the United Kingdom 1908-16 and Diana Rigg, actress famous for appearing in The Avengers both attended Fulneck school.

We were heading the other way back to Bradford, so after a short rest to catch my breath Lou and I once again set off. I was quite a distance from home at this point and had decided to test my stamina on what I knew would be fairly level ground after we had cleared Black Carr Woods and reached Pudsey. I was going to walk what was something of a liner route all the way back to Wrose. Left right left right that kind of thing. So with that notion in my mind I left Bankhouse and took Scholebrooke Lane down the valley towards The Banks and Black Carr Woods.

Lou Parson has this habit of being ever so brave when she comes upon other dogs that are behind a gate or fence and cannot reach her. No matter the size of the dog she goes crazy at them from the safety of her side of the obstruction. It is a different matter if the dog is coming straight for her unrestrained of course, then she's not so hard. So when we came to a Dog boarding kennels just along Scholebrooke Lane she was at the gate giving it large to four massive hounds behind it in the yard. Two Airedales and two Rhodesian Ridgebacks just sat there sunning themselves and didn't give a damn despite her best efforts to rouse them. One of the Airedales just looked at her and seemed to say in a dog way "oh go away little dog I can't be bothered Iam sunning myself". Oh to observe the pantomime that these wonderful canine creatures sometimes exhibit for us humans.

We were now almost at the valley bottom and the track narrowed considerably and became no more than a footpath. It snaked along the side of Tyersal Beck through the ancient Black Carr Woods on one side and The Banks on the other. Black Carr Woods is the only wooded area in the Bradford area which is situated on coal geology as opposed to the otherwise predominate Gritstone. The shallow valley we were now crossing is drained by Carr beck and Pudsey Beck. This area is considered to be one of the most natural Oak and Birch woodlands in the United Kingdom. Amongst the other tree species that grow wild here are Alder and Willow. The woods were silent apart from only the occasional distant birdcall as Lou and I walked immersed in the secluded peacefulness of the place.

We meandered through the wood till we came to a stone railway bridge and its abutment. This lonely stone structure stretched over a redundant railway cutting. This track was installed in 1875 after much negotiation with several railway companies. Until this point, the growing population associated with the cloth manufacturing industry in Pudsey had been dependent upon their nearest station at Stanningley. In 1870 a local committee was formed to petition the London and North-Western Railway Company to continue their line from Wortley to Bradford via Pudsey. The request was, however, declined on account of the difficulties of crossing the Tong valley and obtaining a site on which to build a station at Bradford.

The committee was determined, and took their appeal instead to the Lancashire and Yorkshire Railway Company. The application was favourably received, but during surveying of the land for construction, the Great Northern Railway Company also obtained permission in parliament to branch from their Leeds-Bradford line to Pudsey. Further negotiations ensued, and after consultation with 32 landowners, a route was agreed. The ceremony of the first cutting took place on the 24th March, 1875 and the railway opened for passenger traffic on the 1st April 1878. Two hundred feet to my left the track passed through a tunnel on its way to Greenside Station. The track was finally dismantled in 1964 as part of the Reshaping of British Railways, or the 'Beeching Axe' as it is sometimes known. Oh Doctor Beeching what have you done?

After passing by two small disused quarries Lou and I emerged at the side of The Fox and Grapes pub on Smalewell Road, and it was but a short walk from here to the main Waterloo Road in Pudsey. By now my feet were stinging and my calves throbbing but at least it was a level and normal surface from here until I arrived home in Wrose. I had no idea just how far it was or even how far we had come but it was even at this point one of the longest walks I had yet done. Sometimes you have to test yourself so you can determine your limits in case you need to reach them in an emergency. So pulling my black historians cap down I took a deep breath and marched on towards Bradford.

Waterloo Road became Galloway Lane which then brought us to the main duel carriageway of Bradford Road. Heading towards Bradford Lou and I turned off onto Gain Lane at the side of the now sadly demolished pub The Junction. Bet you didn't know this was a Smithy in years gone by long before it was a public house? Here I could smell the wonderful aroma of freshly baked bread emanating from the nearby massive bakery. It seemed to waft down Gain Lane towards me and drift over the playing fields near Daniel Peckover's old house and grounds. More on this man in another chapter if I get home to write it that is. All I needed now was for it to snow and I'd be feeling like Captain Scott crossing the Beardmore Glacier in Antarctica.

We passed by the huge Morrison's head office with its turnstile entrances and hundreds of parked cars. I stopped to reminisce outside "Robbie's" famous tiny motorbike and Reliant workshop where, many years ago either of these two identical brothers would produce just about any spare second hand part you would need from within a motley assortment of crumbling sheds. These two blokes were legends in their own lunchtime, and the third identical brother used to run "Mr Boot" at the lights at the top of Leeds Road.

Crossing from Fagley into Undercliffe we took Leeds Road past the site of the long gone Springfield Works and the Freemasons Hall to reach Harrogate Road. My feet were numb by now and I had the distinct early throbbing of an attack of the dreaded Gout which I sometimes get in my right big toe. I have inherited it so I am told from my Mother's side and when it comes on which is not often it hurts like hell, and it was starting to right now. But I knew I was on the last leg and a huge mug of sweet Earl Grey tea awaited me at home and this heavenly notion drove me forward and drove the pain of my big toe from my mind.

Continuing along Leeds Road I passed the site of the long gone Manor Potteries factory and turned down Bolton Road towards where the tram depot used to be. Maybe only twenty minutes more then I would be home I thought as I limped on pulled gainly by the stout and still fresh Lou Parson. She will come right in the house, pick up one of her pulls and want to play when we get in I thought. Down through the Swaine House estate and past one of my ex-wives house (I've had three but that's another story altogether). I must have looked like The Elephant Man as I limped past her house. Gawd I hope she doesn't come out now and see me like this I thought. The image of her laughing at me made me quicken my step and I hobbled on towards home.

The Earl Grey indeed tasted sweet as it passed my parched lips. The warm water in the bowl that sloshed around my feet felt good. In fact I felt damn good as I had tested myself manfully and walked thirteen miles that day. It may not sound like a great number of miles but when you consider all the trekking up and down the valleys and becks that I had done, and add to that handling a boisterous young Jack Russell along the way it's not bad going. I was exhausted and spent and would sleep like a dead man that night. I looked down at Lou Parson with her big brown eyes and the pull in her mouth and you know what........I really just couldn't be arsed.

Eccleshill to Spink Well Lock Canal Road

Lou Parson and I started this walk with my back to St. Lukes church on Harrogate Road. St. Lukes church was built and consecrated in 1848. It was designed in a largely Gothic style with a spire, this spire however was removed in the 1970s and was rebuilt in a more modern style when the stonework began crumbling. Just behind the church on Fagley Lane is Fagley School which was built in 1842. I crossed the road towards a solid looking row of 18th century Weavers cottages called Armscliffe Place and made my way along Victoria Road towards the village of Eccleshill. Victoria Road was formerly known as Mill Lane and was given its present day name in 1887 in honour of Queen Victoria's Golden Jubilee. Parts of this area was quarried in the 18th century for stone which was used in the construction of many of the local fine mills and buildings.

I soon passed Old Mill on the left, an early 1800's woollen mill which was rebuilt in 1816 after being destroyed by fire. The present building on the site is dated 1863 although parts of it date back to the early 1800s. I carried on towards Eccleshill village and after passing a few modern build semi-detached houses, Lou and I soon came to The New Inn pub. The place was busy with early afternoon drinkers and the familiar aroma of well-kept beer wafted through the open windows as we passed by. After a few minutes the now sadly disused and derelict Hutton School came into view.

This fine but presently boarded up Victorian building was built in 1886 by local mill owner John Hutton on land where Old Eccleshill Hall once stood. Today only the gateposts of the Hall situated in the wall surrounding Hutton School remain. John Hutton bought the land in 1884 for £2000 and donated it so the school bearing his name could be built there. The world famous artist and former Eccleshill resident David Hockney studied here in his youth.

Directly opposite Hutton School is the well-known local landmark known as the "Monkey Bridge". Sitting underneath a stone paved walkway in a large stone wall the Monkey Bridge was a 19th century village lock up for drunks and a public urinal. Just in front of here was a grassy triangular junction upon which stood the village stocks. Presumably the drunks served time in the stocks as well as the lock up. The stocks were moved in later years to nearby Hodgson's Fold. We carried on Victoria road towards the old Methodist Chapel which sits just at the rear of The Victoria Inn at Bank Top. The steep road leading down to Harrogate Road from Bank Top, known as Bank, is an ancient road that dates back to Roman times.

Lou and I stopped for a short while to admire the old but still used Methodist Chapel at Bank Top. In 1775 this small Chapel also known as Bank Top Chapel was constructed on Lands Lane off Norman Lane. The famous Methodist John Wesley (1703-1791) preached here in 1776 it is said. The building was in use as a chapel until 1854 and today it is one of the oldest buildings in Eccleshill. It was the third Methodist Chapel to be built in the city of Bradford. On the opposite side of Norman Lane is the Chapel burial ground which was created in 1823. I have strolled around this burial ground on a few occasions and one grave in particular has always caught my attention.

This particular grave contains the mortal remains of one Donald Jowett. Sgt Pilot Jowett died aged 20 aboard a Consolidated PBY Catalina MK II AM269 BN-K flying boat aircraft, which crashed shortly after take-off near to Stranraer in Scotland. Jowett was a member of 240 Squadron RAF which was based nearby at Loch Ryan. Jowett is a famous Bradford name and is one that I would come across many times during my rambling around these parts.

Further along Norman Lane directly opposite The Lane Ends public house is a building which is obviously a converted cinema, or Picture House to use its correct term in the period that it was constructed. Despite today being used as a gym and health centre it has that particular aesthetic appearance that old cinemas always seem to have.

The Palladium Cinema was opened in 1929 by Ralph Dickinson and upon construction had 1,000 seats in stalls and circle levels. In 1931 the new owner John Lambert of Modern theatres changed the name to The Regal and reduced the seating capacity to 900. The Regal Cinema was closed on 23rd November 1966 with the final offering being the great Peter Cushing and the majestic Christopher Lee in "The Hound of the Baskervilles", and Leo Genn in the film "Steel Bayonet". The building was then changed into a bingo hall, which operated until 1988 when it was converted into a Snooker club. In 2008, the snooker club closed and this area was taken over by the gymnasium in 2009. Today it houses an independently run fitness centre named Flacks Fitness.

I wanted to once again visit the magnificent Bolton Old Hall at the end of Wood Lane, so I made my way through the sprawling Swaine House estate.

What remains of Wood lane was once part of the ancient packhorse track from Idle via Idle Moor down to Bradford. The farmers and merchants would use this trail to transport their goods and livestock to the market in Bradford. After a short distance it ends as a road and becomes more of a footpath which still winds its way down the side of Bolton Woods quarry to the site of the long dismantled set of locks for the Bradford Canal which was known as "Oliver's Lock". At the point where it changes to a footpath I stopped for a second or two to admire a quaint 18th century farmstead building.

This solid structure of typical vernacular Sandstone construction was built in 1857 by the local Jowett family. No doubt some distant relations of Sgt Pilot Donald. The building was converted into four separate cottages sometime in the early 19th century, and was then home to workers from the estate of the nearby Bolton Lodge. Taking a short detour through the fields at the edge of the quarry we soon arrived at the aforementioned Bolton Old Hall. This Grade II listed coursed Gritstone timber framed hall house was built in 1627 for a wealthy wool merchant. The north front has a large mullioned-transomed window lighting the staircase. The Doorway has a date panel inscribed "TW over Anno Doi" above the date 1627. According to local legend the house is haunted by "Blue Mary". This apparition appears at the circular window in the upper wall of the main gabled front section of the house. Past residents of the house have said that she was causing the decline in the local cow's ability to produce milk and what little milk was produced was rancid, so they hung up horse shoes and needles to placate her. Just how this would have helped things escapes me but you know local people and their local legends?

A short distance away we joined Bolton Hall Road on its way down to the village of Bolton Woods. We took a small detour off the side down into a small gully, where at the bottom one of Bradford's "Holy Wells" breaks the surface. Today this tiny trickle of water known as Trap Sike dribbles it's almost pathetic way down the valley side to ultimately join Bradford Beck on Canal Road. Rejoining Bolton Hall Road we walked down the steeply narrow heavily tree lined road, past the entrance to Bolton Woods Quarry and a small row of former quarry workers cottages to emerge in bright sunlight by The New Vic public house. In the early days of Bolton Woods village this was The Conservative Club and was subsequently owned and run by Walkers Bradford Breweries. On the wall at the side there remains a faded "ghost sign" promoting this famed local brewery.

Lou and I were now on Stanley Road heading out of the village in the general direction of Canal Road. On the first slight bend in the road almost on the edge of what was once a small but quite dense plantation named Bolton Woods there stands one of the ventilation stacks for the Frizinghall to Esholt sewage tunnel. This is one of three such stacks along the length of this three mile long tunnel linking the long gone Frizinghall sewage treatment works with the newly built facility at Esholt. The second stack is a short way back past Bolton Woods village and the third is behind the clubhouse of the cricket ground on Westfield Lane at Idle. This tunnel was started in 1913 but was interrupted by WWI before being finished in the 1920's. The Frizinghall plant which treated the raw sewage was closed in 1926 and only a few huge pipes running along Bradford Beck remain today.

Walking up Poplars Park Road towards the site of the part built new housing estate I climbed over a stout stone wall to enter the small wooded copse that once contained the farm and house named Hollin Close. Over the years since the demise of these buildings nature has reclaimed the area and today the trees are tightly packed forming a dense canopy that blots out the sunlight. This gives it a gloomy and somewhat edgy atmosphere despite it being so close to a modern day building site. The thickness of the trees and vegetation seem to form an impenetrable wall that keeps out the sounds of the nearby human and mechanical endeavours.

The house and farm was once owned by the Jowett family and then in turn by the Rawson family, before being leased in the latter part of last century to the corn dealer William Oliver. During his time at Hollin Close some of the land was required for the soon to be built Bradford Canal. The land was to be used for the construction of one of the canal locks. This lock, which was one of ten such locks on the canal came to be known as Oliver's Locks. Bradford Canal closed to navigation in 1922 and the site is now home to various industrial units and a group of gypsy caravans. A small stream which runs down the valley side from Old Hill behind The Horse and Farrier pub to Bradford Beck is known as Oliver's Beck. In 1852 Hollin Close was leased to a tea dealer named John Tordoff who manufactured starch in the outbuildings. Today apart from a few small walls almost nothing remains of the house and farm that once was Hollin Close.

After stumbling through the undergrowth of the Hollin Close site for a while I found the scant and faint outline traces of the carriage drive and followed this for a while. Somewhere in this area there is reputed to be a number of very old gravestones lying flat in the soil. These cover a burial pit containing some victims of a long ago Smallpox epidemic. Needless to say I didn't fancy scrabbling around in the dirt searching for these so with a shiver down my spine I pressed on. After crossing over the culvert across Oliver's Beck and skirting around what remains of Brow Wood I emerged at the bottom end of Bolton Lane. Turning uphill Lou and I walked the short distance to Kings Road making for the small nature reserve which runs alongside towards the site of the former Spink Well Locks.

This nature reserve was created in the early 1990's from derelict land and is a haven for a variety of wildlife species such as Long Tailed Tits, Greenfinch and even Orange Tip Butterflies. Kestrels nest on the site each year and can often be seen hunting over the hillside. But what I was searching for was more tangible and solid than any of these. I had heard rumours from the typical "man in the pub" that most of the original huge carved stone blocks which formed part of the Spink Well locks had been dumped in the dense thick undergrowth somewhere in this area when the lock had been dismantled in 1922.

Today the Citroen car dealership on the very end of Kings Road covers the site of the lock. It didn't take us long to discover the two massive piles of moss covered blocks of carved stone. They simply lay at the side of the path under a canopy of overhanging wild trees. Due to their immense size and weight I doubt they had moved since they were placed there nearly a century before.

The whole area around here has changed immensely in that time. The huge Power Station on Canal Road and the massive gas holders next to the canal bridge have long gone. Numerous modern and brightly lit car showrooms have replaced these dour and grimy industrial buildings. But sitting alone atop the dismantled canal lock stones in this inner city haven of peace I could almost hear the greetings of long deceased canal boatmen as they approached the lock. In 1939 many years after the canal had fell into disuse, a local lad aged 10 named Leonard Partridge drowned when he fell into the disused Spink Well Lock. By then the lock served no purpose and sometimes tempted local children to play in and around it. Leonard laid on a plank and tried to reach a piece of timber that was floating in the middle of the water and sadly he slipped in.

By this time the sky had turned a dark and brooding colour of grey and was threatening to discharge a heavy downpour, so we made our way out of the nature reserve and down the cobbled remains of the road that once led up to the locks to catch the bus back up Kings Road and home.

I have walked through many wooded areas during my walks. Some are dark and dense and some are light and open but they all have one thing in common. With a little imagination I can feel the past and the history of these places, and with a little knowledge I can almost see how the people from centuries past lived and worked in these most noble of surroundings. Woods and forests are alive even though there apears to be not much going on. They are the habitats of many living creatures and of course even the trees are alive. They grow slowly and relentlessly but they are alive all the same.

Even the present day fields that surround my cottage were thick with forests four hundred years ago. Wild Deer and Boars roamed through the thick trees. They hunted and were themselves hunted until man laid the forests bare to make the fields I see around me today. A wood tells a story not only of evolution but of innovation. A story of man's quest to progress and better himself. A beck that runs through a wood powered a waterwheel. The waterwheel powered a saw that cut the trees that had been felled by a man's labour. Where there was a wood there was always water and where there was water there was always power. Man learned to harness it all to his advantage. A wood tells a story and on this walk I wanted to visit Ravenscliffe Woods, an ancient wood which told many stories.

I had to take Lou parson to the Vets on the roundabout on Harrogate Road at Eccleshill for her annual inoculations so it was there I started this walk. Starting by the magnificent St. James church we set off on our journey and almost immediately Union Mills was before us. Built by James Johnson in 1816 this steam powered two storey mill was constructed for the Woollen trade. Sometime later Jeremiah Scott added a further three storey extension. From 1892- 1983 John Pilley and Sons operated the mill and so it became known as "Pilley's Mill". In 1905 a serious fire destroyed much of the building but it was rebuilt and manufacture continued. Today the buildings are a mixture of commercial and light industrial units.

We passed through the housing estate beyond the mill to make our way to join the old railway track bed that would lead us down to Fagley. The railway passed over nearby Harrogate Road by a bridge on its way over to Quarry Gap junction in Laisterdyke. The bridge was demolished many years ago when the road was widened. In 1874 the Great Northern Railway opened its Laisterdyke to Shipley branch railway, a six mile double track branch line from Quarry Gap to Shipley and Windhill railway Station. The line passed through Eccleshill, Idle and Thackley stations on its way from Quarry Gap. Eccleshill station opened in 1875 and was located just north of the bridge over Harrogate Road, but like the other stations it was demolished many years ago when the line was closed. Today only the embankment and the abutment of one side of the bridge remains. The line was closed to passengers in 1931 although goods traffic continued until 1964. Sections of the former track bed survives today though and it was part of this route that I was searching for.

I found the rear of the old folks home where I knew I could jump down the short banking onto the track bed. Squeezing through a gap between some dustbins I dragged Lou through the fence and down the slope onto the track bed. As we walked along the narrow corridor of dried packed mud I started to imagine the steam Locomotive chugging along here on its way to Quarry Gap junction. Pulling three or maybe four packed carriages of dark suited people, it laboured along the line. The steam rising upwards as the metallic noise of wheels on rails reverberating between the embankments alongside. Excited children on perhaps their first train journey, laughed and cheered with joy at the novelty of it all.

But today a century and a half later all was quiet. The only children I could hear were those playing in the nearby council house gardens that backed onto the former track bed. Lou sniffed intently at a blossoming wild Raspberry bush and I made a mental note to return here at the summers end to pick them. Wild Blackberry bushes are all around these parts but seldom have I seen wild Raspberries. Homemade Blackberry and Apple crumble made with fruit picked by my own hand is a joy I simply have to experience each and every summer.

After a short distance I noticed in the bushes part of a small stone wall. I dragged Lou over and upon closer inspection saw that it was the top of a bridge. There was a trail leading down from the side of the embankment so we both slithered down it onto a track below. The bridge ran underneath the former railway line giving access to fields on both sides. This was built upon construction of the line to enable the local farmer to lead his cattle or sheep from one field to the next and so avoiding the railway line. How very pleasant and thoughtful of The Great Northern Railway Company. I was somewhat dismayed to see the tunnel was used as a doss depot and drug den by yobs from the nearby Fagley estate.

Lou and I left the line a little further on and let the path meander on towards Thornbury. We joined the bottom part of Fagley road and headed towards the spot where we could begin our trek through Ravenscliffe Woods. We passed by the magnificent Ravenscliffe Farm cottage with its old barn and mullioned windows before arriving at a building that was obviously a former lodge. In the garden of this small lodge was the most admirable cast iron lamppost. Standing the height of two men with four individual ornate lamps at the crown it wouldn't have looked out of place in Kensington but here on the edge of one of Bradford's most notorious council estates it looked distinctly out of place. I also noticed the most wonderful antique Victorian Post box stood silently and somewhat forlorn in the garden. The things you can see in the most unexpected places when you wander around Bradford.

This lodge was one of four built as entrances to a new estate of luxury villas designed in the 1850s and to be sited in Calverley Wood. The others were Apperley Lodge, or "The Needles Eye" as it was known, Carr Lodge and South Lodge. The Needles Eye was demolished in the 1960's on safety grounds. With the 19th-century expansion of the region's manufacturing industries, nearby Calverley's situation within reach of the centre of Bradford made it a popular place for wealthy Bradford industrialists to live. Fred Foster, Lord Mayor of Bradford, lived for a time in Ferncliffe House, while the great industrialist and innovator Samuel Cunliffe Lister was born at Calverley House Farm. The houses of Elmwood and Brookleigh were also occupied by prominent families.

In an effort to capitalise on this trend, in the 1850s the Thornhill Estate devised a plan to lay out portions of land in Calverley Wood to be developed as a select housing development for wealthy industrialists. Expressions of interest were received and the roads were laid out, but just two plots were sold and developed before the scheme was abandoned. However, the scheme had a considerable impact on the appearance of the village, as stone quarried from Calverley Cutting was used in the construction of some of the village's houses.

Passing through the open ornate wrought iron gates beside the lodge we entered the wood. The track before us was once the carriage drive which linked this part of the abandoned estate to the other on the far side of New Line at Greengates. It was more than just a simple track though as I could see the remains of low sturdy walls which once lined the sides as it wound its way down through the woods. Back in the 1850's this area was nothing like it is today with the nearby Council estate running alongside. It will have been a rich and sumptuous wooded area where the wealthy industrialists of Bradford came to relax and enjoy the peacefulness within its boundaries. There lies the reason for the proposed development of the luxury villas.

As Lou and I passed through the woods the trees rose up alongside a huge soil banking to the right. This was held in place by a stout wall running for hundreds of yards. Here the wood supports a number of species of trees- Sessile Oak, Silver Birch, Sycamore, Beech, Rowen, and Ash to name but a few. To the left down a gully Fagley Beck seemed to follow us silently watching our every move. I noticed a small series of stepping stones over the beck. Smooth and well worn by tens of thousands of feet over the centuries, the flat stones laid across the beck as they had always done. The clear water trickled away on its journey to join the river Aire as we waved it goodbye.

As I carried on along the side of the beck the trees thinned out in front of me to reveal an open meadow. Flat in nature but still surrounded with trees I knew this was the site of a long gone reservoir. It belonged to Bradford Corporation Waterworks and formed part of a nearby sewage farm. Today the stone lined side walls and spillway are still visible through the vegetation. It was known as Low Rein reservoir and was filled in after a series of drownings some years ago. Today nature has reclaimed the area and it has reverted back to woodland and the meadow I saw before me.

Lou and I followed Fagley Beck away from the meadow and towards Round Wood. Here I believe was the site of a Medieval Ironworks. At this point the beck was dammed to provide a head of water which was then used to power drop hammers to forge the iron into basic implements of all descriptions. The woods, the water, the power remember? Charcoal for heating the metal to the high temperatures needed was made from wood collected from the surrounding forest.

We rejoined the former carriage drive as we entered Bill Wood which would lead us to Ravenscliffe Mill. Built by James Harper in 1872, this mill specialised in the manufacture of cloth for Army uniforms. Initially this included scarlet tunics such as those worn by the British Army during the Anglo-Zulu conflict, but as the nation entered the Boer Wars production changed to Khaki and continued up to 1957 when production ceased due to lack of demand for such cloth. The mill is till operational today and has a number of uses including a gym.

I was now approaching another of my beloved "time bubbles", the tiny hamlet of Carr Bottom. Tucked away at the end of a small lane just off New Line and Carr Road, this collection of two cottages around a ford over Fagley Beck is but a world away from the modern hustle and bustle nearby. The two small stone houses either side of the ford are listed buildings dating from the period 1650-1700, a time when building outside Calverley village and along the Carr was just starting. Both houses have unusually large lateral chimney stacks. Fagley Beck runs under the track between them and over this is a structure which is no more than a footbridge. In fact it is marked on the 1847 Ordnance Survey map as such. Down this track would come all the traffic, pedestrians, carriages and carts which passed up and down the valley between Leeds and the towns and villages in the Aire Valley. It was an awkward stretch of road and was probably unsuitable for stage coaches until the New Line at Greengates was constructed 1826.

There are no satellite dishes, no parked cars nor any sign of modern life whatsoever within this tiny hamlet. The water from the beck rushed at some speed below my feet and made a tremendous roar. This only added to the ambiance of this quaint tucked away piece of the past. I sat on a large stone on the grass verge and tried to picture an old man in his Grandad collar shirt tending the small garden of his cottage. It was the year 1860 and the nearby Ravenscliffe Mill had yet to be built. The surrounding area was thick with mature trees and the air was silent but for the sound of his digging. He was sowing potatoes that would feed him through the autumn. Simple peasant food but tasting all the better for being planted then harvested by his own hands. He would feel good as he roasted them in his open fire in a few weeks. The peas he picked yesterday would taste sweet as they filled his belly that night. The hearty broth and the simple bread he baked was all he would need that day. The fire would still be crackling in the grate as it died down in the early hours, an he would sleep well tonight and rise early to begin another day. I wondered if he had an imagination as vivid as mine.

Lou had been resting in the grass at my side whilst I had been day dreaming. She sprang to her feet as I moved off up the slight incline away from the hamlet and towards Carr Road. Crossing over I approached another fine lodge of the Thornhill Estate. The Lodge, Carr Lodge, was the second of the four lodges built just after 1850. The road from Carr Lodge was called Eleanor Drive, after Thomas Thornhill's second daughter, Eleanor Frances. I wanted to walk along part of the famed Calverley cutting so made my way along Clara Drive which I knew passed over the cutting. This wide avenue is lined by massive detached houses all private and secluded behind gated entrances. Lou and I walked for a short distance passing by the rear of Ferncliffe which is now used as a Cheshire home. We reached a small bridge spanning the cutting. Below in a deep ravine I could see the steep sides of Calverley Cutting, and noticing a footpath to the side we left the avenue to descend downwards.

Calverley Cutting was created in 1856 by the Thornhill family to replace the old packhorse track through Calverley to Apperley Bridge. It was a passage blasted through the deep rocks and some local people at the time complained that it was too hard for "sickly folk" to navigate. Upon landing in the cutting from above I was glad it ran downhill from there as although I cannot be termed sickly I still would not have liked to travel upwards in it.

As I stood there in the center of the cutting I cringed at the raw spookiness of the place. It was only mid afternoon and the sun was high and bright in the sky but the cutting emitted a feeling of pure malevolence. Down here on the floor it seemed like midnight but up above the sun still shined. It really was a weird place. On each side the high craggy rocks towered above blotting out the sun everywhere but the sky above. Thick dense trees grew from the rocks and ivy rolled down the rocks to form a carpet around me. The walls of stone seemed to close in on me and the sense of oppression was almost too hard to bare. I had no time to imagine men and horses toiling up and down the cutting pulling the stone on the wooden bogies to the canal below. I had to walk downwards through the long chamber of darkness to escape and see the sun once again.

Hoping that nothing or no one jumped down on me from the heights above I peered at the tiny sliver of light that I could see at the bottom of this unholy place. The dog snarled at some unseen entity, her tail pointing stiffly downwards. I steeled myself, breathed deeply and started to march like Colonel Nicholson in The Bridge on the River Kwai. Hoping I didn't trip over my stiff upper lip I urged Lou Parson on and hoped for the best.

Ten minutes later, sat on a rock at the bottom smoking a cig in the sunshine I thanked whatever God it was that gave me safe passage through the cutting that day. A young couple so in love walked past me to start the climb up through the cutting. I nearly stopped them and begged them to reconsider their foolish and naive action. Guessing they would have just laughed at me I smiled and dragged my shaking sweat stained limbs from the rock and started off towards Apperley Bridge.

Lou and I crossed Harrogate Road and walked towards The George and Dragon public house. Standing proud opposite the stone bridge over the river Aire, this former Coaching Inn dating from 1587 is currently a Grade I listed building. Engraved on a lintel over a fireplace in an upstairs bedroom are the words "Not for the purpose of making a show but of necessity Samuel Hemmingway and Mary his wife enlarged this house AD 1704. These things are cherishing; victuals, drink, warmth, shelter, which of thou possess, remember to gratefully give thanks to God".

Sat in the beer garden with a pint of Wobbley Bob in my hand and the warm sun on my bald head I raised my glass and did exactly that. And cursed damn Calverley Cutting to hell vowing never to return.

City Centre to Tong Village via Raikes Lane

Usually I have a plan for these walks that I do. Each walk has a beginning and an end and hopefully plenty to interest me in between. I know it may seem that at times I simply wander about gazing at old buildings but all my walks do have something of a structure. But for this one today I fancied a change. I decided I would simply set off from Bradford City centre and see where I got to. The disadvantage of walking in this manner is that I may miss things that I would have known about had I done my usual military style research beforehand. This notion mattered not as I packed my food, donned my historian's flat cap and went to catch the bus.

Thirty minutes later Lou and I jumped from the bus in the busy Interchange and headed towards Wakefield Road to start our journey to where ever. Wakefield Road is one of the main arteries running out of the city centre and it would take me to the ancient Roman road of Tong Street. From there I could escape the inner city industrial grime and once again immerse myself in open countryside. Almost immediately I came upon the location of the long gone Adolphus Street railway station. This station stopped serving passengers before even my Grandfather was born never mind my Dad.

In the heady mid-Victorian days of railway fever, Bradford had no less than three terminus stations operated by three different companies; Kirkgate station (later Market Street, then Forster Square), operated by the Leeds & Bradford Railway (LBR), Exchange station, operated by the Lancashire & Yorkshire Railway (LYR) and Adolphus Street station, operated by the Leeds, Bradford & Halifax Junction Railway (LBHJR). The terminus at Adolphus Street was well laid out and spacious, but was inconveniently placed. It was further out of the city centre than the other termini, and passengers had to endure a steep uphill climb to reach the station.

The station was provided with a substantial train shed over six lines. There were four platform faces made up of two side platforms and a central island. Between each pair of platform lines there was a central road for running round. A concourse at the west end of the train shed and at the back of here was a substantial range of office and passenger facilities including waiting rooms, a telegraph office and the booking office. The facility also had a goods yard to the east of the station with numerous sidings, two of which passed through a substantial goods shed. There was also a large coal depot on the north side of the yard with an engine shed, turntable and coaling stage on the south side of the goods yard.

The main station building was demolished in the 1970's to allow for the realignment of Wakefield Road. The access ramp to the goods yard on Dryden Street still exists, together with a substantial part of the side wall, including a bricked up entrance. This remaining section of wall still looks as good today as the day it was first laid by the hard working mid Victorian stonemasons. The heavy modern wagons thundered up the road alongside oblivious to this superb piece of history. Only a short distance up Wakefield Road Lou and I passed the Railway Club which as the name implies is a nod to the former station. Walking steadily up the gradient of the road we continued towards Tong Street. The area here was distinctly industrialised and showed a certain level of deterioration. Side streets of tightly packed back to back houses peeled off from the far side. These fine old built to last houses have seen better days now but they still offer accommodation to the great unwashed of today.

I passed under a box section former railway bridge spanning the road. The line it served is long gone but the fenced off bridge remains although access is impossible due to the razor wire around its edges. I wondered what its iron walls above me contained as I walked underneath. Up ahead I saw a building I knew well from my Tropical fish keeping days. QSS Aquarium Centre is still there after all these years and housed in a former Police Station looks good for another few years yet. As I passed by my mind went back to the Saturday mornings that I spent in there choosing new fish to care for. That certainly is a hobby that can become addictive and expensive. The boarded up former pub The Napoleon stands a few feet away. One of many former public houses in this area now surplus to local requirements and the same can be said for many others in Bradford in the 21st century.

The tall straight spire of St. Johns Church of Bowling beckoned me towards it. The clock on the spire seemed to wink at me and invite me to sit on the stone steps again just as I did one night with my second ex-wife many years before. The beer in the nearby Gallopers pub had gone down well that night and we were experiencing a rare few moments of closeness. Shuddering at the recollection I pull my cap down further on my head and pressed on. Only a few yards past the church I noticed a few moss covered old stone steps at the side of the pavement. Later investigation told me these once belonged to a whole series of shops that once stood here on what now is waste ground. There was even a quite sizeable swimming baths situated here until the whole row was demolished sometime in the 1960's. The learned souls in my history group came up with a whole raft of old photos and information when I brought up the subject some time later.

Modern industrial units and massive roadside advertising hoardings passed by as Lou and I slogged up Wakefield Road. These gave way to a small row of early 18th century cottages at the junction with Fenby Avenue. Standing still proud amongst the industrial wasteland these sandstone buildings are a timely reminder to Bradford's heritage. I was rather pleased that I had decided to take this route as it gave me a somewhat welcome contrast to the usual countryside that I walk in.

Approaching Dudley Hill roundabout my senses were sharpened by the recollection of a quite marvellous if little known building which lay on the far side. The roundabout is always busy with the fast moving heavy traffic so Lou and I took the underground subway to emerge on the far side directly opposite the former Dudley Hill Picture House. Today a carpet warehouse I didn't even have to look closely to quite easily appreciate its former stylish purpose.

Designed by Cleckheaton Architects Howarth and Howarth for Walter and Percy Goodall, this red brick fronted gem stands alone in a surrounding sea of urban industrial decay. The Goodall brothers had four other cinemas; The Picture Palace in Heckmondwyke, The Pavilion in Dewsbury and The Picture Palace and The Savoy picture House in Cleckheaton. Howarth & Howarth had previously worked for the Goodall's on their other cinemas and came up with a superior design of red brickwork combined with white faience type decoration of LEFCO 'Marmo' tiles made by the Leeds Fireclay Company.

The interior featured a raked (sloping) floor, tip-up seats with better quality seats at the rear and in the small balcony. Goodall was quite ahead of his time by instructing his architects to include a sloping floor in all his cinemas. The Goodall's also claimed to be the first to use 'bucket' seats in their cinemas for better comfort. The vaulted ceiling with plaster moulded decoration led to a similarly curved proscenium arch approximately thirty feet wide with a stage depth of about ten feet. The interior plasterwork was by John Theabold & Sons of nearby Wakefield Road. The stalls seating capacity of almost six hundred was arranged in two blocks with centre and side aisles with the front row fourteen feet and six inches from the screen. The straight fronted circle was unusual in that the projection room was in the middle thus dividing the circle into two parts with five rows of seats each side of projection room - a total of just 88 seats.

The first film to be shown at Dudley Hill was "How's Your Father", a black and white American film on the 9th December 1912. The final film to be shown was "Thunderbirds Are Go" and it closed on Saturday 1st April 1967. The premises were then sold to a new owner for use as a Bingo club, but when that ceased the building was unused for a time prompting one Fred Atkinson, Curator of the Beamish Open-Air Museum, to consider the possibility of dismantling the cinema brick-by-brick and re-erecting at Beamish for further use as a cinema. Sadly the idea did not develop and it became the present day carpet shop. Despite these two diverse occupancies, the Picture Palace building remains virtually unaltered and is a time capsule of a 1912 vintage picture house.

Leaving this fantastic building behind Lou and I walked on along Tong Street passing by the site of the former Dudley Hill Railway Station. This station served The Leeds, Bradford and Halifax Junction Railway and opened to passengers on 20th December 1856 and to goods traffic on 1st January 1857. The station closed in 1952 but passenger services continued on the line until 4th July 1966. Today the site is occupied by a series of industrial units. This station was but one of many in the Bradford area that no longer exist today.

I was now entering an area that once contained many small coal pits, factories, mills and foundries. Today many of the mills survive as industrial units but the coal pits are long gone and resigned to the history books. I smiled wistfully as I wondered just what the Romans would have thought of it all. Passing by the only pub left on Tong Street, The Holme Lane, I turned down Holme Lane itself a little further on to wander past the edge of the massive Holmewood Council Estate to hopefully reach some airy and welcoming countryside beyond. Rows of dirty early 19th century terrace houses mingled with giants mills along the roadside. Sprinkled with the odd cottage it seemed very much a miss matched area. I had enough of industrial grime by this point and was looking forward to the open fields and country lanes that I knew were not far away.

The unmistakeable style of 20th century social housing became evident as Lou and I trekked down Holme Lane. Skirting the estate I came to a long bank of thick bushes along the roadside. A gap opened in the bushes and through here I could see a great expanse of open land. This was the site of Tong

Colliery's massive Number One pit. This pit and numerous other small pits were served by its own tramway which ran between two engine houses, one quite a distance back on Tong Street and the other on Tong Lane close to the village.

Holme Lane had now taken on a distinctly countryside feeling, and at the junction with Raikes Lane I saw a tiny babbling beck running under an earth banking at the roadside. I was back on my favoured walking ground. Trees and becks, horses in fields, crows fluttering from the trees, it was a relief after the sometimes dark foreboding industrial landscape I had journeyed through so far today. Filled with new energy and optimism my pace quickened as I passed the old and historic Raikes Hall farmhouse. This late 17th century two storey farmhouse of coursed Gritstone is today home to a famed riding stables and carriage hire centre. I stopped for a while to watch the horses being trained in the fields alongside the farmhouse. Yes I was defiantly home as I find it a pure joy to observe even the most humble equine in motion. The head rises and the strong muscles ripple as these noble beasts move gracefully across the ground. There is little to be seen in a Cow wandering around a field chewing grass but when it moves a horse portrays a sense of beauty that few creatures can match.

As I turned away from this exhibition of equine excellence my gaze fell upon another of this areas magnificent and historic residences. Constructed in 1669 on the site of an older timber framed house, Ryecroft Hall has a south facing entrance with five mullioned windows, some retaining their original leaded glazing. Inside it even boasts its own original 17th century Minstrels gallery similar to the one in The Stansfield Arms pub at Apperley Bridge.

We carried on walking down Raikes Lane following Kit Wood Beck as it trickled alongside us. The water was stained with the familiar tinge of orange from the ironstone that was disturbed by the activities at the many local coal pits. This phenomenon is widespread amongst the watercourses in the Bradford area and I have seen it many times during my walks. Raikes Lane had narrowed considerably and was flanked on each side by wide open fields and meadows. Stout fences kept the grazing cattle and sheep in their rightful places as the odd isolated cottage flashed by. The comforting aroma of muckspreading filled my nostrils as the farmer contentedly worked his magic upon his fields some distance away. The hedgerows were alive with tiny birds fluttering and making nests for their young. Out here in places like this time can stand still if you want it to. I shook my head in wonder that I was but a mere three miles from Bradford city centre.

I consulted my well crumpled map and it spoke to me. It said "thou must journey to Tong Village and all will be well". Remembering that when a map speaks you listen I turned off Raikes Lane and started up the long and steep ancient packhorse trail of New Lane. The lane narrowed once again as it climbed the hill towards the farmstead of Calverley Clough and Shackleton Wood. The tiny trail was fringed by tall Hawthorne bushes for perhaps half a mile then broke out into wonderful open countryside once again. The surface was broken and uneven after centuries of use by the merchants that walked this route to ply their trade and make their living long ago.

Calverley Clough was the first building of any kind we had come across for perhaps two miles. The farmyard was open to the road, the yard awash with the evidence of recent cattle movements. The comforting smell of beasts and nature was all around me. It invaded my senses like an old friend, the calling of cattle in a nearby shed filled my ears, I was intoxicated. Stirring myself we walked on towards the massive Shackleton Wood. Along with the nearby Park Wood this forms itself on the boundary of The Tong Park Estate.

By far the largest open space within this area is Tong Park which covers much of the north side of Tong Lane. It is known that prior to the remodelling of Tong Hall in 1773, there was a formal garden directly in front of the building, bounded by high stone walls, with a similarly enclosed garden to the rear. Tong Park surrounded the Hall and is gardens and probably took the form of a grid of pathways bounded by formal planting and lawns. It is unknown whether the remodelling of Tong Hall also involved large scale changes to the nature of the surrounding parkland, but it is known that the square front and rear garden walls were demolished, meaning the Park itself became the setting for this unique landmark building.

During the last century, the Park covered an area of 32 acres, but under the ownership of Eric Towler between 1941 and 1943, 20 acres of the Park was given over to pasture, leaving a reduced area of formal parkland in the vicinity of the Hall, which by this time had probably lost much of its rigid grid layout. Today, Tong Park provides an attractive mixture of well-maintained areas of grassland and woodland which provides Tong Hall with an attractive setting. The boundary wall and railings to the Park at Tong Lane are beneath the canopy of densely packed sycamore trees. The gateway is set behind a neat tapered grass verge which contrasts with the tightly packed wall of foliage on the other side which makes for an interesting tunnel-like vista of Tong Hall, situated some 200m from the gateway. Passing through the gateway a regular line of shrubbery below the canopy of the deciduous woodland reinforces the straight line of the drive and encloses it. The entrance lodge and the large rectangular fishpond behind it are the only interruptions to the woodland, but are more or less swamped by branches and leaves.

But I was to see none of that as I continued on along New Lane past the farm of Gil Stubbing and the tiny wood named The Shrog. The road widened a little at this point and the flatness of the terrain was welcome after the long haul up from Raikes Lane. Before long Lou Parson and I reached the junction with Tong Lane and we turned left to head towards the ancient and historic village of Tong. After only a few hundred yards we came to The Old Vicarage. Built in 1739 this beautiful Grade II listed building has the usual mullioned windows and inside boasts part panelled walls and window seats. The nearby St. James Church was not deemed large enough by the then Lord of the Manor to have a full time Vicar so the house was lived in by the Curate.

The site of St. James Church, Tong has been a place of Christian worship for close on a thousand years. The church as it stands was re-built in 1727 by a team of stone masons that included John Nelson. Nelson was later to experience a dramatic conversion through the preaching of John Wesley in London, and became a significant Methodist leader and preacher. The re-building was instructed by Sir George Tempest of Tong Hall, who had rebuilt Tong Hall in 1702, and was to later build the Village School (now the 'Schoolroom'). The church replaced an earlier building that had been built in c. 1140 A.D.

The Tempest family continued to live at nearby Tong Hall (rebuilt in 1702) until 1941. They were the Lords of the Manor of Tong, and they owned most of the village and surrounding farms. In 1980, during an extensive restoration of the church building, important archaeological discoveries were made which showed that there had been a Saxon church building on the site before the Norman church of 1140. The foundations of this early church were uncovered and its rough shape identified. The archaeologists also found fragments of Roman pottery and a flint barbed and tonged arrowhead from Bronze Age times. This latter confirmed the likelihood of there having being some kind of settlement here for close on 3,000 years.

There was little change to the life and fabric of the church during the Victorian era. Bell ringing continued to be popular, and the present stained glass window at the East wall was added. The Church is a Grade 1 listed building, and is visited by large numbers of people, especially in the summer period. The interior of the church is largely the same as when it was re-built in 1727, and so includes a Georgian style three decker pulpit, and box pews.

I sat myself on a wall opposite this wonderful typical country village church. Across the road in front of it I noticed a set of double sided stone steps pushed up against the surrounding church wall. They formed what would have been a mounting block for the carriages of the day, although I don't think this was their original position. Perhaps they had been there the day Alice Tempest married her young rich lover at St James church in Victorian times. The dark carriage drawn by four shining fine horses stopped here right in front of me. With a steady hand the driver brought them to a steady halt by the block. His accomplice jumped down to open the door for the bride. Decked in her beautiful and fine white wedding dress she waited till he opened the door. The church entrance was surrounded by the invited well to do guests. A sprinkling of local village well-wishers stood gathered just where I was now. Her father offered his hand to hers and helped his daughter step down from the carriage. The Groom waited nervously inside the church with his best man. The Vicar John McStay stood hands clasped in front of him nodding respectfully as he greeted the bride. As the group followed the Vicar inside, the watching Poacher with the Jack Russell touched his flat black cap then melted away into the trees.

A speeding cattle truck brought me firmly back into the 21st century with a jolt. I checked my watch and saw Lou and I had been sat there for over thirty minutes. Time to get moving little dog I said to Lou and jumped down from the wall and together we started to walk back along Tong lane towards Westgate Hill where I knew I could catch the bus to Bradford.

Later that evening as I sat before my fire in Magpie Cottage I went back over the events of the day in my mind. This I always do as I think it is an important part of my walks. The pre walk planning is one part, the actual walking is another and the post walk bit is another still. Not for the first time one single thought came to me strongly. I always seem to picture myself as a common man. The village boy sitting on the wall at the side of the carriage drive in the grounds of the Knoll at Baildon, the ne'er-do-well stood outside the long gone

Canal Tavern at Thackley, the Poacher stood watching the wedding in Tong Village. Always a simple working class man never a member of the Landed Gentry. I have never given much credence to the notion of reincarnation or anything like that, but sat there that night, I did wonder if stranger things did happen at sea.

Denholme to Bingley via Harden

I have always been impressed by The Victorians. They ushered in a great age of innovation and expansion. Technological, social and military expansion which made Great Britain the greatest and most powerful country on Earth. They created an empire like no other before or since. The area around Bradford is steeped in The Victorian's influence as the many fine buildings and structures prove. It was one of these fine structures that gave birth to the idea of today's walk. It is situated out in the green and pleasant countryside surrounding Bradford, and it was to here that Lou and I travelled to start our journey to pay homage to surely one of the local Victorian's finest architectural legacies.

Denholme is just the same as the other villages in these parts that were created by local wool barons and industrialists. Like the villages of Saltaire and nearby Queensbury, Denholme still has the shadow of its creator and benefactor hanging over it. One only has to look at the names of many of the streets and even the park to appreciate the impact that the Foster family had on the village and its people. The entire Victorian housing sites of Denholme were built by the Fosters who also built the old textile mills in the village. The houses were constructed for the workers of the mills. It was common in Victorian England for wealthy businessmen to build entire towns to house the workers of their mills.

The village sits astride the old Roman Road from Manchester to Ilkley, though there is no evidence of any settlement there. The line of the road is visible on the ground to the south of the village, not far from St Paul's church. The first evidence of habitation in the area dates from the 13th century. There is a grant of land, dated 1239, whereby Thomas de Thornton gave grazing land at Denholme to the monks of Byland Abbey. It is likely that the monks would have built a Grange in the area and this may well have given the village its first occupants. The Monks grazed sheep as the fleeces were a valuable cash crop at the time. By the 15th century the land belonged to the Tempest family who held it for many years until it was gambled in a game of cards and lost to The Saville family of Halifax by Sir Richard Tempest.

In 1822 the main occupations in the village were mining, farming and hand loom weaving. Coal, fireclay, iron pyrates and York stone could be found in reasonably plentiful supply and there were good sources of water. These natural resources attracted industrial interest, and the Foster's arrived on the scene. Recognising the economic potential of the village they started building their mill on the only level plateau of land available in the valley, with easy access to water. The first mill, started in 1838, was never completed. It was blown down in January 1839. The second was larger than the original, and was a profitable concern until it burnt down in 1857, a common fate for these industrial buildings

The third mill, larger still, also thrived, but on September 6th 1873 there was a strike which lasted 14 days. An agreement, to employ only weavers in the new shed, which held 1,000 looms, had been broken, leading to industrial action. In 2005 any employment on the site of the old mill ended with the closure of Pennine Fibres. The mill building has subsequently been demolished and plans have been approved to build approximately 96 houses on the site.

Today the village is quiet and pretty much of a backwater in places. Many if not all of the 18th century former workers cottages survive and are inhabited by local people. The late Saturday morning summer sun was high in the sky as Lou and I walked confidently along the main road through the village. Passing by rows of these sturdy workers cottages huddled by the roadside we made good time in our journey to Bingley. But Bingley was miles away and there was much of the local landscape and history to see before we reached the ancient market town in the valley below.

We turned off the main road taking the narrow track named Carr Lane. My map told me this was a dead end with what appeared to be a tiny cottage right at the end. Next to it was a stream or a beck and this small area conjured up a vision of pastoral remoteness in such a way that I simply had to visit it. It was actually a small farmstead with a tiny cottage tucked away at the side. The stream was no more than a spring which emanated from the field a few yards from the cottage. The old G.N.R railway line used to run but a short distance from this tranquil place and the cottage would have shaken like the barley in the wind when the trains roared past. It looked rather run down but it was lived in by some lucky soul. This simple but hardy Sandstone dwelling was home to someone as there was a small motorbike in the front garden which had been used only a few minutes before as I could smell the faint exhaust fumes hanging in the still air around me.

Turning around I made my way back up the lane and took a small footpath which would lead me across the fields to nearby Whalley Lane. The path crossed the site of a tiny delph. The scaring of the landscape was evidence of the toil and the backbreaking work of the tough local men who raped the land for a living. From here I could clearly see the line of thick trees that now grew along the former train line. Nature always reclaims the land once man has finished with it even if it sometimes takes many years.

I climbed over the drystone wall onto Whalley Lane. Lou had already beaten me to it and was stood in the lane waiting for me. As I dropped onto the tarmac she pulled me with a jolt across the road towards a farm gate. Behind the gate staring at us were six beautiful Collies. These dogs were identical in size and colour and simply sat behind the gate in a line just staring at us. This breed of dog is in my experience never aggressive in nature but playful and very intelligent. Like the Jack Russell they are a working breed and this they had obviously been bred to do at Buck Park Farm. They watched us intently as we disappeared past this late 18th century hammer dressed stone farmhouse on our way to Hewenden reservoir and viaduct.

The famed viaduct was the main reason for our walk today. I had seen and admired it many times whilst driving through the village of nearby Harecroft but never had the pleasure of walking along the pathway on the top. Like the other viaduct on this former train line at Thornton, it is now part of the Sustrans railway trail and can be enjoyed in a way it was surely never intended when it was constructed by the Victorians.

The narrow lane wound down the hillside flanked by open fields to both sides and the trees of the track bed stood proud up ahead. A hay cart and tractor chugged up the hill towards us, its load piled so high I thought it would surely topple and cover us as it passed. It didn't and with a cheery wave the red cheeked farmer went on his way up the hill. The lane passed under the train bed via a road bridge. This small but tall bridge with its twin abutments was built to allow the railway line to cross Whalley Lane. Even though the road is but a mere country lane The Victorian engineers designed and constructed this bridge with as much care and attention to detail as they had with the nearby Hewenden viaduct and other such structures along the line. As I stood for a moment to admire this humble bridge the thought occurred to me that these fine people took attention to detail to a new level when they laid their railways all those years ago.

The early afternoon sun was baking as we followed the lane as it snaked around the valley bottom to cross Denholme Beck at Meal Bridge. Here the beck was wide and powerful and would have had to have been to power the saw mill that once stood nearby in Park Wood. Close to Park Wood was Buck Park Quarry so I suspect it may have been stone and not timber that the mill processed. My map had told me there was a small track leading off Whalley Lane a little further on and this would lead Lou and I through the woods towards Hewenden Reservoir and the viaduct beyond. We passed by a large rabbit warren on the field at the side of the track. The many visible entrances gave me an idea of the scope of the underground labyrinth that the rabbits made their home. If Lou had been unrestrained I would never have seen her again as she would have been lost forever beneath the soil. That is just one reason why she is never ever unrestrained. She is a most obedient and loyal dog but given full unfettered access to her primeval instincts, of which chasing down quarry is but one, she would lose her head and my commands would fall on deaf ears. So she stays on the extendable lead wherever we go, and fifteen feet is long enough for the both of us.

I looked up ahead and just above the tree tops could see the ridge of the viaduct. It stood perhaps half a mile away and I couldn't wait to reach it. The reservoir appeared magnificent the night before on Google maps and that was an added bonus, I simply could not wait. The track skirted along the edge of the woods, underneath yet another fine old railway bridge and through the light covering of trees. This was a welcome change after the recent dense, heavy wooded areas that Lou and I had tramped through. The scenery was light and airy as we passed the house of Wood Nook. What a splendid place to live, isolated amongst the trees with the reservoir on the doorstep almost.

The fields swept down the towards the water's edge, cattle grazed everywhere but paid us no attention as we walked among them towards the site of the long gone Wilsden railway station. Built in 1886 for The Great Northern Railway it is actually two miles from Wilsden and closer to Harecroft. It closed in 1955 and only the Station Masters house survives today as a private residence. I climbed up the banking above the fields towards the former station site and from here looked down upon the magnificent 1.16 Kilometre long Hewenden Reservoir. The sun shimmered on the water's surface as Whooper Swans and Yellow Legged Gulls flew overhead like a squadron of Spitfires would have done in 1941. I sat there enjoying my packed lunch for what seemed an age gazing at the massive body of water before me and thinking of the men that constructed it all those years ago.

The magnificence of the reservoir was so captivating that I hardly noticed the viaduct standing guard away to the north. The pleasure of striding along its high seventeen arches was yet to come once I had digested my customery cheese and onion sandwiches. Crossing Hewenden Beck, the viaduct stands at 123 feet tall and spans 576 yards with 17 arches each of 16.5 yards.

The viaduct originally formed part of the Keighley and Thornton Branch of the Great Northern Railway and, together with the mile-long Lees Moor Tunnel, opened to passenger trains in 1883. Engineered by Richard Johnson from Hammer-dressed and rock-faced stone, it served as a railway viaduct along the Queensbury Lines and it now forms part of the Great Northern Railway Trail for cyclists and walkers. This grand structure is a Grade II listed building and due to shifting sands in the earth below the foundations go as deep as the height of the structure. It was constructed from stone prised from the ground in the nearby Manywells quarry. The last locomotive traffic crossed this superb structure in 1963, and since then many thousands of people have walked its length high up in the sky. Today it was my turn and I had waited many years for this opportunity.

As I opened the gate at the east end of the viaducts top I had no sense of the length of the structure due to the curve which was built into it. It is almost like a massive stone banana and was built this way due to the topography of the land below. The stonework was unaltered by the passing years, the surface and corners as sharpe as the day they were cut by the Victorian stonemasons skilled hands. Standing there looking down upon the wide expanse of rolling fields and hills I wondered if the men that built it ever considered they were creating something that will surely last a thousand years. As a rule I don't like heights but as I stood up there in the heavens I felt almost privileged and honoured to have the chance.

The spell was broken by the bell of an approaching cyclist who had not seen us due to the bend and nearly took my arm off as he passed. Hell it would have been worth losing a limb for this experience. Silently thanking The Victorians for their ingenuity and sense of grandeur I pulled Lou into the centre of the tarmac walkway and started to wander to the far end. Here I found a small area with an information board that told the story of the viaduct and afforded me a view back along its whole length from the side almost. From here I could truly appreciate its stunning architecture as the seventeen arches unfolded across the valley below me. From here it was easy to imagine the dense clouds of steam pumping from the locomotives funnel as it swept majestically around the bend towards the nearby Cullingworth station.

Lou and I re-joined the trail on the former railway bed and were soon at the site of the old Cullingworth station. Cullingworth railway station was a station on the Queensbury Lines which ran between Keighley, Bradford and Halifax. The station served the village of Cullingworth, West Yorkshire, England. It opened for passengers in 1884 and closed in May 1955. Goods traffic continued until 1963, when the surviving line closed completely. Today nothing remains apart from some modern buildings on the site of a former goods warehouse. The stout locked steel gates to this area made any investigation impossible so Lou and I moved on through the village towards the open road which runs to Harden. We took the Halifax Road past the Vicarage and its ancient stone horse drinking trough. As in Denholme earlier that day the road was lined with early 18th century mill workers cottages.

Cullingworth itself stands in the eastern foothills of the South Pennines. Manywells Beck flows through the village, leading into Harden Beck, a small tributary of the River Aire. The centre of the village still retains a distinct rural feel, despite the extensive 20th century residential development around the older core. The original core of the village, located around Station Road and Georges Square, contains many listed vernacular structures. These include farmhouses, converted barns and commercial buildings as well as smaller cottages. The more formal style of architecture of the church and chapels provide an interesting civic aspect. These buildings all provide a unique record of the early development of Cullingworth into a thriving agricultural hamlet and later into a busy cloth-manufacturing village.

Several other mills were built in and around Cullingworth. A corn mill and tannery were active at Cow House Fold, to the northeast of the village during this period. However, the largest mill in the area, constructed by 1852, was the Worsted mill on the western side of Halifax Road. This mill, built around a courtyard with an unusual gate and entrance, was run by the Townend Brothers, an eminent and wealthy local family. The mill was extended in 1823, 1840 and again in 1860 and was the first maker of Worsted heald yarns in the Bradford district as well becoming the main source of employment in the village, at its peak employing 800 workers. The Townend family also worked the coal pits at Denholme, Dene Brow, Hazel Crook and Hollin Hall. These collieries supplied high grade coal for the gas works, which were located within the Cullingworth Mills complex and supplied gas not only to the mill but to the whole village.

People were attracted to the village to find employment in the mills and during the 19th century the population of Cullingworth expanded. This increase necessitated the construction of more buildings, mostly in the form of back-to-back and terraced housing. The settlement developed southwards towards Cullingworth Gate and east of Halifax Road. Improvements were undertaken in the village such as the widening of the roads (including Station Road) and the demolition of some older properties. Today part of the giant expanse of Cullingworth Mill survives along with the foreman's house and the entrance lodge.

We dropped down the hill into the gully alongside Ellar Carr Beck. Here the road was steep and I had to take great care with Lou Parson as there were no pavements and the traffic was whizzing by at speed. But after a short distance a pavement did appear and I could relax. The road was lined with the dense woodland of Ellar Beck on one side and a large earth banking on the other as we made our way towards the cottages of Cow House Bridge in the gully bottom. This short row of former workers cottages was pristine in appearance belaying their great age. Built to house the workers in the nearby mill Woodfield Mill, they were now homes to local people who commuted into nearby Bingley and Bradford to make their living.

Bingley Road had now become Hill End Lane as it swept uphill towards Hunters Hill and the site of a former Tannery at Hunters Hill farm. Catstones Moor with its ancient quarry and even more ancient Ring stones stood guard above us. The road was long and straight as it wound up the side of the moor towards Harden. The almost square plantation of Hunters Hill Wood appeared to my left and over to my right were the open meadows and fields towards Wilsden. After maybe two miles of hard slog up the hill we entered the edge of the village of Harden. Passing Leech Lane where excavations in the 1980's suggested a Roman settlement and villa once stood, we descended the slight gradient into Harden itself.

The main road through the village is once again lined with pristine former mill workers cottages. Every summer the village holds a medieval "fayre", with jugglers, jousting and other entertainments. Medieval tents are set up on the top field and demonstrations show how simple tasks like the washing up and making a tent peg would have been done. There was no sign of maidens in long white flowing dresses or knights on horseback so I guess Lou and I were a little too early for the summer festivities. A game of Cricket was being played on the pleasant pitch on the outskirts of the village though. The sound of lightly oiled Willow on leather is always a joy to hear and the little fat bloke bowling way too fast for his stature amused me as we walked by towards Bingley.

The long straight road passes very close to the famous St. Ives Estate as it winds its way down towards Bingley. The St. Ives area is known to have been inhabited from at least the Neolithic or Bronze Age from artefacts left behind. Up until the Dissolution of the Monasteries in 1540 the land was divided between the monks of Rievaulx Abbey and Drax Priory. In 1540 the land was purchased by a Walter Paslew and was subsequently owned by the Laycock and Milner families and the St. Ives mansion house was built in 1616.

In 1635 the Ferrands purchased St. Ives at the time known as Harden Grange, and it was in 1858 that the names of Harden Grange and the local St. Ives were interchanged. There are stories of a local connection with General Fairfax and the Civil War, but little is known with any certainty. Sarah Busfield (née Ferrand) inherited St. Ives from her uncle and she and her son William changed their family name to Ferrand and, when she died in 1854 her son William Busfield Ferrand inherited the property. The estate and mansion were bought by Bingley Urban District Council in 1929.

A granite obelisk close to Lady Blantyre's Rock north west of Coppice Pond commemorates the career of William Busfield Ferrand (1809–89), a Member of Parliament, magistrate and one time owner of St. Ives Estate. Coppice Pond was built as a feed water supply for what is thought originally to be a fulling mill, later landscaped by the Ferrands and used for boating. Today it is stocked with a variety of fish for angling and has a bird hide and duck feeding pier. On the north side of the pond is the archery club while east of Coppice Pond is the mill. A mill has been recorded on this site since the early 14th century and it is probably the oldest building on the estate, although modified since then. To the south of Coppice Pond near Cuckoo Nest Cottages is the restored Baxter's Pond, fed by both Coppice Pond and the mill. East of the mill is Home Farm with its cafe, coach house and stables, and to the rear a Dutch barn and a car park.

Lou and I had been walking for what seemed hours and time was getting short so a visit to the St. Ives Estate would have to wait for another day. My pace picked up as the road descended down the hill between Bell Bank Wood and Holme House Wood. The ancient and historic Ireland Bridge and the small town of Bingley was not far away. From here I could catch a bus back to Shipley and then the local bus up to Wrose and be home for the Manchester United game on Sky Sports. I'd had enough history for one day and besides I wanted a culture fix of a different kind as I ate my tea that evening.

High Eldwick to Baildon via Weecher Reservoir

An old woman I once met at Keelham crossroads near Thornton asked me how I came up with the ideas for my walks. I told her that I didn't bother doing the official Council leisure walks as these were usually boring and straight forward. I prefer to invent and plan my own. Yes they do sometimes take in certain aspects of the well known local walks but I twist and fine tune them to add my own slant on things. I have access to many old Ordnance Survey maps spanning over a century from 1847 up to the 1950's. Sometimes I burn the midnight oil as I pour over these and other maps looking for inspiration.

More often than not it is just a single word or perhaps two that catch my eye and make me investigate deeper. Then I work on the potential walk further and open it up to include other places that interest me and before long a complete walk has been constructed so to speak. This walk is a prime example of this method as it was born from just two words. The words Hydraulic Ram might not stir the minds of most folk but when I saw them on the 1889 Ordnance Survey map one evening, my interest was aroused and just a short while later I had a complete walk organised.

A hydraulic ram, or hydram, is a cyclic water pump powered by hydropower. It takes in water at one "hydraulic head" (pressure) and flow rate, and outputs water at a higher hydraulic head and lower flow rate. The device uses the water hammer effect to develop pressure that allows a portion of the input water that powers the pump to be lifted to a point higher than where the water originally started. The hydraulic ram is sometimes used in remote areas and the fields between the mills of East Morton and the nearby Alma Terrace could perhaps be termed "remote". What was its purpose? Was it still there? I had to go and find out, and so this walk was born.

So on a bright Wednesday morning in May 2015 Lou and I set off to head for Shipley to catch the Eldwick bus that would take us up the slopes of the valley opposite Bingley to Heights lane. Heights Lane was long, straight and level which was a good start as we had plenty to see along the miles we were to do today. Passing by open fields and paddocks with the occasional horse we made good time in the mid morning sun. After a short distance the small number of houses along the roadside faded away to leave an uninterrupted view of fields over both sides. The disused Height Sandstone quarries went by in a moment as Lou and I walked the road in silence. Smaller disused quarries like this and tiny old coal pits are dotted all around this area and the wider area of Baildon Moor in general.

We had officially left Eldwick at this point and the drystone walls rolled on in splendour as they had done for hundreds of years. Crossing over the road I stopped to admire the isolated farmhouse and lush mature gardens of Croftlands. Now heading towards an area known as The Riggs we passed the site of the former Bingley Sanitary Tubes and limeworks with its associated lime pits. The tall red brick chimney could be seen from quite a distance and the land around the site was scared with the evidence of the previous activity. Further over to the west past this area I could see Deer Park, a small wooded area where Deer will have roamed since antiquity and most likely still do. Although we were climbing upwards towards The Riggs the gradient was only a gradual increase and both Lou and I took it in our stride. The signpost said one and three quarter miles back to Bingley but we seemed to be in the middle of nowhere such was the seclusion and isolation at this point. I passed Drake Hill Cottages and wondered why the name carved on the stone gateposts read Harfleet but gave it no heed as country folk do strange things at times.

The junction with Otley road was not far away when we passed Prospect House and looking further beyond there I could see the banking of the massive Graincliffe Reservoir. Lower down the hillside the smaller Compensation reservoir is fed from here via Eldwick Beck. This reservoir also controls the flow of water into Loadpit Beck as it flows to its journeys end at the river Aire far below. The modern buildings of the filter beds stood in contrast before the rising Baildon Moor far beyond. Lou and I reached the junction with Otley Road and turned left down the sharp, winding steep hill towards the ancient village of East Morton and the Hydraulic Ram. This road has been the site of many traffic accidents and even the odd fatality over the years due to its steep nature. The high drystone wall to the right rises up to further enhance the steepness of this road and I reeled Lou all the way in on her lead and proceeded with caution.

The wonderful row of 18th century sandstone terrace houses that is Alma Terrace stood proud along the right hand side just as I entered the village. The seventeen or so houses date from the late 18th century and are marked on the maps from 1889 onwards. As with many streets in England they were named after the famous battle of Alma in The Crimean War. The Battle of the Alma (20

September 1854) is usually considered the first battle of the Crimean War (1853–1856), and took place just south of the River Alma in the Crimea. An Anglo-French force under Jacques Leroy de Saint Arnaud and Fitzroy Somerset, 1st Lord Raglan defeated General Aleksandr Sergeyevich Menshikov's Russian army, which lost around 6,000 troops.

Beyond these houses was open fields and the Hydraulic ram, and beyond that Botany Mill, Providence Mill and Upper Mill. I walked to the very end of Alma Terrace as I knew there was a footpath alongside the last house which would lead me to where I thought the ram may still be. I say still be as I didn't know if it disappeared or not but I was going to have a look and find out regardless. Finding the narrow footpath flanked by high drystone walls I lifted Lou over the metal gate and walked along it into the fields. The path led me to a triangular shaped piece of patchy scrubland where the maps indicated the ram was. I wasn't even sure what I was looking for to be honest. A cylindrical metal object stuck in the ground perhaps. I scoured the piece of ground looking for this mysterious object but sadly found nothing that could fit the description. So sadly after maybe an hour of scrabbling around in the dirt and weeds I gave up and took to the footpath once again to walk back to Otley road and begin the climb out of the village.

By the time I reached the small wood that once contained the long gone Todmore Stones I was gasping for breath. Sweating like a man seeing a Police car in his rear view mirror, I rested at the side of the road and started on my packed lunch. As I dined on my Peanut Butter sandwiches a taxi driver with a death wish came flying down the hill at an obviously illegal speed. He had to break sharply as he got to Alma terrace and only just made it. The smell of burning rubber from his tyres nearly put me off my dinner.

At least from here it was a straight level road along past the wood of Little Graincliff and the famous public house Dick Hudson's beyond. Formally known as The Fleece this pub takes its name from a previous Landlord named Dick Hudson. Situated on the old packhorse trail from Ilkley to Bingley it was a resting place for weary travellers just as it is today. It was originally a tavern attached to an old farmhouse called The Plough boy which lost its licence when the new Eldwick road was built. The first Landlord was Thomas Hudson in 1809 and he was succeeded by his Son Dick who held the licence from 1850 to 1878. I have eaten there on many occasions in the past and it is always a delight to visit. The beer is good, the food is great, and history pervades every nook and cranny of the old place. It really doesn't get much better.

Otley Road took us right past Dick Hudson's and on towards Harvey Smith's farm and horse training centre at Craiglands Farm. Harvey Smith is a well known local Showjumper famous for his "V" sign. He stood out from the ranks of showjumpers because of his broad accent and blunt manner. His career was often controversial; in 1971 he was disciplined (overturned on appeal) after he gave a "V sign" to the judges following a near perfect round which won him the British Show Jumping Derby for the second year in succession.

Eldwick Crag and its disused quarry rose up like a demon on one side, open fields on the other as I navigated the busy road with great care, stopping every few feet to let the passing traffic flow by. We passed a couple of roadside barns and cottages before reaching Eldwick's first Methodist Mission Room and Sunday school. This beautiful tiny building dating from 1815 stands right on the roadside as looks as good today as they day it was built. On the hillside just above this building Hog Hall once stood. Today only a few stones lay on the hillside as evidence of this fantastically named dwelling.

The moorland fell away to reveal open land and fields on both sides as we approached Smith's Craiglands Farm. The flat land across the road from his farm is ideal galloping and training land for his horses and Lou and I just had to stop and observe a group of them for a while. When they finished the three quite magnificent beasts and their riders trotted across the road in front of us from their training area. Now walking slowly, their work for the afternoon done the leading rider nodded a greeting at us. I returned it and thanked them for allowing me to watch such fine animals at work.

I place I knew well was not far away. A place where I had spent many Saturday nights house sitting whilst the owner was away climbing and caving in the Dales. Mark Southam used to look after Weecher Reservoir and a bonus of his job was that he got to live in the cottage alongside it. This small dwelling in its isolated position had the habit being burgled whilst he was away so myself and another friend would ride over on our motorbikes, stay overnight and party to keep it safe. This we duly did on quite a few occasions but don't worry Darren Whitaker our secret is safe as Iam saying nowt more. I remember one summer Saturday night many years ago when Mr Southam erected a marquee on the large front lawn overlooking the reservoir and invited a couple of local bands to play and a load of people to come and party. A band from Keighley named Whipping Post entertained us that balmy Saturday night. There were cars, vans and motorbikes parked all down Sconce Lane, tents were pitched everywhere on the front lawn. Forget Woodstock, the music festival Salstock was born that night and Iam saying nowt more.

With some relief I turned off the main Otley Road and headed down the track alongside the reservoir. There would be no traffic from here to the end of the walk at the foot of Baildon Moor so both Lou and I could relax a little and enjoy the passing scenery. The narrow country land snaked down the side of the vast body of water high above. The high banking and stout wall kept it in place and before long we arrived at Little London Farm. In centuries past this place was an important meeting place for traders and salt markets were sometimes held on a flat plateau of land below. All through history the availability of salt has been pivotal to civilization. The word "salary" comes from the Latin word for salt because the Roman Legions were sometimes paid in salt, which was quite literally worth its weight in gold. In Britain, the suffix "-wich" in a place name means it was once a source of salt, as in Sandwich and Norwich.

We were now on Sconce Lane and this would take us to our journeys end. Flanked on one side by tiny disused delphs the narrow lane wound along through the countryside to take us to Faweather. In the 13th century the land for many miles around belonged to the Monks of Rievaulx Abbey. They built the original Grange on this site to serve their medieval estates. The Monks also farmed Sheep on the surrounding hills for their milk, meat and highly prized fleeces. There is evidence too of iron workings nearby dating from the 13th century. The lane led us past Great Wood, Gill Beck and Faweather Quarries. This quarry was operational from the early 18th century and stone was carted from here to Otley for church building. Like many other small local quarries it became disused at the end of World War I.

Passing Ash House Farm Lou and I walked towards the former hamlet of Sconce itself. This collection of thirteen cottages was built in the mid-18th century for local miners, but was reduced to just one in 1934. Many of the small hamlets in this area were demolished by Baildon Council due to sanitation concerns. Today it is owned by Shipley and Baildon Scout Council and used for camping purposes.

The night before when I was planning this walk I noticed a small square of land opposite the site of the cottages at Sconce. Marked "Aviary" it drew my attention and now I was stood right beside it. It was perhaps the size of half a football pitch and was surrounded all the way round by a drystone wall. A small metal gate gave me access to what appeared to be simply a patch of tree lined grass. The maps did seem to indicate the presence of a small building in the centre with spokes radiating outwards to the outer walls. It turns out that it was an artificial hatchery to produce bird eggs for exhibitions. Owned by a Mr Lambert he employed Mr and Mrs Allpress to relocate from Peterborough in 1904 to manage it for him. Later it became a small holiday camp until it burned down in the 1930's. So that's what it was thought I as I left the field and closed the gate behind us.

Lou Parson and I walked on and arrived at the end of Sconce Lane at the point where it meets Hawksworth Road. Turning right to start the climb up the moor side towards Baildon to catch the bus back into Shipley, my thoughts went back to Sal Southam's Reservoir side cottage at Weecher. Many years had passed since I sat alone on his doorstep and watched a dark blood red sun slowly creep over the horizon towards Bradford. My friend, the venerable but lightweight Mr Whitaker was asleep on the couch and had been for some time. It was perhaps 4.30am and I was wide awake and buzzing. Why come to a place like this and crash out at midnight? As usual I wanted to make the most of it and would sleep the next day.

As I sat there on the step, the Incantations album by Mike Oldfield drifting out around me through the open door, I recall a peaceful easy feeling coming over me enveloping me like a trusty old coat. Now a quarter of a century later I still listen to that great Oldfield album and it takes me back to that blood red sun and that same feeling. Mr Southam is and was indeed a lucky man to have witnessed that sight whenever he wanted. He still lives there now. How do I know? A van with his name on the side was parked on the gravel drive in front of the cottage when I walked past. Maybe one day all the great friends and characters from that period in my life ought to get it on again and Sal Southam can host Salstock II.

Greengates to Thackley Corner via Little London

The bus dropped Lou and I on the outside of the Thorpe Edge Estate on the Dudley Hill, Killinghall and Harewood Trust Turnpike Road. Today this long stretch of road is known as Harrogate Road and as its name suggests runs all the way to the North Yorkshire spa town of the same name. Walking past the former site of Holybrook Mill and Oak Lee Mill now occupied by Sainsbury's Supermarket, I waited for ages to cross the busy road junction by Greengates superb War Memorial. We were making for the tiny area down Harrogate Road known due to its profusion of Dye Houses as, strangely enough, Dyehouse Fold.

It was common in former times for the mills of Bradford to be grouped in the same vicinity according to their purposes, and following this trend the mills adjacent to the canal at Apperley Bridge were predominantly used for the dyeing of wool and cloth. The area between the mills and the New Line road at Greengates was used for "Tenterhooking", and one of the streets of the new build estate on the site pays homage to this former use with the name Tenterfields.

Tenterhooks are hooks in a device called a tenter. Tenters were originally large wooden frames which were used as far back as the 14th century in the process of making woollen cloth. After a piece of cloth was woven, it still contained oil from the fleece and some dirt. A craftsperson called a fuller or waulker cleaned the woollen cloth in a fulling mill, and then had to dry it carefully or the woollen fabric would shrink. To prevent this shrinkage, the fuller would place the wet cloth on a tenter, and leave it to dry outdoors. The lengths of wet cloth were stretched on the tenter (from Latin tendere, meaning "to stretch") using tenterhooks (hooked nails driven through the wood) all around the perimeter of the frame to which the cloth's edges were fixed, so that as it dried the cloth would retain its shape and size. In some manufacturing areas like at Greengates, entire tenter-fields were once a common sight.

The history lesson over, Lou and I strode purposefully down the hill in the direction of the canal and slightly beyond that, the river Aire. We crossed over the river using the bridge constructed in 1936 to augment the original bridge which still survives a few metres to the west. Here to the east during the

Football season the mighty Bantams of Bradford City train on fields which are often waterlogged in the winter. But today was during the off season and the only activity on the playing fields was some children pretending to be their local heroes. This area was also the site of Bradford's first and so far only Aerodrome in the early years of the 20th century. The lure of a lunchtime pint of well-kept locally brewed ale was suppressed with some difficulty as I arrived at The Stansfield Arms. Built as a Coaching Inn in the style of a farmhouse and barn and dating back to 1543, this fantastic ancient place once housed the soldiers of Lord Halifax as they waited to cross the nearby river Aire en route for Leeds during the English Civil War. The beamed historical public house with its vintage wooden floors was also used as a gatehouse for the Stansfield Estate at Esholt. I have dined there on many occasions in the past and have always admired the Minstrels Gallery in the old part of the building. But today I had no time for drinking ale as there was serious walking to be done.

Harrogate Road had now become Apperley Lane as it started its climb up the valley side in the direction of Rawdon and Little London. Carrying on up the incline, Lou and I passed the lodge of Woodhouse Grove School and the Wesleyan Methodist church before turning off along Woodlands Drive. Here lies the location of the original Apperley Bridge railway station, which was finally closed by the British Railways Board, as a result of the Beeching Axe, at about 9.30pm on 20 March 1965.

The Leeds and Bradford Railway opened on 30 June 1846. At first, there were no intermediate stations, such had been the haste to get the line opened. Temporary stations were quickly provided, including Apperley Bridge, which opened some time during July 1846. A permanent structure followed about a year later. It comprised two platforms, partly covered by an overall roof. The main building ran parallel to the railway on the south side up at road level. A principal customer of the station was Woodhouse Grove School, whose land had been crossed by the Railway. About 1849, the Railway agreed to purchase gas from the school in order to light the station. The Railway was widened to four tracks in about 1900, taking more land from Woodhouse Grove School, who used the money to build a swimming bath. The station was enlarged to four platforms, with a distinctive wooden building above at road level. The original station building was swept away when the cutting was widened to accommodate the new "fast lines" on the south side.

Woodlands Drive was to take me up the valley side towards Cragg Wood. This area covers a rural suburb of fine Victorian Villas set in spacious wooded grounds that was developed in the 1850's. The surviving woodlands of the area and the vernacular buildings of the farmsteads and cottages recall an earlier landscape. We were now walking along the former carriage drive of the estate across the contours of the valley as it rose up towards Rawdon and Little London. I looked back across the open fields and meadows below me as the carriage drive took me past substantial Victorian mansions commissioned by the wealthy industrialists of the growing nearby city of Bradford. Views of the villas are limited from the roadside as they are set back in private grounds surrounded by mature trees of all descriptions, but their elaborate gateways and lodges acted as focal points as we walked along.

These Victorian mansion houses feature high walls of architectural ornamentation in the Gothic Revival, Tudor and Elizabethan styles. The high quality materials used in the construction included local Gritstone and squared and coursed masonry. These magnificent houses of the wealthy were built on the varying terraces on the valley side, allowing each to benefit from the open views across the valley.

At the junction with Cragg Wood drive I found a tiny footpath flanked by massive stone walls that ran along the edge of the grounds of Buckstone Hall. This path had something of a tunnel like appearance as the walls were themselves topped by the overhanging branches of the mature trees which lined the grounds of this fine house. Designed by the Bradford Architects Lockwood and Mawson for Herbert Dewhirst, Buckstone Hall was nicknamed "Little Windsor "or "The Castle" due to its dominant tower which was clearly visible for miles around. The Dewhirst family lived here until 1911 when the property was sold to Sir Arthur Croft of The Thornbury Engineering Company. The house became a casino in the 1960's.

Lou and I walked along Cliffe Drive, passing by the houses of Crag Head and Daisy Hill. This superb mansion was owned and occupied in the 1860's by Henry Brown, the Mayor of Bradford and co-owner of the well-known store Brown Muff and Co. As I took yet another footpath towards Buckstone House I glanced back down the valley and could just about see the outline of the mansion named Summer Hill. This fine Victorian Gothic revival residence was at one time occupied by William Henry Salt, the Second Baronet and eldest Son of Sir Titus Salt.

Today Buckstone House is known as Apperley Grange. Now the location of Rawdon Golf Club Apperley Grange is situated one hundred and fifty yards from "Buckstones Rock". This rock is a significant local landmark and is thought to have been the secret meeting place for 17th century Baptists and other none conformists in the area before their chapel was built a short distance away. The famous Preacher John Wesley was reputed to have preached here on a number of occasions. This whole area gives an idea of the wealth and privilege that the Victorian industrialists enjoyed. The estate was a forerunner of what the aborted estate of a similar nature across the valley at Calverley was to have been. I was used to seeing and admiring the humble cottages and farms across the Bradford are during my walks, but now I was walking amongst the former grand residences of their wealthy paymasters.

Once again dodging the flying golf balls and sour looks and gestures from the golfing fraternity, we carried on the footpath to pass by Kent House. This house was once owned by the Granage family who lost a Son at the Battle of Arras in World War One. Lieutenant William Briggs Granage of 235th Brigade of The Royal Field Artillery died of his wounds aged 37 on the 14th May 1917. He was killed by a shell as he walked to the headquarters of an infantry brigade near Swan Chateau and was buried in Lijssenthcek Military Cemetery.

We were now approaching Little London, and crossing Micklefield Lane Lou and I walked along London Lane to once again be amongst the humble old cottages that I had come to know so well. The designated conservation area of Little London occupies a spur of high ground in a somewhat dramatic position above the Aire valley. Cragg Wood tumbles down to the south and to the west can be found the Esholt estate. To the north east the land rises gradually and culminates in the nearby Billing Hill and the moors above Yeadon.

Little London probably originated as a small farmstead but quickly grew into the form we see today in the late 18th and early 19th centuries. This was largely due to the local weaving industry. Here the streets were narrow and the cottages close together as I passed through to cross Apperley Lane making for a lane which would take me across open fields and down towards the Esholt estate. Here at the head of the tiny lane stood the oldest house in the Little London area. Lane Head House dates from the early 18th century (1710-20) and is thought to have been built as a steward's house connected to the Esholt estate. The former service cottages to the house also survive as does Smithy Hill cottages (1750), The Grove (1797) and The Folly (late 18th century).

The small track led me down the valley side past huge allotments filled with just about every vegetable I could think of. Down at the valley bottom I could see the railway line and my map had told me to head for it and skirt alongside it to the east for a while to arrive at a substantial stone bridge. I was glad that I had come this way rather than the other and was traversing down the valley side. This ancient packhorse trail from Rawdon to Esholt was steep and narrow in the extreme and the remaining setts were uneven and troublesome due to the wear from the many horses and humans who had walked it over the centuries. As we neared the railway line the trail turned sharply to the right before disappearing into a thick wooded area that flanked the line. The railway bridge stands upon Gill Lane and this track leads into the Esholt sewage plant. Even though we were still quite a distance from there the smell was indescribable and didn't bode well for what was to come. I tried not to think of the nature of what was stirring around in the tanks and filter beds as I continued along Gill Lane in the wooded area that flanks it.

The tiny beck of Yeadon Gill ran alongside us in a gully as we walked down the track towards the junction with The Avenue. Turning left here we took this wide modern open road for a short distance then turned off along Coronation Avenue. I knew this road led straight through the centre of the sewage plant like a dagger through the heart and officially I should not be going this way. The only other alternative was to take the long way round and cross the river Aire by way of the small iron footbridge some distance away. This in turn would bring me out near Bottom Farm and Thackley Canal Bridge. Only the week before I had walked that way and noticed a small hole in the perimeter fence near the Press House, and if I was not noticed by any of the plants workers I could use this as a short cut. The official name for the Press House was the Sludge Disposal Building. Inside here 128 steam filter presses compressed sludge to recover grease (lanolin) which could be used for a variety of applications, and the press residue was sold as fertiliser to meet the cost of operating the plant. After Bradford's woollen textile industry declined, the Press House became roofless and derelict.

So trying not to appear subversive like the Russian Mafia I walked confidently along Coronation Avenue, over a bridge spanning the river Aire and into the plant itself. Past rumbling and gurgling filter beds and tanks we went, eyes peeled all the time looking for any workers hanging around. But I saw no one and we were never challenged as we reached a large car park next to an area my map had indicated as Strangford Hall. All the time I was breathing through my mouth as the stench was simply overpowering. How these men can work here day upon day baffled me but I assumed they just got used to it and got on with the job. I made for the derelict Press House and found the hole in the fence that I had spotted the week before. Pushing Lou Parson through it and followed her, crawling through on my back to emerge on the canal towpath. It had saved me perhaps thirty minutes of walking so I was well pleased with my foresight to remember the tiny gap in the fencing. I crossed the turn bridge to start the walk up Ainsbury Avenue which would take me to Thackley. At the far end of Ainsbury Avenue is the site of a former open air school. I had noticed this area more than once on the Google Maps and it interested me as I thought there may still be some surviving ruins indicating its former use.

In the years between 1908 and 1939 sickly children from the dense working class areas of Bradford were brought in from the city centre to attend this ground breaking school. In the early part of the 20th century Bradford's progressive education authority quickly saw that the open air, good food and exercise would benefit the districts disadvantaged children. These children of humble working class parents normally lived in cramped conditions with poor sanitation. Bradford Council had recently bought Buck Wood as part of the land belonging to the Esholt Estate, which they needed for the development of their new sewage plant. Part of Buck Woods seemed ideal for the open air school.

In 1908 40 pupils were brought to the school by tram from the city centre to be fed and schooled in the south facing, open fronted classrooms. Close to the main entrance to Buck Wood on Ainsbury Avenue is a plateau that was created from waste material from the first railway tunnel under the woods. This flat raised area was used as a playground by the children that attended the school, and foundations of some of the school buildings can still be seen leading down from the north east edge of this plateau. Soon after another row of chalet style buildings were added taking the number of available places up to 120. By the time the school closed in 1939 thousands of children had benefitted from the special care and atmosphere offered by the school. During WWII the buildings were used by the Army and the Home Guard. The raised plateau became the site for an anti-aircraft gun due to the areas proximity to the Avro aircraft factory at Yeadon. The buildings were finally burnt down in 1966 and most of the site cleared allowing it to return to nature.

Upon reaching the end of Ainsbury Avenue I turned into Buck Woods through a large gate. After walking only a few metres I came upon the raised plateau which was used as the playing field. Just to the side I noticed a set of stone steps leading down into the woods. Lou and I walked down the twenty or so steps and emerged into a clearing in the trees where foundations for some of the schools buildings could be seen. The locally cast bricks still laid in the soil as they had done for over a century. Tracing the outline of the open fronted buildings it was easy to picture how they were arranged in the clearing. I stood there alone in the mid afternoon sun, the wood silent and still. Maybe it was my imagination but I swear I could hear the distant excited babble and chatter of children as they played their games on the plateau. Filling their young lungs with the fresh air instead of the coal dust and smog of the inner city most would remember their days here with affection. Thinking back to my own school days in the late 1960's, Iam still not sure if it was boiled cabbage or Esholt sewage plant I could smell as I walked off towards Ainsbury Avenue and headed for home.

High Eldwick to Crossflats via Bradup Bridge

Ancient standing stones and cairns have always stimulated my imagination. Images of Druids enveloped in hooded robes, hands flung upwards in reverence to their God and chanting strange incantations to the darkening heavens filled my mind as I read about the famed Twelve Apostles on Bingley Moor. Perhaps people from times past really did know things about the Earth, spirits and the Gods that we do not. I felt compelled to follow their prehistoric path to find out for myself. So pulling out my trusty maps and consulting the oracle of Google Earth I made my plans.

The bus driver stopped at the penultimate stop to let the only other traveller decamp. Turning around to me he asked if I wanted this stop as well. "No man Iam going right to the end of the line" I replied as he shrugged his shoulders and with a hiss closed the doors. The end of the line was still a short walk through the countryside before Lou and I reached Dick Hudson's pub on Otley Road. We were to take the well trodden Dalesway Link towards the summit of Bingley Moor. We were to follow the path that many pilgrims had struggled along before us, and now it was my turn.

I stood at the entrance gate and filled my lungs with air to help propel me up the daunting pathway before me. The path was clearly defined due to the stout drystone walls on either side so it was simply a case of tramping upwards towards the horizon. I reeled Lou all the way in to help pull me over the uneven stones, lowered my head and arched my back and set off.

After fifty metres I turned and looked back. The pub was still there but I felt like I had walked to the moon already. Leaning forward hands on my knees I draw yet another large lungful of air to try and stem the pounding feeling in my temples. Wishing I had chosen to walk the flat even streets of Manningham I staggered on once again. At least the surface of the path had changed from random broken half sunken rocks to flat stones making it easier on my ankles. The bleak open moorland opened up around me as I started to walk with a little more pace. My breathing was not so laboured and the pounding in my head subsided a little. Looking down at Lou Parson I noticed she was intelligently avoiding the swampy bog that lined each side of the pathway. I was not so lucky as my foot slipped off the edge of a stone to sink into the sucking mud. Forget the dog she'll sort herself out I told myself as I once again focussed my attention on the tiny milepost on the horizon.

The moorland seemed to stretch forever around me as I reached Spy Hill. At one thousand feet above sea level I knew I had done most of the climbing. I rewarded my sweaty efforts with a short rest atop a large rock. Pulling out a sandwich I tore off the crust and offered it to Lou. She dropped it in the mud but ate it all the same and thanked me by jumping up for more and covering me with whatever it was she herself was covered in. Although still muddy at least from here the terrain was flat and even. I could now start to enjoy the bleak and windswept Hog Hill Flat. Images of grizzled old men leading packhorses loaded high with cloth filled my mind as we passed the milestone that pointed the way to Ilkley. The track had changed to hard packed sand at this point and we started to make good time towards the summit of the moor. Passing through Peat Edge we climbed another two hundred and fifty feet as the trail snaked on and on through the banks of heather.

I was consulting my map every five minutes as I really didn't want to get lost up here. To seasoned moor walkers it may not be the outer edge of nowhere but I had never been anywhere quite like this as I normally walked through areas not as remote and windswept as this area was. Eventually after what seemed an age we arrived at The Twelve Apostles stone circle on the very top of the moor.

The Twelve Apostles is probably the most visited prehistoric site in West Yorkshire. Dating back to The Bronze Age (2000BC) it is also the most damaged and unfortunately the stones have been moved about quite a bit in the last century. Even so they still attract quite a lot of speculation from different faiths, cults and religions. The dozen up righted stones are just over a metre in height and appear evenly spaced with no obvious entrance to the ring. Descriptions from the 19th century suggest there may have been as many as twenty stones at one time. An earlier earth bank that surrounded the stones is also mentioned. There have been theories that suggest the stones were used to observe the movement of the Moon and other celestial bodies-indeed it was once known as a "Druidical Dial Circle". It is also said that from within the stone circle the rising summer solstice sun appears exactly above the White Horse at Kilburn.

The stones were erected close to the crossing of the two most important trackways crossing these moors, marking an event of some importance. These trackways face the four cardinal points, or airts, and one of them is believed by archaeologists to have been a major prehistoric trade-route that crossed the mid-Pennines. Around 1800 BC – the academics guess – the ring of stones took form. The all-but-forgotten Black Beck Well, two hundred yards south of the Twelve Apostles, was an important water-hole for the prehistoric traders and travellers and may well have had some function relative to this megalithic ring. Certainly, the well was being used by traders late into the 19th century.

One thing I was sure of was that the circle in front of me today bears little resemblance to the place when it was first constructed around four thousand years ago. The scattered woodland which covered most of these now-barren moorland heights have long since gone and the stones have been moved and overthrown so many times that it would be very difficult indeed to gain an accurate picture of what the circle originally looked like.

Leaving the circle I walked on for a few metres then took a track that ran off to the left. I followed this track across Rombalds Moor towards Whetstone Gate. On the horizon to the west I could see another tall stone cairn, which was unmissable in this treeless landscape. A straight line through this cairn will strike The Swastika Stone and is said to mark the point of the major Lunar standstill, the maximum moonrise on the north western horizon, an event that only occurs once every nineteen years. Next to this was a Trig point which marked the highest point on the moor. The large stone slabs I was now moving along were laid perhaps only a century ago to prevent soil erosion by the many boots that tramp across this part of the moor.

Continuing along this path I passed by an imposing group of boulders known as the Thimble Stones. These appear to have also been a stone circle at one time. Here lies two huge chunks of millstone Grit with a recumbent boulder forming a natural altar. It is quite likely these stones had some relevance to the Prehistoric inhabitants of the moor. Once past this point the path took me towards then along a massive centuries old drystone wall on the western boundary of the moor. Apart from the Trig point and the mile stone markers this wall was the first sign of any sort of modern human activity I had seen since leaving Dick Hudson's. Half a mile further on was Whetstone Gate which marks the former main Keighley to Ilkley road. The name originally denoted the presence of a stone in the area used for the sharpening of knives.

I had now reached Whetstone Gate and my attention turned to the small village of East Morton way below. Walking quickly past the small building with its attached Police radio relaying mast I joined the narrow tarmac road alongside. This would lead me down to East Morton, and here I knew I would find modern evidence of past human endeavour and this lifted me and gave my aching body new life. Whetstone Gate is an area north of Riddlesden where a narrow lane leads down towards the beautifully isolated cottage of Bradup and then East Morton beyond. The lower slopes of the moor provide pasture for sheep farming and this gives way to an expanse of heather moorland which forms the south western part of Rombalds Moor. This area is rich in bird life with breeding pairs of Meadow Pipit, Skylarks, Lapwings and Curlews. Birds of prey are also often seen here circling the sky waiting to pounce on their prey.

Lou Parson didn't have to pull me down the road as it dropped quite sharply as I passed the disused and abandoned Whetstone Quarry. Just past here at the side of the road I saw a stone drinking trough that was being filled at a high rate by a natural spring. It carried the inscription "T11 XS 1858". The water was crystal clear and burbled away in the silence of the moor as it filled the trough. In times of antiquity any decent source of water was held in high regard and this spot will most certainly have been one of the most revered on the whole moor.

I could see the isolated cottage of Bradup just a short distance down the road. As I approached it my attention was drawn to a series of small enclosures in the field opposite. These were sheep pens where the local sheep which grazed on the moor all their lives would be brought to be sheared of their woollen coats. The thin narrow chambers which constrained them whilst they were being relieved of their fleeces had something of a "Heath Robinson" look about them and it all appeared to be a small scale operation. Artisan craftsmen at their best no doubt. I was sorely tempted to have a close look at the adjacent cottage as it seemed to be totally deserted but just as I was about to cross the road towards it, a farmer came trundling down the road on his tractor and I thought perhaps I was not as alone in this wilderness as I had thought and passed on the idea.

I found this little area to be beguiling in the extreme. The deserted cottage, Bradup Beck and its ancient bridge made me want to stay sat there on the wall for a whole week. I tried to imagine what it would be like to live right here in the winter. How isolated, secluded and alone I would be. There would be no Sky TV or Broadband, no mobile connection for my phone. But the fire would glow from the peat blocks I had cut from the nearby moor in the summer and that would be recompense enough.

Shaking myself from my daydream I jumped down from the wall and continued down the road past the rolling heather tinged fields till I reached the farmstead of Upwood. The Roman road from Manchester to Ilkley passed close by here and the most preserved section was broken up by William Busfeild in 1848 and used to construct nearby drystone walls. My map had told me to take Upwood Lane which ran alongside the farm. This is no more than a footpath in reality and would lead us through open fields to eventually reach the north side of East Morton. As Lou and I walked along here I could smell for the first time the familiar aroma of the countryside. Cattle and sheep filled the nearby fields as I made our way along the high walled flanked track. I glanced over to the south and the tiny cosy hamlet of West Morton came into view.

The path turned to skirt along the grounds of Manor Heath. The secluded gardens of this fine house lay behind a massive stone wall that was only interrupted by a small wooden door. A secret door to a secret garden where fairy's and pixies held court amongst the water lilies of the pond perhaps? Who needs drugs to invoke such a vivid and colourful imagination?

Back in the real world the pathway took me to Green End Road and the disused Upper Mill. This Cotton spinning mill was constructed in 1798 but was destroyed by fire in 1899. This whole area was dotted with cotton, Worsted and paper mills at one time, a veritable hive of industrial activity all powered by Morton beck. Oldside Mill at Alma Hill was built in 1792 and believed to be the first Cotton mill in the area. Sunnydale Mill which manufactured bank notes and stationary was thought to have the biggest waterwheel in Britain at one time. Built in 1833 this mill closed in 1878 and was finally demolished in 1935. The largest mill was the Worsted manufacturing Botany Mill which closed in 1938. Manufactured goods would have been transported to the south of the valley where a warehouse and wharf on the Leeds-Liverpool Canal was conveniently situated.

To house the workers rows of 19th century cottages were constructed near the mill sites. These included Providence Row near Botany Mill and Upper Mill Row adjacent to Upper Mill, and the now demolished cottages near Sunnydale Mill. Alma terrace on Otley road, built in the 19th century was also owned by Botany Mill.

Despite industrialisation and growth a number of farmhouses and cottages dating to the 17th and 18th centuries survive to the present day. Some of these are grade II listed and include Laurel Bank which contains a date stone dated 1669. Situated on the main road, Green End road similarly contains two surviving farmhouses and cottages of this date, and one farmhouse with a date stone dated 1664.

Today Sunnydale is a place of solitude, however this cannot be said of the last two hundred years or so. At the end of the 1700's the industrial revolution arrived in East Morton with something of a vengeance with mills and factories springing up all along Morton Beck. This was to take advantage of the ready supply of water from the beck to drive the waterwheels and later the steam engines used to power the mills. Although the workers cottages can still be seen and indeed are still lived in, the same cannot be said of the mills as these have long since disappeared. Strangely enough the remains of the engine house at Sunnydale Mill can still be seen hiding amongst the undergrowth.

I spent the next two hours simply wandering around the tiny streets of former mill workers cottages in this area. Dreaming of hardy men with whiskers and flat caps coming home after a hard days graft at the local mill. Trudging along the street in their clogs as their children ran along to greet them, it will have been a hard life but one that may have had a meaning that has been lost forever today.

The small Methodist Chapel on Green End Road will have been packed every Sunday with the men and their wives dressed in their finest clothes. The starched white collarless shirts worn by the men only on this day, the bright floral dresses shimmering in the summer sun as the women left after the sermon. They were simple people who possessed only simple things but as I walked around I wondered if it was in some respects a better life than we have now. The spell was broken when my mobile phone rang. It was a friend of mine who enquired as to where I was. I replied to him that although I was not that many miles from home I was indeed far away.

It was downhill all the way as Lou and I walked through the village heading for Morton Lane. This long road winds down the valley side and would take us to Keighley Road where I could once again catch the bus back to Shipley. Passing by a myriad of old cottages and a handful of grand Victorian houses we crossed Morton Swing Bridge near the aqueduct that carries Morton beck over the canal. Sat on the grass at the bus stop I mulled over what I had seen and experienced this day. I had witnessed the ingenuity of industrial man and felt the spirituality of his Prehistoric forefathers all in the same day. I had been on a journey across the ages and through the past in the space of a few hours.

How could I not share it with others?

Keelham Crossroads to Scarlet Heights

Today's walk was always going to be special. I was going to visit and walk along one of the Victorians greatest feats of engineering not just in this area but in any area. Thornton Railway Viaduct stands proud alongside Salts Mill and Listers Mill as marvellous monuments to the Victorians ingenuity and expertise even to this present day.

Lou and I started this walk at Keelham crossroads and the history of law breaking speeding drivers on this road was immediately apparent. The warning signs for the speed cameras stood at the roadside and there was also a dedicated "Police Only" layby carved out of the kerbside. I have never noticed one quite like this one apart from on the motorway. Needless to say the passing traffic stayed within the legal limits so perhaps the warnings are being heeded. The wide open expansive fields opened out on each side, dotted only with the occasional farm as we strode along the kerbside towards the historic village of Thornton.

Although I had driven through the village on many occasions I had never walked around the area, so all of this walk was on new and unknown territory for me. Thornton is a village with a rich history of mills, railways and not least the famous Bronte family. The Rev Patrick Brontë became the incumbent of Thornton Chapel in 1815, and Charlotte, Branwell, Emily and Anne Brontë were born at 74, Market Street, Thornton before the family moved to Haworth. The remains of the church where the father preached, known as the Bell Chapel, can be seen in the restored old graveyard off Thornton Road opposite the current church.

The preserved centre of the village retains the character of a typical Pennine village, with stone built houses with stone flagged roofs. The surrounding areas consist of more modern housing, still isolated from the rest of the city by green fields. Its elevation, poor soils, isolation from major transport routes, and rainfall of over 34 inches a year limited farm production. Resources such as coal, iron and sandstone, the development of turnpike roads, and the coming of the railways enabled Thornton to share in the prosperity generated by the 19th-century wool worsted trade. The increasing use of steam-powered mills (at the expense of the former cottage-industry production methods) concentrated production in the valleys of the city centre. Foreign imports, the

Second World War, and closure of the railways, all contributed to the decline in manufacturing. Today Thornton is a residential suburb of Bradford but still retains some wonderful cottages dating back to the dawn of the Industrial Revolution.

But as I walked along Thornton Road back towards the village my thoughts were firmly fixed on the one single item of history that I wanted to see and experience above all else. The week before I had walked around the Denholme area and visited the magnificent Hewenden Viaduct and today I was intent on walking along the top of its more famous sister, the Thornton railway viaduct. The only thing was I had no idea how to gain access to this Victorian engineering marvel, but as it turned out this would lead to a most unusual meeting with possibly the nicest Satan's Slave you could ever meet.

Walking along the main road Lou and I passed the farmstead of Lower Bottomley Holes and the imaginably named cottages Top of the Row. The passing traffic was still just on the legal limit and I could see on one motorists face the ire at having to drive legally as he plodded past at 30 MPH. At Pearson Place I stopped at the crumbling roadside shell of a former warehouse. Looking sad and forlorn with its boarded up windows and half its roof missing I wondered exactly what noble activities were carried out here in the past. The rotting wooden boom above the upper loading bay windows hung out from the building like the Grim Reapers thin boney finger apportioning blame to those who had abandoned the building.

I walked on and almost immediately saw the upper rampart of a railway bridge across the road. The line passed underneath Thornton Road at this point to carry the line into the southern entrance portal of Well Heads Tunnel. Glancing over the wall on my side of the road I could see the deep tree filled cutting leading to the portal. I spied a small path running through the undergrowth and leaping over the wall dropped down to see how far it went.

The portal entrance was only just visible and I could see it was bricked up and had hefty metal gates securing it. The path was so densely packed with thick bushes and brambles that even Lou Parson would go no further than a few feet so reluctantly I gave up and returned to the road. A shame as a visit to the inside of a Victorian railway tunnel is always a treat due to the magnificent largely preserved stonework that is usually found within.

Constructed between 1878-1881, the tunnel boasts a vaulted stone roof and stone portals and buttressed sides but contains no air shafts. When built this tunnel was some 662 yards long but the removal of the northern portal has reduced this by forty yards. The inside contains regular refuges in the walls and on one grim stormy evening some years ago a man was found dead huddled up inside number thirteen. The line was closed to passenger trains in 1955 but remained open for goods traffic until 1961. From the direction and layout of the tunnel and line I judged the former station and the viaduct would lay on the south side of the main road so at least I had an inkling of the direction that I should be taking when I entered the village.

The road was long and straight at we approached Simmonites Land Rover dealership. Opposite here stands the massive and impressive Thornton Cemetery with its seventeen Commonwealth War Graves. I had always thought that living over the road from a massive old cemetery would be a bit scary, but the new build block of apartments across the road occupy such a great position I could certainly live there. A track up the side of the graveyard leads past an old abandoned water Filter House then onto the Bottom of the Row farmstead. The Filter House was built in 1926 by Bradford County Waterworks to serve the villages of Denholme and Thornton before closing in 1975. Most of the tucked away farms in this area have wonderful and evocative sounding names, Top and Bottom of the Row are but two and another named simply Squirrel can be found not far away.

The sun started to come out from behind the clouds for the first time today as the open fields turned into rows of roadside bungalows and houses. Mostly late Victorian houses of a middle class nature on one side with the odd rundown warehouse on the other. We were now entering the built up area on the edge of the village. The road to my right fell away to reveal the gully where Pinch Beck runs. Beyond that the distant hills climbed up towards Queensbury and the windswept hamlet of Mountain. There I knew was my journeys end after I had sampled for the first time the delights of a walk along the viaduct and the former railway track bed.

I turned and looked back along the road that I had walked along. Perhaps a thousand yards away I could just make out the trees around the southern portal for Well Heads tunnel. The fields between the trees climbed up towards Close Hill Lane where beyond the northern end of the tunnel broke through the heavy soil. The tunnel itself ran through this giant hill in front of me, and as

I stood there I pictured in my mind the hundreds of Victorian navvies and labourers toiling and sweating to burrow like tiny ants through the earth to create what was at the time a subterranean marvel. I shivered as the hairs on my neck stood up as thoughts of the yet to be seen viaduct filled my head.

Lou and I had now entered the village and this was apparent due to the build-up of the roadside housing. Looking across the road I saw cobbles and stone walls that are the only remaining signs of the long gone Thornton Railway Station. No other parts of this large station remain. The station had an island platform and was reached from the road by a fifty foot iron bridge. The site has been occupied by Thornton Primary School (previously Royd Mount Middle School) since 1977. The original goods platform and a large retaining wall are still visible and have been incorporated into the school's grounds design and it was here that I now stood. The area of the goods yard is now occupied by the schools playing field. A large stone warehouse measuring 130 feet by 50 feet once stood here. It handled coal, wood, livestock and animal feeds. It is down the side of the school via a pathway that one gains access to the viaduct but at this time I didn't know that and Iam so glad I didn't as will become apparent shortly.

Walking on past the school and completely missing the viaduct entrance path Lou and I passed the Great Northern public house. Obviously named after the company which ran the railway and not the Rugby League team this pub is fronted by what appears to be a massive sea of impressive stone setts that could no doubt tell a few tales if they could speak. As we passed through the village the road was flanked with stout terrace houses, take aways and fish shops. Side streets and alleyways snaked off at almost every angle to lead to courtyards lined with tiny cottages. Providence terrace must surely have led to Providence Mill and been home to the workers who grafted in the grime and dust to earn their pittance of a living. A Chinese, a Barbers, the Co-op, a Methodist Chapel (there's always a Methodist Chapel), we passed them all looking for the road to take us down towards Pinch Beck Valley and the viaduct.

I turned down Lower Kipping Lane as the excitement in my bones reached fever pitch. The viaduct was so close I could almost smell it. I felt like it was drawing me in, compelling me to feast my eyes upon its magnificent structure. I hardly noticed the tight roadside cottages as they flashed by. Walking downhill in the middle of the road towards the valley floor we picked up speed.

The absence of pavements bothered me not one bit as I rounded the last corner, and then stopped and stood silently as the viaduct presented itself before me in all its Victorian glory. Pulling the dog to the side of the road I could hardly believe what I was seeing. Never had I witnessed a structure as beautiful as this in all my walks around this area. I felt humble and privileged to stand before this marvel of Victorian ingenuity and engineering. Yes I was that impressed!

Thornton Viaduct opened in 1878 as part of the Great Northern's route from Queensbury to Keighley - arguably, the most engineered section of railway in West Yorkshire. It is Grade II listed, incorporates 20 barrel vaulted arches - each with a span of 40 feet - and its 300 yard length incorporates a rare S-shaped curve to allow access to Thornton Station. The old track bed crosses Pinch Beck at a height of 120 feet. The structure is formed of 17,000 cubic yards of masonry as well as 750,000 bricks. I felt like staying right where I was and counting every single one. It is supposedly haunted by the ghost of "Fair Becca", who fell from her horse whilst riding along the top of the viaduct. Local folklore says that if you call her name three times she will appear.

I sat there atop a drystone wall for what seemed like hours just gazing at the viaduct. The warm sun beat down upon my head, the birds twittered in the nearby trees, and all was well for once. Although it stood perhaps two hundred feet away my eyes examined every stone, every arch, looking for imperfections, but I saw none. Was it really built 137 years ago I said to Lou, it could have been built yesterday. I simply had to get on the top and drink in the scenery below. I knew it was part of a dedicated walking trail but how could I gain access. I noticed the arches disappeared into the hillside away to my right. Below this were gardens or open ground I was not sure which. Climb that wall down there and get underneath its belly and have a look from there I mused.

Five minutes later Lou and I stood on what appeared to be someone's well tended lawn. The underneath of the arches stood as tall as the heavens above us. The silence was broken when a voice boomed "Oi, what you doing man you're on my lawn". Thankfully it wasn't God but a bearded shaven headed man in a black leather waistcoat and jeans. I'd seen his type before, they usually smoke drugs, wreck pubs and ride motorbikes. But somehow I was not scared of this Satan's Slave as he walked towards us pointing his finger up the hillside. "If you want to get up there you have to take the proper path by the school not through my garden" he said.

Then the strangest thing I have ever seen happened. Out from the open door of his cottage some twenty feet way came two Jack Russell's running at full speed. They came charging straight for us, snarling and spitting with lips curled. I feared for Lou as quite often this breed of dog does not get on with others of the same, and never mind Mr Slave these feisty little buggers were out for a fight big time. Picking Lou up into my arms I braced myself for the inevitable onslaught that would surely come when they launched themselves towards her and my upper torso. It all happened in a flash then it was over. The dogs came to a stop just like in the cartoons (cue screeching of brakes) and stood in front of us, heads tilted to one side with an almost enquiring look on their faces. The male dog stood up on his hind legs and sniffing, offered his nose up towards Lou. The female did the same as Mr Slave crossed his arms and asked me where I had got my dog from. "A young couple in Idle village, Darren and Kelly I think it was" I replied "Why?" His laughter broke the ice and my heart once again took its rightful place in my chest. "They're Brother and Sister to your dog mate that's all". Never again will I ever doubt the intelligence of our wonderful canine friends as that was the weirdest thing I have ever seen in twenty years of living with these creatures.

Lou Parson's brother and sister Sam and Ella

To cut a long story short I stayed there with Douggie, Sam and Ella for an hour or more. He and I used to move in the same circles years before when I was a bad assed biker and we knew a lot of the same people. The dogs of course played in the garden and got re acquainted after their parting when the litter was split up. Another of Lou's siblings, a male named Midget lives in Bolton Woods near to our home and we see him on occasion so that leaves only one other male from the litter whose whereabouts are unknown. I was pleased for Lou that day as it must have been nice for her to once again meet her brother and sister. Douggie bought his cottage underneath the viaduct with compensation he received from a bike accident and I envy him greatly. The garage alongside the cottage was once a wash house for the Great Northern railway company where they cleaned the staff uniforms he told me. A nice bloke in a great place I am glad he has a tiny part to play in this book.

It was time to move on after a while and making our farewells Lou and I departed back along Lower Kipping Lane. I found the path by the school and started to walk along the former track bed on the top of the viaduct. The vista of pinch Beck Valley and the golf course below was stunning, the stonework unrivalled in its complexity. Seven hundred and fifty thousand stone bricks held together with mortar and Victorian sweat. We walked the tarmac former rail bed as the viaduct curved along the contour of the valley. I could clearly see Lister's Mill and its fine chimney far away amongst the bustle of Bradford city centre. The bright green dome of its neighbouring Mosque shone in the early afternoon sunlight. Away to my right were the hills leading upwards to Queensbury and it was there we were now walking towards. Only two miles away it looked a lot further as the viaduct ended and the track towards the massive high Birks Embankment began.

Before reaching the embankment I came to Upper Headley Hall. This fine unaltered hall was built by the Midgley family in the reign of Elizabeth I in 1589. Constructed of coursed Gritstone and stone slate roofs this building has a gabled west wing of moulded Saddle stone. The front entrance has a particularly good square of chamfered mullioned transom windows which most unusually retain their original leaded glazing and wrought iron casements. The interior retains tarred oak doors and panelled partitioning.

Almost immediately we were along the top of High Birks Embankment. This 104 feet long, 900 feet long structure was constructed from 250,000 yards of tipping material dug out from the nearby tunnels. Constructed to span the

Birks valley below subsidence was a huge problem for the Victorian engineers when it was built. Crossing over Cocking Lane the trail was flat and the surrounding countryside just purred by. Lou was startled by a compound of chickens by a small farm. This was right along the side of the trail and if it was not for the wire fencing she would have been in there and no doubt be in her instinctive element. Crows and Magpies fled the nearby treetops when her high pitched screeching awoke them from their slumbers.

We were now approaching the famous "Queensbury Railway Triangle". We had been walking along the former track that took the line over Thornton viaduct and on to Keighley. The Queensbury Lines was the name given to a number of railway lines in West Yorkshire, England that linked Bradford, Halifax and Keighley via Queensbury. All the lines were either solely owned by the Great Northern Railway (GNR) or jointly between the GNR and the Lancashire and Yorkshire Railway (L&YR). The lines opened piecemeal from 1879 and it was not until 1882 that a full service was available. Passenger services continued until 1955, most goods services continued until the 1960s and the final part of the line to close lasted until 1972.

The lines were marked with a number of major civil engineering works including several viaducts and tunnels. A feature of the line was the unusual station at Queensbury which until the latter part of the 20th century was one of only two stations in the United Kingdom that consisted of a triangular junction with platforms on all three lines forming the junction. It boasted a triangular layout with inner and outer platforms on all three sides, as well as a signal box at each corner. The first train pulled in during the spring of 1879. The line north snaked its way to Keighley, embracing viaducts, tunnels and lofty views over the industrial sprawl - earning it the affectionate title of 'The Alpine Route'. To the south-west, via the glorious gloom of Queensbury tunnel, lay Halifax whilst Bradford nestled to the east, also linked by a hole through the hill. Much to the annoyance of locals, Queensbury itself was perched high above its station, connected by a steep, meandering lane which the Great Northern Railway grudgingly lit after some protest. Today, the triangle has lost its shape and the platforms have been engulfed by twenty feet of landfill. A lonely rusting footbridge rests below the station house, next to the spot where the signal box once stood. The tunnel underneath Queensbury is blocked by metal gates but access can still be gained as I heard tales of midnight ravers holding parties inside during the summer months. This tunnel was opened in July 1878 when the link to Halifax was completed. The tunnel was 2501 yards long and almost a quarter of a mile under the village of Queensbury. It was the longest tunnel on the Great Northern rail system and took nearly four years to complete. Queensbury itself stands on top of the hill the tunnel cuts through, part of it about 1,000 feet above sea level. Apart from its unusual platform arrangement Queensbury station had a sheer drop of over 50 feet behind one platform. When seen from this side it has rather a Swiss appearance, fostered perhaps by the massive timber supports on the steep hillside. As a change from tunnels, the Keighley line beyond Queensbury provided passengers with some wonderful open views from Thornton Viaduct. By 1970 only the degraded remains of the platforms and station subway under the Halifax to Keighley platforms could be seen. Apart from the rusting metal footbridge the only visible remains today is the former Station house nearby. Even the subway was demolished in 2004 and the valuable Yorkshire stone spirited away for use in other building projects.

As I sat down in the long grass at the side of what was the Thornton branch of the line I noticed a broken gravestone nearby. A gravestone here, why? I wondered. It belonged to John Dalby who worked for The Midland Railway for forty years. The 1881 census told me that John Dalby was married, age 64, a Railway Canvasser that lived at number 66, Four Lane Ends in Bradford. He was buried at St John the Baptist in Clayton which was the nearest church to this spot I understand. But exactly why his headstone rested here amongst the tall grass at the former site of the Queensbury railway triangle I never did find out.

Due to the length of time I had spent chatting with Douggie and his dogs in Thornton I had to get a move on and leave this somewhat lonely and forgotten place. I decided to make my way up the steep Station Road and then take a footpath which would bring me out onto the main Bradford Road at Scarlet Heights. During the hike uphill I could appreciate just how the locals felt when the station was built down in the valley. Lugging bags and trunks up the gradient will have tested even the most athletic and agile late Victorians. No doubt the station forecourt was filled with horse drawn cabs every night as the trains pulled into this strange and unusual station. The final stretch of the day up to Scaret Heights damn near killed me that's all I'll say, but the view from the top as I looked back down into the triangle and across the valley to Thornton was well worth it.

The snooze on the back of the bus as it trundled down into Bradford was well earned.

Cutler Heights Lane to Greengates via Calverley

The bus dropped Lou and I off at the junction of Cutler Heights Lane and Wakefield Road. For a change I had nothing of the walk worked out only the end point at New line in Greengates. It was going to be simply a case of making it up as I went along. A blank canvas so to speak and this kind of excited me. Crossing the road we had to walk past one of Bradfords most ugly and depressing disused former public houses. The mostly wooden Kingswood Arms has been boarded up for many years now and is adorned by a host of flyers, billboards and stickers. Empty inside it is the haunt of junkies and dossers and just how it is still standing is a mystery. Bradford Council do something, knock it down, burn it down but do something with it please. I tutted and shook my head as I walked quickly past this sad place towards the former location of something more worthy.

The huge Morrison's depot on Cutler Heights Lane stands just where the Greenfield sports stadium once stood. Today not a trace of Bradford Northern's first home remains but from 1907 to 1969 it hosted not just Rugby League but also Greyhound racing and Speedway. In 1907, the newly formed Bradford Northern rented the ground for £8 from Whitaker's Brewery, who also agreed to sponsor the club. It became Northern's first permanent home and the club set up its headquarters at the adjacent Greenfield Hotel. Bradford's first match there was against Huddersfield on 7 September 1907 and was watched by around 7,000 spectators. The club gained a significant scalp later that year when they beat the New Zealand touring side.

In 1926, the venue was converted to a greyhound racing stadium, one of the first in the UK, opening in October of that year. By now the facilities were much more developed than they had been in early days. There was a main stand made up of covered terracing on the School Street side, opposite the starting gate. There was also covered terracing along the back straight on the Cutler Heights side. At one end was a huge tote board but no terracing and at the other end, a concourse with betting and a club house overlooking the dog track. Greyhound racing continued throughout the following decade's right up until the stadium's closure. In 1961, a 320 yard Speedway track was laid inside the dog track and the city's speedway team, Bradford Panthers, relocated to Greenfield from Odsal Stadium. The first meeting was opened by famous speedway promoter Johnnie Hoskins. Success was short lived and the last meeting at Greenfield Stadium was a double header against Sheffield and Leicester on Tuesday 9 October 1962. The Panthers folded soon after. The stadium was closed for business in March 1969 and was sold for industrial warehousing. The last sporting event was a greyhound meeting on 5 March, attended by 4,790.

I love old disappeared sports grounds as for some reason the ghosts of the flat capped Hurrah shouting mainly male crowds invoke powerful images in my mind. As I passed by this famous old place I made a mental note to visit the most famous of Bradford's ghostly sports grounds on my next walk. Hopefully I could gain access and shout hurrah for the spirit of the Clown Prince of Football himself, I'll have to see.

From here Cutler Heights Lane leads all the way along to the massive Thornbury roundabout but I was not going that far as I had decided to turn off into the countryside at Tyersal Lane. The road itself is flanked with a mixture of modern houses, old grimy cottages and the odd fish shop here and there. Lou and I passed by another pub from my distant past, The Travellers Rest. Not having been anywhere near it for nearly thirty years I don't know what it is like today but back in my day it was a place where you could buy just about anything as long as you didn't ask where it came from. I was once witness to a very nasty knife fight in there and shuddered at the memory as I urged Lou along to pass it rather quickly.

The old train line from Dudley Hill Station used to run parallel to Cutler Heights Lane and the track bed can still be walked along in places. Just after I turned onto Tyersal Lane I crossed an old iron bridge that once belonged to the line. It was one of those kind of bridges that no one ever gives any attention to but the huge iron rivets still bare the marks of the foundry that cast them over at Low Moor. Bridges like this one and parts of the general infrastructure of Bradford's long gone rail system still stand all over the area. People simply pass them by and never give a moment's thought to the skill and ingenuity of the fine men that created them.

As I made for Tyersal Gate I glanced over across the fields on my left to see the largest herd of horses I have seen. These obvious Gypsy horses were untethered and simply stood grazing there in the open fields. The horses were all sizes and colours and I wondered what was in store for them when their usefulness was exhausted. Even though I was walking alongside the edge of what was once the largest council estate in Europe I felt free due to the large open expanse of fields on one side. My pace quickened and my strides lengthened as I reached Tyersal Gate and realised I was heading towards pure open countryside.

My map told me that Tyersal Mill was disused but it appeared to be a hive of activity with various car repair shops doing brisk business as we passed by. The former workers terrace houses attached to the mill are still occupied and in good shape. The farmstead of Harpers Gate stands slightly away from the lane behind the mill. It too was busy as a tractor pulling a muck spreading machine behind it trundled past us. The wonderful aroma of the country was defiantly with us as the tractor covered the lane in leakage as it passed on its way to the fields. This is more like it I said as I looked down at Lou. She just sneezed violently in agreement. Over across the fields I could make out the huge dense Black Carr Woods dominating the skyline through which Carr Beck runs to join with Tyersal Beck a little further on.

The lane had narrowed considerably by this point, the drystone walls hemming us in and funnelling us towards on one the finest and most historic houses in the area. The large late medieval timber-frame Tyersal Hall was constructed in 1691 of thin coursed hammer-dressed stone with a stone slate roof. The four room front has six first floor windows and a single-storey porch with double-depth Quoins. All the windows are double- Chamfered mullioned with almost square reveals. A gabled porch with Tudor-arched doorway and chamfered surround contains a lintel initialled and dated " RT 1691 ". The interior hall is open to the roof with a mid-19th century elaborate Gothic stair with turned balusters and low panelled walls. The hall is flanked by parlours with plaster ceilings and moulded cornice running round the spine beam.

I stood in front of the ornate iron entrance gates and wondered just who lived here. More to the point who had lived here in the past and what stories would they have to tell of days gone by. The gates are flanked by stout thick carved stone posts and from these runs a wall alongside the grounds. The wall is dotted at irregular intervals by strange carvings that jut out from the wall. The thick trees inside the grounds hides the building from prying eyes. A sign warning of CCTV coverage told me this was not a place to intrude upon and with that Lou and I walked briskly down the lane and towards the dismantled railway bridges at Black Hey farm.

Black Carr Woods had encroached over the fields towards us and the boney woodland finger of Stubbs Rein pointed across to meet us at the edge of the lane. I stopped for a moment as I noticed a small car park to the side of the lane. Next to the road is a small fishing lake which was not marked on my map so I assumed it was a recent development. The small handful of Anglers were sitting and waiting for their next catch in the mid-day summer sun. All were completely silent as they scanned the water's surface for activity. Looking up I noticed the huge embankment at the far end of the lake. Now heavily wooded it once carried the Pudsey and Low Moor branch line of the GNR train line from Tyersal Junction over Tyersal Beck through to Greenside Station in Pudsey. It was not hard to imagine the dark metallic beasts laden with coal spewing out vast clouds of steam as they roared across the embankment towards the dismantled bridge further down the lane. Leaving the fishermen in peace Lou and I continued on along the narrow lane heading for Black Hey Farm. As we approached the farmhouse and barn which stood alongside the lane a Collie charged out from the yard. Normally this breed of dog are not in any way aggressive, more intelligent if not a little daft at times.

This Collie was obviously something of a guard dog which considering the secluded nature of the farmhouse this did not surprise me. Lou didn't disappoint me though as she lunged forward with lips curled to see the dog off. The lead in my hand extended all the way out and nearly tore my arm from its socket but at least the Collie backed off and ran off into the yard.

The old bald headed man sat in the farmhouse watching television a few feet away never stirred. I guessed that as he was old he had the volume on Sky News turned right up and never heard a thing. Walking away down the lane I shook my head as I tried to make sense of the concept of receiving Satellite TV in such a secluded place as this.

The huge abutments of the dismantled railway bridge stood still proudly on either side of the lane a little further down. The stonework untainted by the passing years since its construction it stood to usher us along down through the woods towards the stone Clapper bridge that fords Tyersal Beck. From here the lane climbs steeply up towards the former busy little area of Smalewell Mill. To the east of Gibraltar Mill, this woollen mill was first constructed in 1821, but on the night of 9th November 1867 a fire broke out in the boiler house. Despite the attendance of Pudsey's brand new fire engine which was successful in extinguishing the fire, the roof fell in and £500 worth of damage was sustained.

Turning off the lane at this point Lou and I walked along a track through the woods. The wood was lightly packed with trees allowing the light to penetrate down to the rich undergrowth flanking the track. I strolled by small overgrown long forgotten delphs as I passed the site of the wonderfully named long gone old cottage of Buffy Lump. The track straightened out and away in the distance I could see a figure walking up the slight gradient towards us. The man greeted us as he walked past and carried on up the track and I gave him no further thought. A few hundred yards on I reached a wooden gate at the end of the track. Here stood one of my favourite cars, a blood red Heinkel Kabine Bubble car no less. It was obviously the property of the bloke we had just passed as there was no one else around. The engine was still warm and I could smell the faint whiff of the engine oil and hear the faint ticking of the metal parts as they cooled. It was a rare treat to see such an iconic car close up even if the surroundings were a little bizarre. As I left the car I looked up and from here I could see the outline of Black Hey Farm up on the hillside and I knew that Pudsey lay up the other side in the direction we were travelling.

We walked along Waterloo Road and over Hillfoot tunnel to arrive at the bottom of WoodHall Lane just as the heavens opened with a giant crack of thunder. I took refuge under the canopy of the changing rooms of the University playing fields and waited for the rain to subside. Only five minutes later it stopped and the sun once again came out so Lou and I carried on. As we walked up Woodhall Lane we passed by what was once The Woodhall Estate of The Quaker banker Daniel Peckover.

Daniel Peckover resided at `Woodhall` which stood on the opposite side of Woodhall Lane to Woodhall Lake. The house was built in the latter half of the 18th century by the Gott family who were the owners of the land in this area from 1755. Daniel Peckover seems to have been one of the great and good of Bradford. Was on the town council and various committees, and often donated money to help get public schemes off the ground. He commissioned the construction of a huge lake on his land mainly to give gainful employment for the unemployed men of the area. By the side of this lake stood Woodhall Grange, a large Victorian villa. By 1901 (and still in 1911) Woodhall Grange was occupied by Cornelius Metcalfe, a retired waterworks contractor, aged 53. His brother Reuben (also retired) and two sisters (living on their own means) were also present. The Grange is now long gone and apart from a few stone steps no trace of it remains today.

Lou and I walked steadily up Woodhall Lane towards the tiny ancient hamlet of Woodhall Hills. This timeless small conservation area is centred around the small, nucleated settlement of Woodhall Hills Hamlet, which was originally a collection of workers cottages around Old Hall Farmhouse. A small, central village green still survives. The more recent extension to the west of the conservation area repeats this pattern with a small, central grassed area within the courtyard. To the north of the conservation area is the old Ravenscliffe Farm which is now part of Woodhall Hills Golf course.

The character of the conservation area is influenced by the near universal use of sandstone. In the medieval era there appears to have been a small community in the area. The current village is the probable site of the documented medieval settlement of Wood Hall. There are several buildings which contain elements which appear to date from the early modern era. The nineteenth and twentieth century have not seen significant change within the conservation area. The expansion of housing and industry seen within much of Leeds has not occurred and the size and layout of buildings are similar to those on the 1848 Ordnance Survey map.

Several farm buildings have been converted into residential dwellings and this domestication has undoubtedly shaped the character and appearance of the village. The largest change has been to the setting of the conservation area. The two nearby golf courses have impacted upon the landscape surrounding the village and the addition of Priesthorpe Road and Woodhall Road have changed the relationship of the village to its surroundings.

Lou and I continued along and down Woodhall Lane as it swept down the valley side towards Calverley. Fine green meadows and pastureland opened up to each side as Calverley presented itself to us with open arms. It was welcoming us but we were to only skirt along the edge of this ancient and historic village on our way to its equally historic woods. The name Calverley is of Anglo-Saxon origin. A ley was a clearing in a woodland, and is widespread in this part of West Yorkshire (e.g. Farnley, Bramley and Armley). In this case it translates to 'a clearing in a woodland grazed by calves.' This would suggest woodland has existed here since at least the 7th Century, but there is also documentary evidence to prove that within these woodlands, trees were being felled for timber as early as 1336.

I entered the woods via strangely enough, Wood Lane. This narrow muddy track was uneven with stones set in the mud and was quite difficult to walk on for a while till it got a little better near the small lodge that guards the lane. Once past here it opened out and the trees fell back a little. The air was deathly silent and the only sound was the sound of my footsteps and Lou lunging into the undergrowth at every opportunity. As usual there was nothing there she was chasing shadows once again. Away from the track I could see some red bricked building remains. Not very high perhaps three courses but they peeked up above the low and thick undergrowth. I knew these were the remains of an old WW2 army camp where a military training camp was constructed and used to train troops for the D Day landings. These buildings later became Guy's Fireworks in the late fifties. Very unfortunately there was a massive explosion at the factory on June 19 1957.

Local people remembered hearing a bang and a small mushroom cloud appearing over Calverley two or three miles away. Three people died and four others were injured. An inquest was told the explosion occurred when a worker had been drilling into rockets and a spark from a steel bit ignited gunpowder stored in the same hut. The factory consisted of 16 huts in the woods which were formerly an Army and European Volunteer workers camp. The factory which opened in 1953 and employed up to 80 people at peak production periods was closed on December 31 1957. The three people who died after the explosion were Peter Lunnis, Elsie Thompson and Mary Conroy.

I took the route of Clara Drive on through the woods past a series of massive, gated modern houses. They were so big they had letterboxes on the road by their gates saving the Postman a trip to the front door. We crossed over the dreaded Calverley Cutting via the road bridge and this time I stayed well clear of the damn place. By now I was rather glad the end of my trip was near as the Gout had started to tingle in my toe again. So with that I tip toed carefully past the lodge at the end of Clara Drive and joy upon joy saw that the bus was lumbering down the hill. Nice timing Butler!

Manningham and The Ghost of Len Shackleton

The brief visit to the site of the former Greenfield Stadium at Dudley Hill on my last walk stoked my imagination immensely. A few days later I dug out the old maps, did some research and made plans to visit a place where I spent many happy days when I really should have been at school as a young boy. At this time in the mid to late 1970's the Horton Park ground shared by Bradford Park Avenue and Yorkshire County Cricket Club was still in partial use. The Football club had long since folded and departed but the cricket part of the ground was still used by Yorkshire CC. I would bunk off school and get the bus into Bradford for an afternoon of watching Cricket and messing around in the marvellous derelict relic of Archibald Leitch's double sided stand. Thinking back I recall spending more time sat in the old stand imagining the Stan's plying their trade than watching the Cricket, and it was this feeling I wanted to once again invoke if I could.

So the plan was to tramp around the historic streets of Manningham then make my way over to my boyhood field of dreams. Armed with my trusty bag of cheese and onion sandwiches and my even more trusty Jack Russell I set off on a bright Saturday morning to walk down Kings Road in the direction of Manningham. The first stop was the site of the former Manningham Railway Station on Queens Road. Today this place is a stone reclamation yard and the only remains that can be seen is the station perimeter wall running along North Avenue. The station opened on February 17th 1868 and was the first stop on the Leeds and Bradford branch line of the Midland Railway as it left Forster Square Station. Although today this station is known as Forster Square, in the days of Manningham Station it was known as The Midland Station after the company who ran the line.

The opening of the station brought the middle classes to live in the area during the textile boom in the late 1800's when English and German textile merchants moved in. It was quite a huge site in the days when Bradford was known as "Worstedopolis" and it was the centre of the world's Woollen manufacturing industry. From 1872 there was an extensive network of sidings and sheds to the north of Manningham Station and it was a hive of much activity. The Station Masters house stood across Queens Road where the Enterprise car rental company now have an office. The station closed due to the Beeching axe on the 20th March 1965 and although there have been recent plans to resurrect a station on the site nothing has so far come of it.

I continued up Queens Road towards Manningham and almost immediately noticed a decline in the general appearance of the area. The once proud and immaculate terraced houses lining the road were somewhat scruffy and degraded, the pavement was littered with general detritus. It seemed there were empty Cannabis bags every five paces and coke cans every ten. Lou and I hiked up the steep gradient and crossed over Manningham Lane to continue on towards Carlisle Road. Just for a fleeting moment the scruffiness of the area was lifted when the quite magnificent Apsley Crescent came into view. Built for wealthy middle class Bradfordians the twenty four houses on this curved terrace were designed in fashionable classical and Italianate styles by Architects Andrews and Delaunay and constructed in 1855. My spirits were certainly lifted when I saw one of the few curved terraces left in Yorkshire. Apsley Crescent would not look out of place in the great city of Bath.

Turning off along Church Street Lou and I experienced more poor quality housing and even more poor quality roadsides as we carried on through Manningham making for Oak Lane. Even from here I could see the marvellous giant stone chimney of the great Listers Mill. We were now on the edge of what was once Bradford's famed red light area and one of the haunts of The Yorkshire Ripper Peter Sutcliffe. Opposite Skinner Lane I stopped to admire the former Bradford Children's Hospital. This imposing 1889 Grade II listed stone building with its two storey "turreted" annex is presently a Mosque for the Muslim Community.

We turned up Skinner lane then onto Rosebery Road where one of the area's oldest buildings stands. It is also probably the most unloved and destitute buildings of any in Manningham. The Old Manor House was thought to have been built in the early 16th century as a hall and cross winged timber framed house. This places it in a group thought to represent the type of dwelling adopted by the wealthiest of the Yeomanry. The house has been unoccupied for a number of decades and has fallen into a sad state of repairs.

I joined Oak Lane and turned uphill to walk towards the grand and imposing masterful Victorian building that is Listers Mill. Otherwise known as Manningham Mills it once was the largest Silk factory in the world. Built by Samuel Cunliffe Lister to replace the original Manningham Mills that were destroyed by fire in 1871, the mill is a Grade II listed building built in the Italianate style of Victorian architecture.

At its height, Lister's employed 11,000 men, women and children and manufactured high-quality textiles such as velvet and silk. It supplied 1,000 yards of velvet for King George V's coronation and in 1976, new velvet curtains for the President Ford's White House. The 1890-91 strike at the mill was important in the establishment of the Independent Labour Party which later helped found the modern-day Labour Party. On completion in 1873, Lister's Mill was the largest textile mill in North England. Floor space in the mill amounts to 27 acres, and its imposing shape remains a dominant feature of the Bradford skyline. The chimney of the mill is 255 feet high, and can be seen from most areas of Bradford.

The powering of the machinery switched over to electricity in 1934. Before that huge steam boilers drove the mill. Every week the boilers consumed 1,000 tons of coal brought in on company rail wagons from the company collieries near Pontefract. Water was also vital in the process and the company had its own supply network including a large covered reservoir on-site. During World War II Lister's produced 1,330 miles of real parachute silk, 284 miles of flame-proof wool, 50 miles of khaki battledress and 4,430 miles of parachute cord. The Lister's business decreased considerably during the 1980s. Stiff foreign competition and changing textile trends such as increased use of artificial fibres were the reasons.

In 1992 the mills were closed. Being a prominent structure the mills attracted a great deal of attention and several regeneration proposals came and went. The sheer size of the buildings being a major difficulty. In 2000 property developers Urban Splash bought the mills. They planned to renovate the existing larger buildings and build new ones. Apartments, workplaces, shops and public spaces were planned to be part of Listers. Silk Warehouse, which was completed in 2006, created 131 new homes and the lower ground floor is home to Mind the Gap, a disabled performing arts charity. Velvet Mill is the second phase in the regeneration of Lister Mills. Designed by David Morley Architects, the largest listed building in Bradford has been lovingly restored into new homes and ground floor commercial spaces. Bursting with original features, Velvet Mill combines the best of the old with the best of the new, and the new dramatic curved rooftop apartments are a fine example of how combining old and new architecture can transform an already magnificent building into a modern day classic. As I stood there before this Victorian wonder I could fully appreciate just why The Times had proclaimed that the Mills were as 'breath taking as Versailles' when it was built.

I had needed that injection of class and culture and the next was only just around the corner. A short stroll past the red bricked building of a former Telephone exchange along Heaton Road brought me to a pair of stone gateposts. Beyond these up a narrow lane are the historic "Tradesmens Homes". Termed as Alms houses these buildings were constructed for the benefit of retired local tradesmen and their families who had fallen on hard times. Founded by public subscription in 1867 these houses are arranged around a rectangular green. Local luminaries such as Sir Titus Salt, Sir Isaac Holden and Samuel Cunliffe Lister were amongst the subscribers to this most noble of projects. The high Victorian Gothic style buildings were designed by Milnes and France and are constructed of Sandstone brick with Ashlar dressings and steeply pitched Welsh slate roofs. In the centre of the north range is a Chapel and assembly room with stained glass windows and a projecting canted front. Today the homes and their grounds within this beautiful square are immaculate in the extreme and it was a joy to walk around and admire yet another example of the city of Bradford's Victorian benefactor's finest moments.

But sadly as I left this hidden and almost unknown oasis I had to endure yet more litter strewn streets lined with closed down takeaway shops and motor factors as I walked further along Heaton Road. All the rows of once fine Victorian terrace houses at this point were built to house the workers at the nearby Listers Mill. They were built to last and that they indeed have but the shabby appearance of most of them was disheartening to say the least. From one extreme to another I cannot think of any other area that I have walked through where this is more apparent than here in Manningham.

At the end of Heaton Road at the junction of Bavaria Place and Church Street stands another forlorn and crumbling sad old building. The ornate Gothic structure of the Old Police Station was built in 1877 and designed once again by famed local architects Milnes and France. The two storeys and attic was constructed in Ashlar Sandstone with Mullioned windows. The most striking feature is the rounded corner tower topped by a steep corniced French roof of fine green slate. Next to this building stood until recently a huge underground reservoir. Contained within an area surrounded by stout stone walls this reservoir has now been dismantled and the site cleared for redevelopment. It was actually a huge metal underground tank and some time ago I sneaked into the site and found one of the inspection hatches open. Peering down inside I could hear my voice echoing for what seemed an age around the empty subterranean cavity.

On the far side of the reservoir there once was a public toilet situated in the stone wall. Some years ago a local pub barman was bludgeoned to death in there after his shift. Despite a huge Police door to door search his assailant was never caught, and it became just another of Bradford's unsolved murder mysteries. From here Lou and I walked on to reach Toller Lane which would take us towards the city centre and the White Abbey area. I walked past what was once The Upper Globe public house. The building was of course destroyed in the recent riots and I felt more than a pang of regret as we went past as it was my local when I lived round the corner on Abingdon Street some thirty years before. Then the pub was a lively swinging place and I recall spending many highly enjoyable Saturday nights ensconced in there. Today the building houses a thriving builders merchants business but sadly it is one drinking hole less in the area.

We were now on Whetley Hill moving through a whole avenue of Sari shops, takeaways and carpet shops. My spirits lifted when I remembered that my primary goal of the day was yet to come and with that my pace quickened. Before I turned off Whetley Hill to take City Road I remembered I was right on top of what is most certainly a patch of grass that most people are unaware of. This large triangular shaped section of playing field was once home to the original Infirmary of Bradford. Completed in 1844 and extended in 1864 this hospital was in use until it was replaced by todays modern Bradford royal Infirmary on Duckworth Lane in 1936. It replaced a Dispensary which was established in 1825 and then moved to Darley Street in 1827. Today there is no trace of the Infirmary apart from some strange stone arches in the stone wall that runs along the far side on Lumb Lane.

Taking City Road for only a few hundred yards Lou and I crossed Sunbridge road to join Preston Street. This was an area I knew so well from many great nights in the famous back street pub The Fighting Cock. With its Romany style frontage The Fighting Cock is one of Bradford's hidden gems. Much in the mould of a traditional public house it has been the CAMRA pub of the year on many occasions and rightly so. The ever changing selection of well brewed and well kept hand pulled beers are a delight to sample, and I have done exactly that on many occasions. It is one of those places I always seem to say I will return to but never quite get there. You know what when I finish this damn book I will reward myself and spend an evening in there once again hic hic.

I was now in Listerhills, once home to many railways and great mills. Many decades ago it was a thriving yet grimy environment and many a great fortune was made here on the sweaty backs of the inner city living working class people. Images of flat caps, rolled fags in mouth corners and shiny rain sodden cobbles filled my mind as I walked along past one of the area's finest mills of all. Designed by another of the districts famous Architect partnerships Lock wood and Mawson, Legrams Mill was a steam powered Worsted mill. This mill was constructed in 1873 and was originally designed as an integrated mill complete with combing shed, weaving shed and warehouse. The slump in the fortunes of the traditional Bradford products of Cotton and Worsteds caused the mill to adapt to become a spinning mill and the weaving shed was never built. Today the former mill has been adapted once again to become a series of smart apartments and flats.

Tramping on past row upon row of former mill workers back to back houses we reached the junction with Horton Grange road and we turned along here to make our way ever closer to the one place I wanted to be this day. The road here is lined with middle class Victorian terraced properties with more back to backs spreading out behind. I took a short cut through the back streets here to find myself on Horton Park Avenue just at the point where the railways used to run. Today this spot is occupied by the car park for the Mumtaz restaurant nearby. I stood here and watched the traffic as it passed by down great Horton Road. I was getting myself in the mood for what was to come in only a few minutes as I allowed my imagination to wander and create images of Leyland double decker buses lined up here at the roadside in the 1950's. Waiting with engines running for the throng of passengers to alight at the final whistle at the nearby football stadium, they would ferry the men home to their families and Saturday tea in the greyness of post war Britain.

A blacked out horn hooting BMW crammed with too many Asians stirred me from my daydream and rousing myself I continued along the road towards Horton Park. This public part was opened on the 25th of May 1878 on land purchased by Bradford Council in 1873. From 1980 to 1932 Horton Park Avenue was served by a tramway which ran alongside the park. The main entrance is set back from the road and is flanked by stone gateposts which support two pairs of late 19th century ornate iron gates. A few yards to the right stands a two storey stone lodge which is used as offices by Bradford Council. Just a few yards further back along the road from the lodge is the site of the parks former glasshouses and a fine conservatory. These were removed many years ago but an ornate drinking fountain which once stood in the wall nearby survives, albeit without its fittings and inscription plate.

Almost directly across the road from here is the site of the former Horton Park railway station. This was a station on the Queensbury-Bradford section of the Queensbury Lines which ran between Bradford, Keighley and Halifax via Queensbury. The station was built to serve the nearby football ground. It opened for passengers in 1880 closed for regular passenger trains in 1952 but remained open to special trains on match days until 1955. The station had a large goods yard which kept it open like the City Road Goods Branch until 1972 when it shut and the tracks lifted. The station remained in place along with its concrete sign until only a few years ago when the station was demolished to make way for the new Al-Jamia Suffa-Tul-Islam Grand Mosque. Today very little apart from part of the stone station wall survives of the railway station.

I jumped down from the wall alongside Horton Park Avenue to join the massed crowd of mainly men as they made their way towards the turnstiles at the Powell Avenue end of the ground. It was a cold Tuesday afternoon in April 1941 and Avenue were playing a Wartime Cup game against the then mighty Preston North End. My hero the "Clown Prince of Soccer" Len Shackleton was playing tonight and I was going to cheer him on with typical teenage gusto from the terraces. At fifteen I was not yet old enough for the armed services although my Father was away fighting the dreaded Hun in North Africa. Today I was free to mingle with the large crowd queuing outside the turnstiles to pay my three penny admission fee tonight. Oh to be able to afford the half a crown to sit in Leitch's fine double decker stand and watch in comfort. But then I might miss the camaraderie and closeness of my fellow working class Bradfordians on the packed terraces as Shack twists and turns to beat four Preston defenders to score the winning goal in the last minute. All those flat caps in the air will be a fine sight indeed.

I'd sold a bag of coal that I had scrounged to old Mrs Murphy down the street where we lived on Pleasant Street. I had enough to pay my way into the ground and even some left for a hot Bovril to warm me as I stood on the packed terrace. But the thrill of seeing Shack in action was enough to warm my very soul. Everyone loved a maverick and he was one of the very best. It broke my heart when he departed to Newcastle United for the second ever highest transfer fee of £13,000, but he did bag 171 goals in wartime football for us. The Clown Prince didn't disappoint me and the crowd of 18,000 this day as he did indeed score the winner but it was but a simple tap in at the far post. 1-0 but they all count I suppose I thought to myself as clutching my free souvenir team sheet I made my way back home for my tea.

I had a dream that night. I was in a line of players all wearing the famous Avenue colours. Bouncing the heavy laced ball up and down on the concrete floor as I waited to run out onto the famous old pitch, I glanced nervously across at those bastards in claret and amber from across the city. The number nine on my back felt big, almost as big as the expectations of the massed Avenue supporters who filled the stadium. What I would give to score the winner in the last minute like Shack even if it was only a simple far post tap in. I tossed and turned in my bed as I weaved and dribbled through the City defence. The mud from the heavy ball stained my forehead as I headed against the bar for the third time in the second half. My legs strained with the exertion under the blankets as I lunged to stab the ball over the line for the last minute winner. The cheers of the crowd as I was carried shoulder high from the pitch were silenced as the air raid siren woke me up and Mum came rushing in to usher me down to safety in the Anderson shelter in the back garden.

Although I saw quite a few Cricket games at the famous old ground on Horton Park Avenue I never did get to see a Football match. Today The Dolls House and Archibald Leitch's fine old gabled stand has long since disappeared, half of the pitch is now occupied by a fitness centre, and the terrace has sprouted a small forest of trees. The perimeter wall with its occasional bricked up entrances still remains though, but this is high and topped with barbed wire making any attempt at scaling it a useless exercise.

But I do have the memory of climbing through a small hole in Leitch's soon to be demolished double sided stand during one of the afternoon Cricket games I saw at Park Avenue in the mid 1970's. The Powell Avenue terrace was still there complete with its roof. Even the famous Dolls House stood there withering away in the corner to my right. I recall the seats in the stand were rather small and cramped and at an unusually steep angle unlike what I was used to at Valley Parade. The pitch was complete if rather overgrown and yes it was easy to imagine what it was like when there was a game on and a big crowd present.

Iam sad to say that was the nearest I ever got to seeing any action on this famous old football ground, and that is something for all the great sporting moments and experiences I have had that I will always regret. Anyway besides, man and boy I have always been a City supporter.

Keighley to Haworth With The Bronte's

I had always known this was to be the point where I would finish this series of walks. I wanted to end it with something a little different and I had the idea of a trip on the wonderful Worth Valley Railway for ages and now this was the time. Merge that notion in with some Bronte history, a bit of walking and fresh air, how could it possibly go wrong?

I had to catch the bus down into Shipley and then another to Keighley to get to the starting point for this my final walk. I've always liked Keighley railway station. It has that 1940's look and feel about it. As the train pulled in I half expected Trevor Howard to tip his Trilby at me as he stepped down from the carriage amid the steam. Sadly it was but a mere Diesel train that pulled in and not a steam engine. I would have had a further hour long wait to get on board a steam train, and I knew I had quite a few miles to go today so couldn't afford to waste an hour sitting around.

The station platform is resplendent in its ornate roof girders and supports, all decked in the company colours of cream and burgundy. The sun shone on the people stood at the end away from the canopy. A group children giggled excitedly as Mother handed out sweets. Lou Parson drank from the convenient water bowl as I sat beside her with a feeling of calmness. I felt so laid back I nearly fell over.

We were going to Haworth and from there out onto the moors above and beyond the village following the Bronte trail and all that touristy stuff. The Keighley and Worth Valley Railway is a 5-mile-long branch line that served mills and villages in the Worth Valley and is now a heritage railway line in West Yorkshire, England. It runs from Keighley to Oxenhope. It connects to the national rail network at Keighley railway station. The railway was incorporated by an Act of Parliament in 1862 and the first sod was cut on Shrove Tuesday, 9 February 1864 by Isaac Holden, the chairman of the Keighley and Worth Valley Railway.

The railway was built as single track, but with a track bed wide enough to allow upgrading to double track if the need arose. The rails were completed in 1866, track laying having started at each end and now being joined in the middle. The line was tested with a locomotive from Ilkley, which took nearly 2 hours to get from Keighley to Oxenhope, but just 13 minutes to get back. The opening ceremony was held on Saturday 13 April 1867 and nearly a century later British Railways closed the line in 1962 and their last scheduled passenger train ran on 31 December 1961. A preservation society was formed which bought the line from British Rail and reopened it in 1968 as a heritage railway. The line is now a major tourist attraction operated by 500+ volunteers and roughly 10 paid staff it carries more than 110,000 passengers a year. The railway is currently one of only two preserved railways which operates a complete branch line in its original form. The line and its stations has been used in numerous period film and television productions including the film The Railway Children and the BBC comedy Last of the Summer Wine.

The dark green six carriage Diesel Locomotive pulled into the station and as it waited there for perhaps twenty minutes the platform was filled with the smell that I remembered from my youth. Today's electric trains don't make any kind of smell and smells can be evocative, create images and transport you back in time. This train and its carriages smelt like a train is supposed to smell. As I boarded the train and sat down in the somewhat basic but fully functional carriage I was transported back in my mind and this only served to heighten my feeling of calmness. I stopped short of sitting cross legged on the seat with hands raised to Buddha as the woman sat opposite may have called the guard or had me sectioned. The guard himself was dressed as a guard should dress, he even pulled out a pocket watch then blew his whistle and the train lumbered out of the station.

After only a few minutes the train stopped at the Ingrow West station. Like Keighley and the other stations on the line it is a traditional station with a tiny waiting room and ticket office. Onwards we trundled again at a slow speed but this was fine as the experience could be savoured rather than be rushed. Once again after only a couple of minutes the train lurched to a halt. A voice from the tannoy informed us in a thick Yorkshire accent that we were to wait to let another train pass and as it was only a single line there exists a practise of only one train holding a lever with which to change the points. This is so no confusion arises over who should be on the line and who should be on the passing spot as we now were. Something like that anyway I seem to recall.

Our guard climbed up into the nearby signal box with his small lever. From there the signalman changed the points with a hefty clump. The Keighley bound train past by us slowly filled with smiling waving faces pressed to the windows. There was something quite civilised about all of this and it all kind of made sense. The next stop on this nostalgia trip was Damens station, the smallest standard-gauge railway station in Britain, and lit by gas would you believe? The next stop was the station at Oakworth. Restored to Edwardian condition this station is also lit by gas lamps, marvellous indeed. Within a few minutes the train arrived at my destination, the historic village of Haworth. The station is on the outskirts of the village and so there was quite a hike up Main Street to come. The village of Haworth is a major tourist attraction due to its links with the Bronte family and the Worth Valley Railway, and tourism accounts for much of the local economy. The cobbles wind up past Bed and Breakfast houses, bookshops, cafes and even the odd pub. The Black Bull is probably the most famous as it was here that Branwell Bronte was reputed to have begun his decline into alcoholism and Opium addiction. The street is narrow and lined with rows of 17th century cottages all displaying beautiful hanging baskets of flowers and immaculately scrubbed stone front steps. The people here are proud and they have to be to keep the hordes of visiting tourists happy and spending their money. And why not it's a beautiful and historic place and they should rightly be proud of living here in Haworth.

Main Street turned to Bronte Street but the quaint old cottages just kept on coming. At this point they were very reminiscent of the type of cottages I used to live in over in Laisterdyke twenty odd years ago. As Lou and I walked along the cobbles past them I could imagine the layout and character inside these wonderful but simple dwellings. We eventual arrived at the junction with West Street opposite a small Baptist Chapel and its graveyard. I stopped for a few minutes to admire the gravestones in the small section at the front of the Chapel. The admiration of graves is not a gruesome pastime as some people would think. Even the most humble gravestone can be an object of great beauty never mind history. They can tell the tales of those who have gone before us and when you think about it that's one of the main reasons for having a headstone.

Lou and I strolled out of Haworth along West Street, passing by more rows of immaculately kept terraced cottages, the fields opposite bearing the scars of past quarrying. The road continues on towards Stanbury but I was to take a turn off along Cemetery road towards the moors. Glancing over to my left I could see the rising heights of Penistone Hill with its massive quarries on the other side. Only a short distance along Cemetery Road is the old Haworth Cemetery. Consecrated in 1893 this cemetery contains the grave of Lily Cove, an intrepid but unfortunate female Balloonist. She died aged 21 when her parachute failed to open whilst demonstrating a quick descent from a balloon over the Worth Valley at Haworth Gala in 1906.

I stood here on the road opposite the cemetery gates and admired the view across the valley, over the river Worth and across to Pickles Hill. The patchwork of fields on the far valley side were full of Sheep and their lambs basking in the early afternoon warmth. The tiny specs of the farms dotted over the valley glinted in the sun. It was the kind of scene that you see printed on biscuit tins the world over. The quite magnificent Lower Laithe Reservoir stood proud in the valley bottom. Opened in 1925 by The Marquis of Hartington and constructed by stone heaved from the ground at nearby Dimple Quarry, this really is a huge and impressive body of water. The thick clay that lines it was transported by narrow gauge railway from its source near Top Withens. The small farm of Lower Laithe was submerged during the reservoirs construction and lies somewhere deep beneath the 60 feet of water to this day. Construction on the dam had actually begun before World War I but was interrupted and only completed in 1925.

The narrow moorland track took me past the 17th century farmhouse of Hill Top with its imposing views of the nearby reservoir. Bleak moorland stretched away to my left giving a foretaste of the terrain which was to come in abundance in a short while. Reaching the crossroad with Moorside Road, Lou and I crossed over to continue on towards the famous Bronte waterfall. Here the landscape is dotted with small delphs where much of the stone on which Haworth is built was quarried from the ground by hardworking local men.

By now Lou was in her element chasing the numerous sheep which openly grazed at the side of the track. She may chased but she will never catch as I always keep her on the extendable lead. Besides if she came face to face with a sheep or Ram she wouldn't have a clue what to do. It's all about the chase and any notion of actually catching anything hasn't quite been worked out yet. Passing by the wonderfully isolated Springs Farm I found that the track was rising up gradually as it wound its way along the side of the valley. It was here in the area known as Jos Hill that the valley narrows in and takes on a steeper appearance. Along the valley floor runs South Dean Beck and it is here that I found the famed Bronte waterfall. The picturesque but unspectacular waterfall on the moors above Haworth is fed by Lumb Beck which then joins South Dean Beck. Further on back towards Haworth it then feeds into Laithe reservoir.

I decided to perch myself atop a giant rock and join the handful of fellow walkers here and eat my dinner. It was warm as the steep valley side funnelled the heat down from the moor top. The gentle burbling of the beck as it ran under the ancient clapper bridge gave this small area a pastoral feeling and once again all was well with the world on planet Jackson. I could have stayed there all afternoon but I knew I had quite a bit of walking to do and I still had the unknown moorland across the tops to Denholme to negotiate. We were heading for the long abandoned farmstead of Top Withens, where it is said Emily Bronte based her ruins of Wuthering Heights, but that fact is disputed as she never actually came here.

The problem was I didn't have much idea of where it was only the general direction. Lou and I started to climb up the valley path on the opposite side and almost immediately I became confused as to which way to go. Just up ahead was a young couple both climbing the path with something of a purpose. Ahh right they look like they know where they are going and everyone who walks this way has to be going to Top Withens I thought. So pulling my cap down I scurried off after them. The path eventually levelled off and still following the young couple I seemed to be heading towards a huge copse of trees. In fact just about the only trees around this area, but my instinct was telling me this was this was not the way to be going.

Looking up I saw that the couple had turned around and were heading back towards me. When they passed me they told me they were also lost. As luck would have it another serious walker appeared from behind a large rock, and he pointed the correct way over the hills to the distant shape of Top Withens. It looked so far away and without losing any more time I made my way down the track through the heather. It took Lou and I about an hour of serious walking to reach the ruins as we went up and down the side of the valley.

The ruins of Top Withens certainly are remote and windswept even on a fine day like this. What the area would be like in the depths of a bleak mid-winter I can only guess at. But from here the view across the moors is superb and unrivalled and I could even make out my next intended port of call, the wind turbines on the moors above Denholme. I had to make a start so I left the ruined old farmhouse and took a small rocky path that ran in the direction of the moor top.

The path was uneven and slowed my progress but I once again pulled my cap down and dug my heels in. After perhaps thirty minutes I reached the summit of the moor and turned off onto another tiny path which followed the line of a deep drainage ditch cut in the soil. I was alone once again with only the wind for company. Up here it swept over the moors with an intensity I had not seen so far. With clouds there is always wind and the small cloud which seemed to be following me passed me and headed off towards Bradford. The wind dropped dramatically and the going was so much easier as I walked on the bouncing soft earth.

I saw nothing but the occasional stone marker post in this bleak wilderness. Unlike Rombalds Moor there were no ruins, cairns or drystone walls to break the scenery, only an emptiness containing just a man and his dog. As I walked alone my thoughts drifted back over the walks I had done in the last fourteen months or so. I knew I coming towards the end of my final walk for this book and in a way I was sad. I would of course carry on and do many other walks for any subsequent books I may write but for now this was it.

It had started with the simple walk around my own area in Wrose and was now to end up here on Haworth Moor. I thought back over all that I had learnt about Bradford and its environs, the long deceased people who had grafted to make it the city it is today. The sweat, toil and lives it had cost. The young lad drowning in the still water of the Bradford Canal at Spink Well lock, the man who lost his head whilst digging the Clayton railway tunnel. I once again pictured Titus Salt junior writhing on the floor in his death throes at Milner Field and Matthew Hughes charging the cannons at Sevastopol. All heroes in the story of Bradford and without them the city would not be the place it is today.

Lou and I started to descend from Harbour Hill towards Spa Hill. The vast open moorland began to change to bankings of thick heather. As I dropped down the hillside I lost sight of the wind turbines which had been my focal point so far. The high wire perimeter fence of a plantation steered me further into the heather which by now was enveloping me. It almost blocked out the available light it was that tall. The stems were long, thick and tough, the soil covered with small rocks threatening to turn my ankles at any time. Lou was struggling to fight her way through the roots, I was struggling full stop. I was concerned as all this effort was getting me nowhere and there seemed to be no end to this forest of bracken and heather.

At least I was travelling downhill but to where I had no idea. I had lost all perception of time and all sense of direction. I couldn't go back as it was uphill and the vegetation had closed behind me like an iron fist trapping me with only forward motion as my friend. Lou was scared as she was tucking herself right into my leg as we struggled through this abyss of living and laughing bracken.

Then without warning the earth beneath my feet vanished and I stepped out into thin air and crashed through the bracken down a gully. Lou had landed on my head, her arse on my face as we sped feet first down the gully towards the bottom. I didn't see the large grey rock till it was too late but at least it stopped us falling any further. The rasping of Lou Parson's rough tongue on my face brought me round. How long I had laid there on the floor of the gully I had no idea. A minute, an hour who knows, but I was so glad she was alright and safe. Collecting my thoughts I staggered to my feet and saw the sweetest sight I had seen all day, a reservoir at the end of the gully.

The forest of fern and bracken had decided it was bored of me and ejected me from its side by way of the slide into the gully. What's more as I stood up and brushed myself down I saw what appeared to be part of a conduit. It was only a short climb up the far side of the gully but it would lead to the reservoir and freedom. Ten minutes later Lou and I reached the conduit and started to follow its length along the gully side. Sheep ran for cover as we tottered along clutching onto the cold concrete. At the first opportunity I heaved myself then Lou onto the top and from here I could see a road running down to Leeshaw Reservoir. I ran like Forest Gump making for the road which would surely take us back to civilisation, Lou leading the way like a good Jack Russell always does. The ice cream van by the reservoir gates sold me the best cornet I could ever imagine eating and by far the most deserved. After an hour laid on the grass by the roadside I had enough energy to get myself together and plod on towards the tiny hamlet of Marsh and then back into Howarth. My original destination of Denholme was far away in the other direction and Haworth seemed like far the best option.

The sun came out and its warm rays invigorated me and gave me renewed strength. What little food I had left had been crushed in the fall as had my water bottle but it mattered not as I was going home and the thought of a hot bath was more important. Food could wait and what's more Manchester United were live on the great God Sky later on and with that thought fixed in my mind I opened my stride and headed down the back road into Haworth.

That night I had another lucid and vivid dream. I was struggling in a bog in the fading light, my body slowly disappearing as I was sucked down into the depths of god knows what. I clutched onto the surrounding bracken but it slipped through my sweaty fingers. I cried out for help but no one was there to hear me, no cavers, climbers or walkers came to my rescue. The wetness worked its way up my body to reach my chest. Was this the end, was I to die here alone?. Images of my childhood and friends I had lost flashed through my mind as the cold dampness enveloped and overcame me. Then with a sudden jolt it was all over and I sat bolt upright in the bed.

Lou Parson had been sick under the duvet.

Thanks must go to Michael Murphy (Master Po) of the Facebook group Banter about Bradford, for his patience in the face of many questions.

Kieran Wilkinson, Mick Petty, Tim Brookes and Simon Bean also of Banter about Bradford for their inspiration and knowledge.

Richard Lee-Van den Daele and R David Beale for creating their wonderful book Milner Field, The Lost Country House of Titus Salt Jnr.

Oh yes and a little dog named Lou.

On board The Worth Valley Railway

The author can be contacted at montyw111@hotmail.co.uk

Printed in Great Britain
by Amazon.co.uk, Ltd.,
Marston Gate.